Power without Force

Analytical Perspectives on Politics

ADVISORY EDITORS:

John Aldrich, Duke University
Bruce Bueno de Mesquita, Hoover Institution and the University of Rochester
Robert Jackman, University of California, Davis
David Rohde, Michigan State University

Political Science is developing rapidly and changing markedly. Keeping in touch with new ideas across the discipline is a challenge for political scientists and for their students.

To help meet this challenge, the series Analytical Perspectives on Politics presents creative and sophisticated syntheses of major areas of research in the fields of political science. In each book, a high-caliber author provides a clear and discriminating description of the current state of the art and a strong-minded prescription and structure for future work in the field.

These distinctive books provide a compact review for political scientists, a helpful introduction for graduate students, and central reading for advanced undergraduate courses.

Robert W. Jackman, *Power without Force: The Political Capacity of Nation-States*

Linda L. Fowler, *Candidates, Congress, and the American Democracy*

Ole R. Holsti, *Public Opinion and American Foreign Policy*

Scott Gates and Brian D. Humes, *Games, Information, and Politics: Applying Game Theoretic Models to Political Science*

Lawrence A. Baum, *The Puzzle of Judicial Behavior*

Power without Force

The Political Capacity of Nation-States

Robert W. Jackman

Ann Arbor

THE UNIVERSITY OF MICHIGAN PRESS

Copyright © by the University of Michigan 1993
All rights reserved
Published in the United States of America by
The University of Michigan Press
Manufactured in the United States of America

⊖ Printed on acid-free paper

2004   2003   2002   2001   6   5   4   3

A CIP catalogue record for this book is available from the British Library.

Library of Congress Cataloging-in-Publication Data

Jackman, Robert W., 1946–
    Power without force : the political capacity of nation-states /
Robert W. Jackman.
        p.   cm. — (Analytical perspectives on politics)
    Includes bibliographical references and index.
        ISBN 0-472-10463-2 (alk. paper). — ISBN 0-472-08236-1 (pbk. :
alk. paper)
        1. Power (Social sciences)   2. Political development.
    3. Legitimacy of governments.   I. Title.   II. Series.
    JC330.J33   1993
    303.3'3—dc20   93-24362
                                                              CIP

for Mary

Preface

The political capacity of modern nation-states is an issue that has attracted a good deal of attention in the past thirty-five years. Interest in the problem was initially motivated by two general phenomena. First, the wave of decolonization after the Second World War brought a dramatic expansion in the size of the international community—that is, in the number of sovereign states. And this expansion itself generated a number of efforts to understand the politics and prospects of the new states. Hence book titles like *The Politics of the Developing Areas, From Empire to Nation,* and *Old Societies and New States.* Among other things, scholars were interested in determining the degree to which the new states would follow a historical trajectory similar to that encountered by more established states and the ways in which the two experiences might diverge.

Second, many of these scholars were intrigued by a new behavioral approach to political analysis. Proponents of this general method argued that traditional approaches to political analysis, with their emphasis on the description of the formal properties of political institutions, were insensitive to more informal patterns of observed behavior. Instead of formal descriptions that highlighted the unique elements of particular institutions in specific settings (constitutions, legislatures, and the like), the behaviorists urged the importance of constructing more general statements about political life.

Initial analyses of national political capacity were treated under the rubric of political development. Attention was paid to delineating boundaries between political systems and the broader environments in which they were said to be embedded. Some scholars sought to identify the functions common to all political systems, but performed with varying degrees of success in different settings with contrasting political cultures. Others addressed the role of ethnicity in the process of nation building or the impact of modernization (that is, the changes associated with moves away from subsistence economies) on new political systems. Much of this research appeared in a series of volumes on political development in the 1960s and early 1970s, a series sponsored by the Comparative Politics Committee of the Social Science Research Council. Taking a slightly different tack, Samuel Huntington's influential *Political Order in Changing Societies* (1968) argued that a process of institutionalization is the key ingredient of political development.

During the 1970s the whole idea of national political development came under attack from a variety of quarters, among which two stand out. First, there was a populist attack that argued that the term *development* was itself ethnocentric, teleological, and conservative with its emphasis on order. Second, the dependency/world-systems perspective asserted that the focus on nation-states was inordinately narrow and misguided.

Within the last decade, these criticisms appear to have lost much of their force. Instead, nation-states have increasingly been seen as important arenas, and a good deal of attention has been devoted to the issue of state "strength." Although seldom conceded, this new statism—especially with its emphasis on state strength—has returned us to many of the issues that motivated the original literature on political development. State strength, after all, has to do with considerations of national political capacity. But recent writings on the state have failed to define it in plain terms, and hence the notion of state strength is also undefined. Some analysts describe state strength in terms of the size of the public sector, but this approach rapidly becomes mired in the problems of differentiating the public and private sectors (consider the cases of Japan and South Korea). Others broach the question in a more general way, casting states as "actors." This also raises more issues than it resolves. Not only does the concept of the state (and state strength) remain poorly defined, but, when the state is cast as an actor, the perspective faces overwhelming problems of reification.

Insofar as it has reaffirmed the importance of nation-states as political units, the new statism is an encouraging beginning. What is needed now is a return to fundamentals if we are to make any progress in identifying the political capacity of nation-states. What is to be done? Some suggest that the merits of the different approaches just sketched out are best adjudicated by more empirical research. However, I believe that much useful empirical work has already been completed. Before further empirical analyses are undertaken, it is critical that we stand back and take stock of the theoretical approaches to which I have just alluded and the empirical work they have spawned. What can be gleaned from the earlier studies of development, broadly conceived, and from the critiques of those studies?

Does the new statism offer an improved point of departure, or is it largely a similar tune played by a different fiddler?

This book is an extended essay on the concept of national political capacity (sometimes labeled political development or state strength). My purpose is to explore the ingredients of political capacity and to examine how we might know when a credible national political infrastructure exists. The bulk of this book is therefore concerned with explicating appropriate criteria for identifying the general concept of political capacity. This means that I am primarily concerned with clarifying the meaning of the concept, not with identifying its antecedents and consequences (of course, my analysis does have implications for the latter). It also means that my primary focus is on theoretical issues, although the penultimate chapter does address questions of measurement. These theoretical issues need to be clarified before we proceed to more intensive efforts at data collection and analysis.

The first chapter surveys the analyses of national political capacity that have appeared in the past three decades. I begin with the studies of political development that appeared in the 1960s and then evaluate the reactions they have spawned, concluding that research on the question of national political capacity in the last two decades has not on balance appreciably advanced our understanding of the issues.

Chapter 2 identifies the distinctive features of political life. I argue that the exercise of power rather than force is the key factor, and that this requires an institutional framework that is widely regarded as legitimate. Political capacity therefore involves the creation of legitimate institutions within which conflict can be resolved. This perspective is briefly compared with earlier approaches to political development.

In chapter 3, I consider the implications of recent writing on the state for the analysis of political capacity in light of the discussion of chapter 2. This writing has two general strands: some observers emphasize public-sector size as the key ingredient of state strength, while others more loosely discuss state "autonomy." I conclude that these discussions are of limited use for a variety of reasons, but two problems stand out in particular. First, it is difficult to distinguish the private and public sectors. Second, discussions of state autonomy are typically ambiguous and plagued with problems of reification. Given these problems, a new approach to the question of national political capacity is essential.

My claim that institutions are central to capacity is a general one.

Chapter 4 is concerned with identifying the specific components of institutions that are relevant to the problem. Drawing on analyses starting with Max Weber's that have emphasized the liability of newness, I argue that routinization associated with organizational age is the key ingredient to capacity and that age needs to be considered in both chronological and generational terms. Three elements of organizational age are isolated: the age of the juridical state, the age of the current constitutional order, and the number of top leadership successions that have taken place in that order.

The other element of capacity is legitimacy. While institutional age impinges on the issue, legitimacy needs to be addressed in its own right. This is done in chapter 5. Drawing on the distinction between power and force introduced in chapter 2, I contend that regimes and institutions are legitimate insofar as they are able to resolve conflict or make problems go away without the overt use of force. But legitimacy is a two-way street, and we need also to focus on the degree of compliance or consent exhibited by those who are governed. Accordingly, I also argue that legitimacy is an inverse function of the number of "irregular" or violent challenges to the political order.

Chapter 6 focuses on the measurement of national political capacity defined in terms of institutional age and legitimacy. Here, I link general definitions to concrete operational indicators. Measurement is necessarily inexact, of course, and while the identification of measures reduces definitional ambiguities, it hardly eliminates them all. The data introduced in this chapter involve general orders of magnitude and are intended to encourage broad comparisons of political capacity across nation-states.

The final chapter considers the implications of the analysis for future empirical work and contrasts my approach with that offered by others. My intention throughout is to provide a fresh brief for the study of national political capacity.

A number of people read and reacted to all or much of the manuscript, and I am indebted to Gabriel Almond, Kenneth Bollen, Michael Bratton, Bruce Bueno de Mesquita, Mary Jackman, Letitia Lawson, Arend Lijphart, Seymour Martin Lipset, Terry Moe, Kenneth Organski, Brian Silver, and Randolph Siverson for their very helpful criticisms and comments. While I have not followed all of their advice, the book is immeasurably better for their counsel. Michael Bratton also saved me from an especially lugubrious title, while Bruce Bueno de Mesquita introduced me to the remarkable labors of Bertold Spuler. Readers of Mary Jackman's recent *Paternalism and Conflict* (1993) will recognize that I have incurred a particular intellectual debt, despite our different empirical foci. Ron Roggiero's help in locating data and unusual sources was invaluable. Over the past several years, I have discussed different parts of the argument with many students. While a few sought solace or whatever else is to be found in the *State News* or the *Cal Aggie,* most did not, and the book is considerably improved in light of their individual and collective reactions.

I completed a first draft of much of the manuscript while a fellow at the Center for Advanced Study in the Behavioral Sciences at Stanford, California, with support from the National Science Foundation (BNS 84-11738). As have many others, I discovered that the center offers an extraordinarily stimulating interdisciplinary environment, the impact of which is only partially evident in what follows. I am especially grateful to Margaret Amara and Rosanne Torre for their exceptional assistance in matters bibliographic and to Frances Duignan for ensuring that all the critical things worked. I also appreciate crucial support from the Political Science Department at Michigan State University, and from the Institute for Governmental Affairs and the Academic Senate of the University of California, Davis.

Rachael and Saul Jackman wisely kept their insights to themselves (thus behaving as if they had considered the alternatives) and focused their attention instead on such matters as the Yolo County SPCA and soccer. Whether the book is better for their efforts is a matter for others to judge, but they certainly are.

With all this help, that I have produced such a diminutive egg attests solely to my own deficiencies as a duck.

Contents

CHAPTER 1

Background to the Study of Political Capacity

Most of the change we think we see in life
Is due to truths being in and out of favor.
                    —Robert Frost, "The Black Cottage"

Until the early 1950s, comparative political analysis usually involved the rather narrow study of foreign governments. Comparative studies were limited in at least two important ways. First, they were primarily configurative. They placed considerable emphasis on the history of formal constitutional arrangements and political institutions, in the hope of illuminating the distinctive characteristics of particular nation-states. Second, they were restricted to a small number of states. Typically, a text on comparative government was actually a description of selected aspects of political life in the United States, Great Britain, France, Germany, and, after the Second World War, the Soviet Union.

These two limitations produced a literature that emphasized the importance of case studies and that discouraged attempts to generalize from those cases. The implicit purpose of the study of comparative government was not actually to compare or to generalize about political life, but rather to gain some sense of what political life was like in a few other European countries. Minimally, such a sense might help foster a broader understanding of what American political life was all about. But the case studies emphasized cross-country differences rather than similarities and seldom added up to anything resembling a cumulative body of knowledge (Eckstein 1963). Indeed, that was not their goal.

In the last thirty years, however, much of this has changed. The major impetus for this change was the process of decolonization initiated after the Second World War and the concomitant rise of the "new states," commonly known as the Third World. Although the Indian subcontinent was hardly the first area to achieve independence (consider Latin America), the partition and decolonization of India and Pakistan was most notable in this regard, for two reasons. First, the

British Empire was, as of the mid-1940s, by far the largest empire. Second, India was the "crown jewel" of that imperial estate. The decolonization of India set in motion forces that ultimately led to the dismantling of the rest of the British Empire, along with the other empires (Smith 1978; Fieldhouse 1982; Low 1982).[1]

This process accelerated throughout the 1950s, and the year 1960 saw more declarations of national independence than any other single year before or since. It is easy to forget that at its founding in 1945, the United Nations had only 51 charter members. In the years since, this figure has more than tripled, so that currently, well over 150 states are members of the United Nations. And an overwhelming majority of these are in the Third World. The changes have been so pronounced that today "colonies" are generally regarded as illegitimate. "Nationalism" is now, for better or for worse, the dominant political ideology (Gellner 1983). The United Nations charter specifies the right of national self-determination as the major political right.

It is important to understand that this is a modern right peculiar to the twentieth century. It is also important to recognize that democratic ideology was the crucial ingredient that helped both to legitimize nationalism and to undermine colonial rule. The major grievance with colonial rule was that it did not derive from or represent the people it governed (Emerson 1960, 243). As a result, one way of undermining the legitimacy of the metropoles was to demand democratic institutions. This demand was also a powerful resource for indigenous elites, who used it to legitimize their own status as *representatives* of the indigenous population (Emerson 1960, 242–43; Young 1976, chap. 3; Collier 1982, 32–33). The result was that there were no new states "in which the elites who demanded independence did not, just prior to their success, believe that self-government and democratic government were identical" (Shils 1964, 103).

Decolonization obviously introduced major problems. For the former colonial powers it was not clear how sovereignty should be transferred in a peaceful manner. Although few colonies had been obtained peacefully (to understate the case), the imperial powers did seem concerned after 1945 that they at least give the appearance of exiting in an orderly manner. The Europeans felt that if they had to leave, then, in Mackenzie's words, "it must be with honour, honour

---

1. For an interesting systematic analysis of the precipitants of decolonization, see Strang 1990. Among other things, Strang concludes that decolonization diffused within empires (rather than within regions), with the number of prior decolonization events within an empire accelerating the number of subsequent such events within that empire.

defined by European standards of good government and democracy" (1960, 465).[2]
For the new "states" it was often not clear to whom sovereignty should be transferred. In some cases, of course, there were clearly defined nationalist movements and organizations, while in others there were not.

But even where nationalist organizations were clearly defined, the question of what should be transferred to whom was not always self-evident to the participants. Which nationalist movements were most representative? Of whom? Where were national boundaries to be drawn? The partition of the Indian subcontinent into India and Pakistan is the classic case in point, and as subsequent events revealed, even that partition was not to be permanent.

The Early Development Literature

If decolonization created problems for both the imperial powers and the colonies, it also revealed major lacunae in the study of comparative politics. The field's primary focus on the politics of the major European powers (i.e., the old states) had left it ill prepared for dealing with the phenomenon of the new states. Comparativists were not long in catching up, however. Although analysis of political development had been rare in 1950, by the early 1960s it was a growth stock. Indeed, just as the 1960s represented the peak of the formal decolonization process, they also represented the period in which several seminal studies appeared.

Most notably, 1960 saw the publication of *The Politics of the Developing Areas*, by Gabriel Almond and James Coleman. This collection of essays developed a functional approach to political development, which formed the foundation for the series Studies in Political Development (sponsored by the Committee on Comparative Politics of the Social Science Research Council) that appeared over

---

2. The British, in particular, with their emphasis on "indirect rule," appeared to attach great significance to the idea of preparing colonies for independence. As Schaffer has convincingly argued, however, the doctrine of preparation was used as a bargaining chip to postpone and even prevent independence and to try to ensure that nationalist movements were guided into nonrevolutionary channels. Thus, although "legislative councils" were created in many colonies, their functions were limited. For example, even by 1950 in Uganda only eight of the thirty-two members of the council were African, and only five of those were (indirectly) elected. According to the colonial governor of the time, "All I ask of all African members of the Council is that they will take the pains to acquaint themselves with the facts and will make it their business to pass on the facts in simple terms to as many as possible of their fellow Africans outside the Council chamber" (quoted by Schaffer 1965, 53).

the next several years.[3] Almond, Coleman, and their associates devoted a good deal of attention to the question of the capabilities of national political systems and to the issue of how political processes could be insulated from the wider social and economic environment. In particular, they argued that all political systems share a number of common properties, which they labeled input and output functional categories. On the input side, they identified four functions: political socialization and recruitment, interest articulation, interest aggregation, and political communication. On the output or capability side, they emphasized rule making, rule application, and rule adjudication. Almond, Coleman, and their associates did not suggest that all political systems are equally adept at fulfilling these functions, but they did specify success in fulfilling them as critical to political development.

In the same year, Seymour Martin Lipset's *Political Man* appeared. As part of his synthesis of the field of political sociology, Lipset devoted much attention to the factors that sustain stable democracies. Although a good portion of his analysis sought to explain the collapse of several European regimes after the First World War, Lipset also adduced evidence from the Latin American experience. As is well known, he concluded that economic development and the social changes that accompany it are an important prerequisite for stable democracy. But Lipset went further to suggest that both the timing of economic development and the pace at which democratic procedures were adopted are crucial to democratic performance.

Nineteen-sixty also saw the publication of *From Empire to Nation*, by Rupert Emerson. This was a study of the process of decolonization and the transfer of sovereignty from the imperial powers to the "local" elites in Asia and Africa. Emerson traced the diffusion of Western nationalist ideas throughout the world that followed Western imperial expansion and that, in an ironic twist, ultimately undermined that expansion. He also addressed the implications of the decolonization process for subsequent patterns of political development in the former colonies.

A rapid expansion of the literature occurred in the following years. Most notably, in 1961, Karl Deutsch published a paper, "Social Mobilization and Political Development," which focused on the relationships between the social change that accompanies industrialization and the viability of political institutions, and which developed

---

3. Almond (1987, 427–44) provides a useful summary of this series that places it in the context of other development studies of the time. For a more critical review of this series, see Holt and Turner 1975.

systematic empirical criteria for the measurement of social mobilization. An equally important paper by Clifford Geertz appeared in 1963, "The Integrative Revolution: Primordial Sentiments and Civil Politics in the new states." Geertz's analysis centered on the various social attachments—religious, ethnic, linguistic, and regional—that often compete with national attachments, an issue that has major implications for the study of *national* political development.

Building on these and other studies, Samuel Huntington's *Political Order in Changing Societies* explicitly addressed the question: what is so distinctive about *political* development? Huntington's answer is, first, that political development has to do with the creation of autonomous political *institutions*, and second, that to be effective, these institutions must be able to preserve *order* and *stability* (1968, vii). Some of the earlier literature had tended to equate political development with democratic development, which many critics regarded as ethnocentric.[4] To be fair, the nationalist ideology underlying decolonization was predicated on democratic ideas, as I have already indicated. In an attempt to avoid such an equation, Huntington sought to identify a generic form of political development: "The most important political distinction among countries concerns not their form of government but their degree of government" (1968, 1). Hence the overriding emphasis on order and stability.

The novelty of Huntington's analysis came from his explicit attention to political institutions. Where previous scholars had sometimes blurred the line between broad societal change and political development, Huntington did not. Instead, he defined the concept of political institutionalization as consisting of four components: adaptability, complexity, autonomy, and coherence. In this formulation, development becomes a matter of degree. The more that political institutions can be said to be adaptable, complex, autonomous, and coherent, the higher their capability. States with a relatively capable set of institutions enjoy a comparably high degree of government.

This conception makes a good deal of sense, and, indeed, Huntington's book is generally regarded as the most sweeping treatment of the issues involved in political development. In popular and scholarly discussions of political events, the idea of a political vacuum is often

---

4. Interestingly, the equation of democracy with political development continues. For example, an analysis of political capacity complains about an ethnocentrism in Western conceptions of political development, but then goes on to define political capacity as "the principle of periodic conditional mandate to govern and continuing obligation on the part of the elected deputies to be accountable for their professed policy and performance" (Somjee 1982, 17–18).

used (e.g., Zolberg 1966, chap. 1). At the time of decolonization after the Second World War, many observers argued that the withdrawal of the European powers would leave a political vacuum with no clear lines of political authority. Perhaps the best-known statements along these lines were made by Winston Churchill, who claimed in 1946 and 1947 that the Labour government was proceeding too rapidly with decolonization on the Indian subcontinent. Asserting that there were no representative political groups to whom power could be transferred, he forecast that the only possible outcome of "Operation Scuttle" would be chaos and carnage.[5]

More recently, we have witnessed events in Lebanon following the outbreak of its civil war in 1975. It has been painfully clear since 1975 that no central authority can claim control over Lebanon. Instead, a variety of groups supervise various pockets of the country and compete militarily with each other. This, of course, is the essence of a civil war: at the national level there is a political vacuum because no one faction or group (coalition) of factions has the strength to displace its opponents. A scaled-down version of the same phenomenon continues in Northern Ireland. To be sure, the Protestant majority has the capacity (with British military assistance) to exercise more control than does any group or set of groups in Lebanon, but that control is far from complete. There is thus less of a political vacuum in Northern Ireland, but political institutions remain sharply circumscribed in their capacity. Authorities in Northern Ireland lack the political means to make problems go away, and institutions there are fragile as a consequence.

Currently, we have been confronted with the breakup of the former Soviet Union and its former client states of Eastern Europe. The political viability of many of the new fifteen republics remains very much in doubt and the prospects for civil war centering especially on ethnic claims is high. This has been accompanied by fissiparous politics within such former states as Czechoslovakia and Yugoslavia. By highlighting the absence of widely recognized and accepted political authorities, such cases underscore the fragility of institutions.

Huntington's analysis is important because it explicitly draws attention to these issues. It reminds us that weaknesses in political capacity are not some simple function of socioeconomic development. The population of Lebanon is among the most literate in the

---

5. Portions of Churchill's statements in the British House of Commons are reproduced in Smith (1975). For a more recent argument that the rapidity of decolonization in Africa generated political vacuums in most new states on that continent, see Fieldhouse 1986.

Middle East, and prior to 1975, Beirut was a major commercial and banking center. Indeed, Lebanon was until 1975 widely regarded as one of the most viable democracies in the Third World. Similarly, Northern Ireland enjoys a relatively high degree of economic development when compared with worldwide patterns. Cases like these underscore the proposition that societal modernization does not necessarily induce political development.

Huntington's formulation also reminds us that the process of national political development is not irreversible. Political decay can and does occur: institutions collapse. In other words, political development is not synonymous with or a natural outcome of the social change that accompanies industrialization, as some of the more optimistic modernization studies had seemed to imply. At the same time, the prospect of political decay means that the process of development is likely to be rocky rather than smooth and is not one that proceeds in a simple linear manner.

But Huntington's argument went further than this. Industrialization, decolonization, and other processes have created unprecedented demands for mass political participation, which conflicts with the maintenance of order. If a choice has to be made between (*a*) extensive but unstructured and (*b*) restricted but organized forms of mass political activity, Huntington concluded that the second option is to be preferred because order is ultimately the more important commodity. Participation in a political vacuum lacks organization and continuity and therefore leads to chaos. As a result, mass participation is not to be encouraged where national political structures are weak.

Huntington summarized the argument with his simple and well-known equation that specifies political instability as a function of the *ratio* of political participation to political institutionalization (1968, 55). The ratio is central to the argument. Instability is not generated by low political capacity alone. Indeed, low levels of institutionalization may be associated with considerable stability *if* rates of mass participation are also low. As long as levels of participation and capacity are more or less in mutual accord, instability is unlikely, and Huntington labeled these cases (along with those where participation is lower than capacity) as "civic" polities.

The problematic cases are those where participation *exceeds* capacity, and it is with these cases—the "praetorian" polities—that Huntington was most concerned:

> It is virtually impossible to classify such states in terms of their form of government. We can have little doubt that the United

States is a constitutional democracy and the Soviet Union a Communist dictatorship. But what is the political system of Indonesia, of the Dominican Republic, South Vietnam, Burma, Nigeria, Ecuador, Argentina, Syria? These countries have held elections, but they are clearly not democracies in the sense in which Denmark or New Zealand is a democracy. They have had authoritarian rulers, but they are not effective dictatorships like the communist states. At other times, they have been dominated by highly personalistic, charismatic rulers or by military juntas. They are unclassifiable in terms of any particular government form because their distinguishing characteristic is the fragility and fleetingness of all forms of authority. Charismatic leader, military junta, parliamentary regime, populistic dictator follow each other in seemingly unpredictable and bewildering array. The patterns of political participation are neither stable nor institutionalized; they may oscillate violently between one form and another. . . . Such instability is the hallmark of a society lacking political community and where participation in politics has outrun the institutionalization of politics. (1968, 81–82)

And such instability is prima facie evidence of the lack of any semblance of political development.

Although Huntington was more explicit in his attention to political structures than had been his predecessors, the general argument was anticipated in earlier studies. For example, Deutsch (1961) had suggested that social mobilization in states that lack political capacity is likely to be destabilizing, and that the pace of mobilization should therefore be moderate. A similar emphasis is clear in Olson's (1963) argument that rapid growth causes severe social and economic dislocations that heighten inequalities and thereby lead to political instability. In formulations like these (see also Geertz 1963; Almond and Powell 1966), the problem with growth that is too rapid is that it is unlikely to be accompanied by a corresponding increase in political capacity. Expectations are raised beyond the capability of institutions to channel and process the demands that are thus created.

With twenty-twenty hindsight, and given the dismal economic performance over the past three decades of most African states in particular, one might ask why there was so much concern with rapid growth and the problems involved with mass participation. The answer lies in the comparisons these writers made between the old and the new states. The old states evolved over a long period during which political development occurred in rough if not necessarily smooth sequences. These sequences were not everywhere identical, of course, but in general national territories were consolidated (through military conquest and other means) and institutions began to emerge *before* there were demands for mass political participation. Moreover, the international environment in this century has provided a context within which new states must operate that is fundamentally different from the context within which the old states were forged.

It is important to remember that the nation-state in its modern form is a comparatively recent phenomenon of European origin (Bull 1979; Badie and Birnbaum 1983; Gellner 1983; Hobsbawm 1990). Some have seen it as "the legacy of Europe's now vanished ascendancy" (Bull and Watson 1984, 2), while Elie Kedourie went further in his claim that nationalism was "the European disease" (quoted in Geertz 1977, 249), although Anderson has traced the origins of nationalist sentiment to New World Creoles in the eighteenth century (1991, chap. 4).[6] While the origins of the contemporary international system can be traced back to fifteenth-century Europe, the modern state is less than two hundred years old in the case of Britain and less than half of that in the cases of Germany and Italy.[7] Many European "nations" are even newer (Connor 1990).[8] The principle that all states have equal rights and are in this sense sovereign is less than a century old—it achieved some currency with the formation of the League of Nations and was manifested rather more clearly with the creation of the United Nations after the Second World War (Bull and Watson 1984). The notion that all adults should be citizens draws on parallel principles of popular sovereignty that are equally recent (Bendix 1978).

It is thus not surprising that the experiences of the "new" states have diverged radically from the experiences of the "old" states. Most notably, the new states experienced simultaneously the process of nation and state building, the consolidation of political institutions, *and* demands for widespread political participation. In the words of Almond and Powell, "A major problem in the new nations today is the cumulative revolutions they must face. People demand participation, national unity, economic betterment, law and order—simultaneously and immediately" (1966, 39: see also Rustow 1967, 227–33; Linz

---

6. In its original usage, the term Creole refers to persons of European descent born in the Americas. For an interesting systematic analysis of the growth of nationalist symbols in eighteenth-century colonial North America, see Merritt 1966.

7. Indeed, current ideas of what the state involves are equally modern. The notion that the state is the polity originated in the eighteenth century, and attempts to distinguish the state from "society" came even later (Eckstein 1979).

8. I address the distinction between states and nations more fully in chapter 5.

1978, 7). As I have already noted, the nationalist, anticolonial struggle that created the new states relied heavily on a democratic ideology that emphasized representation, an ideology that ironically originated in the old imperial states. But this emphasis on representation itself gave rise to expectations of high rates of mass participation. In such a context, as it became clear that the history of the old states did not provide a clear blueprint that could be adopted wholesale by the new ones, the question of participation came to be seen as a particular problem for the new states.[9] Hence the concern with participation and the emphasis on order.

The Critique of Development Studies

In the 1970s, the whole notion of development came under attack, from two quarters. First, there was what we might call a populist critique that asserted that the very idea of *political development*—the term itself—introduced an unwarranted teleological element into the analysis. The use of the development label necessarily meant that one had an end in mind, and that end was typically assumed to involve Western institutions. In the words of one critic, "As a result of Western political and cultural hegemony, the ethnocentric notion has been encouraged that only the West's political development represents a valid model" (Kesselman 1973, 153). The idea of development in this view could be no more than one element of cold war ideology. Wiarda subsequently suggested that "such concepts as 'development' or 'modernization' must be re-recognized for what they are: metaphors . . . that have some importance in defining, outlining, or describing reality but that should not be mistaken for reality itself. Not only are they metaphorical devices with all the limitations for describing reality that implies, but they are *Western* metaphors which may or may not (most likely the latter) have relevance to the non-Western world" (Wiarda 1981; see also Janos 1986, 65–66; Somjee 1982, chap. 1).

Along with this, many objected to the emphasis in the development literature on political *order*. As I have already indicated, order is indeed central to Huntington's formulation, as well as to many others (e.g., Zolberg 1966). The objection was that order is not necessarily

---

9. For a good overall summary of the differences between the formation of the old and new states, see Rokkan 1975. Among other things, he noted that the new states have been subject to more pressures from major external centers, including economic pressures and demonstration effects centering on participation and economic redistribution. Further, he argued that this has occurred in a setting where national institutions have not been capable of absorbing or otherwise dealing with these pressures.

the sole value to be maximized. A tyrant may be able to maintain "order," but does that mean we should automatically side with the tyrant? What of those who, in their efforts to eliminate the tyranny, create disorder? For Huntington, disorder was praetorianism, something to be avoided. Without effective political institutions, mass mobilization simply generates crises of overparticipation. Indeed, Huntington went considerably further:

> The existence of political institutions . . . capable of giving substance to public interests distinguishes politically developed societies from underdeveloped ones. *It also distinguishes moral communities from amoral societies.* A government with a low level of institutionalization is not just a weak government; it is also a bad government. The function of government is to govern. A weak government, a government which lacks authority, fails to perform its function *and is immoral* in the same sense in which a corrupt judge, a cowardly soldier, or an ignorant teacher is immoral. (1968, 28; emphasis added)

Critics found this emphasis on order and the conflation of order with morality to be an overwhelming problem. As one put it, "Taking the viewpoint of those in authority has an inherent conservative bias since their *sine qua non* is preservation of their position of power" (Hopkins 1972, 275–76). Another wrote that "Order is imposed from above on the mass, who remain manipulable objects of government policy. . . . The absolute priority accorded to the achievement of political order has, among other things, led to a reconsideration [and denigration] of some of the other objectives emphasized in the past, such as economic development, social reform, and also of course (if more ambiguously) political democratization" (O'Brien 1972, 363, 365). Many found this a particular problem in view of the increasingly conspicuous American foreign policy failures in the Alliance for Progress and the Vietnam War (Smith 1985, 543).

A second broad attack on the development literature emanated from the dependency/world-systems approach that came to prominence in the 1970s. This attack centered on the proposition that nation-states do not exist in splendid isolation from one another but are instead embedded in a broader system. The broader system is one in which dominant classes in strong states exploit weaker, dependent states (see, e.g., Baran 1957; Furtado 1964; Frank 1969 for seminal statements). According to this argument, the development literature is misguided because it assumes that development is a process governed by indigenous forces. Instead, the more realistic approach was to document the ways in which dependent states are systematically *underdeveloped* by elites in strong ones. Dependency analysts sought to redirect emphasis toward the potentially deleterious effects of foreign capital on the economic performance of poor countries, and on the procedures by which institutions like transnational corporations may subvert the political autonomy of Third World states. The parallels with the neocolonial perspective on postindependence Africa are striking (see, e.g., Nkrumah 1965; Leys 1975)—both imply that the achievements of decolonization were more apparent than real.[10]

Expanding this argument further, the world-systems approach associated with Wallerstein (1974a, 1974b) emphasizes the importance of a capitalist world economy, within which core countries (the strong ones) exploit the periphery. In this setting, a few countries are located in an ambiguous and contradictory location labeled the semiperiphery (see, e.g., Chirot 1977). Central to the world-systems approach is the notion that the world economy is an integrated whole. Wallerstein argues that the world economy itself is the basic unit of analysis or "entity of comparison" (1974b), and that current political patterns can only be understood in the light of this system that began in the sixteenth century.

Such a perspective leaves little room for national autonomy. In fact, by suggesting that the world economy is the fundamental unit of analysis, it implies that there can be no such thing. It follows that the study of national political development is misguided because it is either irrelevant or limited in its scope. Nation-states are no more than "partial entities" or "non-systems" (Wallerstein 1974b). National po-

---

10. Note the implicit assumption in the dependency and neocolonial views that the colonies were profitable for the imperial powers. The evidence for this assumption is at best mixed. For example, despite London's insistence that the colonies be profitable and even though there was little economic justification for expansion, there was a significant expansion of the British Empire during the first three-quarters of the nineteenth century. This expansion seems to have been a function of (*a*) slow communications between colonial governors and London and (*b*) governors who, charged with maintaining order, annexed territory more or less continuously to control disorder beyond their borders (Galbraith 1968). Similarly, analyses of British imperial financial data from the half century before the First World War indicate that the profitability of that enterprise was far from uniform (Davis and Huttenback 1986). Fieldhouse (1986) concludes that the African colonies gained independence during the postwar economic boom, the period in which they were economically *more* dynamic than they had been before. However, this profitability of the colonies as markets was offset by the real or anticipated economic and military costs of maintaining colonial rule. For a useful survey of theories of imperialism and their relation to the ideas underlying neocolonialism and underdevelopment, see Mommsen 1980. And for an alternative view that casts imperialism as the outcome of the competition of sovereignties intrinsic to the anarchy of the international political system, see Cohen 1973.

litical institutions cannot even potentially be autonomous, for example, in a world where dominant groups in the core and periphery are linked to each other in unholy ways. Thus, it was not surprising that by the middle 1970s, Wallerstein (1976) asserted that an obituary for the entire "modernization" approach was in order.

Within the last decade, there has been growing disenchantment with this formulation. First, several have argued that Wallerstein's interpretation of European history since the sixteenth century is critically flawed (e.g., Skocpol 1977; Gourevitch 1978; Smith 1979; Zolberg 1981; O'Brien 1982). Chirot (1985) has gone so far as to suggest that the rise of the West is more accurately explained in Weberian terms.[11] At the same time, it is hard to find convincing systematic evidence that the dependency/world-systems argument accounts for national rates of economic growth or for economic inequality within nations in the contemporary world (Philip 1990). For example, investment by transnational corporations does not inhibit economic growth in Third World nations (Jackman 1982; Firebaugh 1992). Nor does the available evidence provide corroboration for the view that non-core status in the world economy increases economic inequality in the states of concern (Bollen and Jackman 1985).[12]

Second, within the dependency/world-systems school, the idea that nation-states have at least some room for maneuver has begun to find favor. Thus, several scholars have emphasized the possibility of "dependent development," according to which many countries, especially those in the semiperiphery, can experience considerable economic development (e.g., Cardoso and Faletto 1978; Evans 1979; Haggard 1990). The dependent development argument still emphasizes a role for foreign capital and transnational corporations, but it

---

11. Indeed, his more recent work offers a striking example of dissatisfaction with Wallerstein's argument. Compare Chirot (1977), which was predicated on the world-systems view, with Chirot (1986), which is not. Similarly, a recent essay by Tiryakian (1991) is titled "Modernization: Exhumetur in Pace," centers on Wallerstein's (1976) "Modernization: Requiescat in Pace."

12. Some observers are unmoved by the contemporary systematic evidence. Thus, Smith suggests that "piddling criticism of the dependency school is a waste of time. A perspective as supple and complex as that of *dependencia* will have no trouble explaining away as irrelevant or as understandable in its own terms, relatively minor points about change in the core, the periphery, or the international system, or demands that its claims be made quantifiable and so readily testable" (1985, 557; for a similar view, see Valenzuela and Valenzuela 1978, 545). This suggestion would be more forceful if suppleness and complexity were the marks of a good theory, but they are not; the danger is that by trying to account for everything, the dependency school explains nothing. If, as Smith and others suggest, the dependency argument can "explain away" all anomalies, then it has no empirical implications for contemporary political patterns and becomes no more than an article of faith (for further discussion on this point, see Jackman 1985, 177–78).

suggests that this role can be modified considerably by actors and institutions in noncore states. It even submits that there may be genuine economic growth outside the core. Some may not regard these ideas as major modifications of the world-systems approach. For example, Smith contends that recognition of the importance of local factors, of a role for the state, and of real economic growth does not involve a rejection of the dependency approach. He concludes instead that "dependency writing is not a simple-minded affair. It is no surprise, therefore, to learn that it has already generated concepts that enable it to pull back into line any potentially fissiparous tendencies leading toward apostasy . . . .Like other coherent *ideologies*, the dependency perspective has self-protecting concepts to deflect all manner of threat and preserve the *doctrine's* integrity" (Smith 1985, 555–56; emphasis added).

But this will not do. What made the original dependency/world-systems argument attractive was its coherence and consistency. Once we accept the three modifications listed above, the whole argument loses that very coherence and becomes as eclectic as the approach it seeks to displace. Indeed, acceptance of the three modifications means that the whole dependency argument has altogether lost its theoretical distinctiveness. If, on the other hand, the argument is to be defended as ideology or doctrine, then it represents no more than a "conversion phenomenon" (Almond 1987, 450; for similar conclusions, see Staniland 1985, 117–47; Packenham 1992) whose validity can only be judged by appeal to theological, rather than temporal, criteria. And that is a task from which social scientists should gladly absolve themselves.

The idea that *states* might be important is now itself the new orthodoxy (see, e.g., Krasner 1984; Benjamin and Elkin 1985; Evans, Rueschemeyer, and Skocpol 1985; and Nordlinger 1987).[13] Not all countries have strong states, of course, but where the state is strong, scholars are increasingly of the view that it plays a major role, even in a world of superpowers and transnational corporations.

Despite the resurgence of interest in the idea of state strength over the past decade, the notion itself remains poorly defined. To be sure, strong states are said to be able to exercise more control over the environment. Such states are in this sense more powerful than weak ones. This suggests that state strength has to do with political capacity or capability—that is, that the current concern with states actually

---

13. According to Binder (1986, 15), this new orthodoxy can be traced back to Tilly (1975).

reflects a renewed interest in the issues that have motivated the study of national political development. Beyond this, considerable confusion remains over exactly what constitutes a state. As I will show in chapter 3, some treatments imply that it is the bureaucracy, others suggest that it includes political figures (like "heads of state" and their entourages), and still others seem to equate the state with institutions or even national-level policies. The variety of conceptions of the state is also reminiscent of earlier attempts to distinguish, in turn, the political community, the regime, and the authorities (Easton 1965). Those earlier contrasts proved difficult to sustain for many reasons, the most notable of which is that their empirical referents were ambiguous. I believe the recent attempts to delineate exactly what constitutes a state will suffer the same fate, and for the same reason.

The Critique of Development Reconsidered

What are we to make of the evolution in the study of national political development over the past thirty years or so? The common answer to this question is that the confidence that pervaded the field in the 1960s disappeared in the 1970s and that the analysis of development was in a state of crisis toward the end of the 1970s (e.g., Hermassi 1978; Smith 1985). Others have argued that the studies of the 1960s constitute first-generation analyses of development, that the dependency perspective represents a second generation, while the new emphasis on states reflects a third-generation approach that seeks to move beyond the earlier debates (e.g., Kohli 1986). In other words, many believe that the general framework that informed the studies of the 1960s has been replaced by a completely new orientation. As one writer phrases it,

> Despite their diversity these [newer state-oriented] studies do pose a challenge to the analytic traditions that have dominated political science in the United States. They see a different political universe, ask different questions, investigate different empirical phenomena, and offer different kinds of answers. (Krasner 1984, 226)

This claim often involves the invocation of Kuhn's (1962) argument that "normal science" is carried out within the context of a "paradigm"—that is, a framework that defines the critical issues. Scientific crises occur when new phenomena are observed that cannot be explained by normal science within the prevailing paradigm. The result is a major paradigm shift. Some have applied Kuhn's idea to the study of political development and suggested that the paradigm of the 1960s was found to be untenable in the 1970s, and that the most recent studies represent a notable paradigm change. Thus, Skocpol writes that "a paradigmatic shift seems to be underway in the macroscopic social sciences, a shift that involves a fundamental rethinking of the role of states in relation to economies and societies" (Skocpol 1985, 7; see also Chilcote 1981; Krasner 1984; Janos 1986).[14]

However, the brief overview of the study of political development since the Second World War that I have provided in this chapter leads me to the quite different conclusion that the wheel has come almost full circle. Although it is seldom acknowledged, current analyses of the state have much in common with earlier treatments of political development that flourished in the 1960s (for a similar conclusion, see Binder 1986). In particular, the emphasis on "state-centered" rather than "society-centered" explanations has a striking resemblance to Huntington's stress on the significance of autonomous political institutions.[15] Consider the evidence.

Proponents of the statist approach argue that the older development studies ignored the state completely and attribute this to a methodological "individualism" thought to inhere in the "behavioral" approach to politics (e.g., Krasner 1984; Skocpol 1985). However, a reading of the development studies in question is not kind to this argument. Central figures in those studies like Emerson (1960), Geertz (1963), and Pye (1966, chap. 1) were explicitly concerned with questions of the state. And Huntington's focus on national political institutions represents a clear implicit focus on states. The suggestion that studies in this genre fell prey to a methodological individualism is also wanting: concepts like political capacity, social mobilization, and ethnic diversity refer to properties of societies and nation-states, not of individuals.

The obvious retort to the above is that such historiographical

---

14. Skocpol goes on to suggest that this new paradigm does not in itself constitute a new, all-encompassing theory:

> The overall aim of this exercise is not to offer any new general theory of the state or of states and social structures. For the present, at least, no such thing may be desirable . . . . Rather, my hope is to present and illustrate a conceptual frame of reference, along with some middle-range issues and hypotheses that might inform future research on states and social structures. (1985, 8)

15. Huntington's analysis centers primarily on the output or impact of political institutions. Other analysts like Almond and Coleman (1960) were equally concerned with the impact of other political, social, and economic factors on institutions. The distinction here is the same as that between state-centered analyses and analyses that center on state-society relations.

considerations ignore the possibility that the new state-oriented studies address fresh issues that were ignored in the earlier literature. However, the record is not clear-cut on this count. First, the difficulties encountered in earlier attempts to define political development have striking parallels in the newer literature. Although the term state *strength* is commonly used, it still awaits clear definition and delineation. Indeed, it remains unclear from writing on the topic over the last decade exactly what constitutes a state. For example, the prominent collection of essays titled *Bringing the State Back In* devotes scant attention to the issue. The only definition of the state that is offered is Max Weber's: "We consider the state to be a set of organizations vested with the authority to make binding decisions for people and organizations located in a particular territory and to implement these decisions using, if necessary, force" (Rueschemeyer and Evans 1985, 46–47). The same usage is proposed by Hall and Ikenberry (1989, 1–2). To be sure, Weber's definition does offer a starting point. However, it also leaves several key issues unresolved. And it is also useful to recall that the earlier studies of development themselves began with Weber's definition of the state (see, e.g., Almond and Coleman 1960, 5).[16]

Second, those studies that do attempt to define the state appear to cover little new ground. Consider Evans's well-known analysis of dependent development in Brazil, which places special weight on the role of the state (1979). Although Evans does not clearly define the term, it appears that he intends the state to refer to national political capacity. For example,

> The capacity of the state apparatus is . . . important. States must have control over a sufficient segment of the surplus so that they can offer incentives as well as support their own activities. Finally, technical expertise and control over information play a role. (1979, 44)

This appears to be perfectly consistent with Huntington's criteria for political institutionalization, although the latter are nowhere cited. Huntington views a strong national political apparatus as a mechanism

---

16. In another essay, Almond noted that the idea of "legitimate physical coercion" was central to conceptions of the political system:

Common to all of these definitions is their association of politics with legitimate heavy sanctions . . . . This is not the same thing as saying that the political system is solely concerned with force, violence, or compulsion, but only that its relation to coercion is its distinctive quality . . . . The political system is not the only system that makes rules and enforces them, but its rules and enforcements go 'all the way' in compelling obedience or performance. (Almond 1965, 191–92).

that generates order and control; in a parallel manner, Evans regards it as an instrument that engenders accumulation and control.[17]

It is interesting that a more precise definition of the modern state had already appeared. According to Finer (1975, 85–86), the contemporary nation state has the following characteristics:

1. It is a territorially defined population recognizing a "common paramount organ of government."
2. This organ of government is subserved by the civil and military services, which carry out and enforce decisions.
3. The state is regarded as sovereign by other states.
4. The nation state forms a "community of feeling . . . based on self-consciousness of a common *nationality*."
5. The population of the state actually forms a community "in the sense that its members mutually distribute and share duties and benefits."

Finer's definition is much more specific than recent treatments. Even so, the parallels between his approach and the earlier definitions of development are striking, in which sense the wheel has indeed come full circle. This outcome led Easton to conclude that the recent interest in the state "is well on its way to becoming a conceptual fad, if not buzz word, that gives a sense of legitimacy and in-ness but not necessarily much else to social research" (1981, 306).

If the wheel has come almost full circle since the 1960s in terms of the substantive focus of recent studies, there is another important sense in which the wheel has traced out a larger circle that returns us to the analytic traditions in favor until the 1950s. As I indicated at the outset, the literature on political development after 1960 was in good measure a reaction against the configurative approach that it replaced. Where the configurative approach had eschewed generalization, those studying political development encouraged it.

Over the past fifteen years or so there has been a resurgence of historicism, where each country is seen as having a unique political experience that is a specific product of its period. For example, according to Valenzuela and Valenzuela,

> The dependency perspective is primarily a historical model with no claim to "universal validity." This is why it has paid less

---

17. In a sense, of course, some of the new statism is an explicit attempt to return to an earlier analytic tradition. But titles like *Bringing the State Back In* are intended to redirect our attention to the substantive traditions in vogue until the 1950s, *not* the analyses that

attention to the formulation of precise theoretical constructs, such as those found in the modernization literature, and more attention to the specification of historical phases which are an inherent part of the framework. (1978, 546)

This statement is very much in keeping with the editorial orientation of the *Review*, an orientation that "recognizes the primacy of analyses of economics over long historical time and large space, the holism of the social-historical process, and the transitory (heuristic) nature of theories."[18] While their substantive concerns are somewhat different, Evans, Rueschemeyer, and Skocpol also stress that one of their major conclusions is that "issues of 'state strength' . . . can be fruitfully broached only via thoroughly dialectical analyses that allow for non-zero-sum processes and complex interactions between state and society" (1985, 355). Approvingly summarizing what he takes to be the historicist position, Chilcote goes even further:

There are a variety of views, not a single view, of the objective world. Distinctive perspectives of the world are found from one epoch or culture to another. Truth is relative to the world view characteristic of the epoch or culture to which it belongs. Thus, world views are temporal and relative, not absolute. (1981, 69)

Most recently, Ragin has proposed that we abandon "variable-oriented" comparative work and adopt instead a "case-oriented" approach that emphasizes the ways in which "different features or causes fit together in individual cases" (Ragin 1992, 5). The claimed advantage of the case-oriented strategy is that "the goal of appreciating complexity is given precedence over the goal of achieving generality. Invariant statements relevant to more narrowly defined categories of phenomena, for example, are preferred to probabilistic statements relevant to broadly defined categories" (Ragin 1987, 54).

It is difficult to see how, with their stress on complexity, inductivism, determinism, and relativism, such statements can lead to (or are even compatible with) useful empirical generalizations (see also Gellner 1985; Kiser and Hechter 1991; Lieberson 1991).[19] Thirty

---

appeared in the 1960s. And as I shall argue below, to the extent that much of the new statism urges us to return to the historicist methodological traditions common until the 1950s, it is regressive.

18. This statement appears in the front of each issue of *Review*, the quarterly journal of the Fernand Braudel Center established by Wallerstein.

19. In a variant on this theme, Somjee (1986) has proposed that future work in the field requires a combination of relativism and universalism. Although some may find the

years ago, Eckstein (1963) urged the need for simplification in the study of comparative politics. Today, his point applies with equal force.[20]

If historicism is a problem with the new orthodoxy, so too is the repeated suggestion that there has of late been a paradigm shift. To be sure, there has been a change in language, insofar as the referent is now state strength where it was once political development. But this reflects little more than a shift in fashion, a change in language without a change in substance. Like the earlier literature, current studies draw their inspiration from Weber, but there is no indication that these studies are drawing us any closer to a resolution of the definitional problems confronted in earlier analyses. Despite assertions that the early development studies were too rigorous and scientific for their own good (e.g., Valenzuela and Valenzuela 1978), the principal weakness of those studies lies in the fact that many of their major constructs (such as output functions and institutional autonomy) were cast in such abstract terms that empirical referents were unclear.

While it may be cathartic to cast the initial studies as evidence of a "confident reductionism and bombastic developmentalism that prevailed in postwar political science" (Tilly 1986, 116), the implication that recent studies represent a paradigmatic shift is vastly exaggerated. Such a shift assumes the existence of a body of literature that can successfully account for one set of empirical phenomena but that cannot account for another. Given the slippery nature of many of their key concepts, the linkage between theory and empirical experience was often loose in the early development studies. But it is important to remember that these studies were charting new courses in unfamiliar territory. Further, they did constitute a serious attempt to make general

---

implicit compromise in this proposal appealing on the grounds that all positions are somewhat reasonable and thus that the truth is to be found somewhat in between them, any such combination is impossible and degenerates into an adoption of a relativist position. And the denial of the feasibility of empirical generalization is itself, of course, an empirical generalization. For a useful discussion of the issues at stake here, see Gellner 1985, especially chapter 3.

20. It also applies to more recent writing by some of the development theorists. For example, Huntington has urged that we direct attention to different "cultures of development." He acknowledges that the concept of culture is "tricky, [that] it is, in some sense a residual category" (1987, 22–23). Nonetheless, he goes on to urge that different "development models" may apply in different cultures. For example,

The need is to generalize from the East Asian experience and derive from that experience a developmental model of a society that is authoritarian, stable, economically dynamic, and equitable in its income distribution. The South American model might be one of class stratification, inequality, moderate growth, political conflict, economic penetration, and alternating democratic and authoritarian regimes. (1987, 25–26)

statements. What is striking about the more recent literature is that its key concepts (most notably, the "state") are *at least* as slippery. Combined with its retreat to historicism, it is not at all clear what kind of useful research program can be generated from this conceptual vagueness.

Instead, the popularity of different approaches to development appears to have waxed and waned with ideological currents that are largely independent of any empirical considerations. As Geddes has recently pointed out,

> When a theory fits with preconceptions and seems highly plausible, scholars feel less motivated to go to what seems like unnecessary trouble to dig up facts to confirm it and, as a result, fail to unearth the facts that would disconfirm it. Ideological predilections have exercised an especially powerful effect on theories in comparative politics because of the absence of subfield norms requiring the rigorous testing of knowledge claims. Where there are no well-established norms for selecting the evidence with which to test speculations and when no value attaches to replicating earlier studies, no countervailing force impedes the natural influence of ideology over the choice of which theories to believe. (1991, 56)

This is hardly the stuff of paradigm shifts.[21]

Laying to one side the issues of historicism and paradigms, the revived emphasis on the state does at least remind us of the importance of the nation-state as a unit of analysis. As I have already indicated, the number of nation-states has proliferated in the last forty years, and nationalism is currently the dominant political ideology. The new states have persisted as geographic entities despite chronically weak institutions in many cases, despite boundaries that are often contrived and artificial, and despite the prominence of secession-

---

21. Kuhn's argument has assumed the status of the received view in many quarters, even though the relevance of his argument to the social sciences is ambiguous by Kuhn's own admission. Indeed, Kuhn's interpretation seems to provide the inspiration for the resurgence of historicism and much of the muddled relativism in recent analyses. There are also those who believe that if a piece of research can be cast as normal science, then it can be dismissed, because only pedants would engage in such activity. However, it is important to understand that the acceptance by many social scientists of Kuhn's argument stands in sharp contrast to the widespread criticism of his interpretation by those in his own field, both as history of science and as philosophy of science (see, e.g., Suppe 1977; Lakatos 1978, especially chaps. 1 and 2; Putnam 1981, especially chap. 5). The continuing fascination with Kuhn's argument in the social sciences has hindered substantive analysis because it has too often been used as a substitute for analysis.

ist movements in several instances. And recent events in the former
Soviet Union and its satellites represent a return to national political
units that were more explicitly defined in an earlier era.

States are clearly the basic unit of analysis in the contemporary
international order (see, e.g., Nettl 1968). It is equally apparent that
this international system is a conservative order whose actors have
a major stake in maintaining the status quo, that is, in conserving
the system of nation-states as juridical entities (Young 1976, 81–83;
Jackson and Rosberg 1982a; Jackson 1990). The preservation of this
system is legitimized by the doctrine of the right to national self-
determination and by the principle of noninterference in the "internal"
affairs of other states. Nation-states have thus come to be defined
uniformly in terms of international law, and in this sense they constitute the fundamental focus of this book. But this definitional uniformity masks considerable variation in the political capacity of modern
nation-states. This is the variation that I seek to identify.[22]

The Purpose of This Book

My goal in this book is to clarify some of the issues involved in what
constitutes national political capacity. The question is a pressing one.
Many states remain weak and ineffective. Others that may not have
appeared so weak have collapsed—witness the Iranian revolution, the
retreats from military rule in some of Latin America, Lebanon, and of
course the remnants of the former Soviet Union and its east European
clients. Although there is some confusion over what political capacity
involves, it is rather easy to have an intuitive sense of the term from
those instances when it is absent—that is, from political vacuums. We
need to move beyond this to a positive understanding of what political
development entails.

My fundamental argument is that institutions are critical to political capacity. Capacity itself is a matter of degree, but to be reasonably
effective, institutions must have a moderate aura of legitimacy. Much
can be learned from the earlier studies of development. While many

---

22. By taking the nation-state as my unit of analysis, I am treating it as the basic case.
Some question this approach on the grounds that the idea of a case is inherently problematic
and fraught with ambiguity (see, e.g., Ragin 1992, and many of the papers he introduces),
but such claims simply obfuscate the issues. Given the dominance of nationalist doctrines in
contemporary politics discussed earlier in this chapter, the nation-state is the major analytic
unit or case with which I am concerned (see, e.g., Kuznets 1951; Jackman 1985). These
cases possess many attributes (I address those that impinge on political capacity) that vary
across different states and, over time, within individual states.

of those studies raised at least as many issues as they resolved, it is important that the wheel not be reinvented too many times. As will become clear, political capacity involves more than simple change. I use the terms capacity, capability, and development more or less interchangeably. Since my focus is on national political capacity, my analysis also deals directly with some of the questions raised in recent writings on state strength. The issue this book addresses is how do we know when a credible national political infrastructure is in place? Let us start at the beginning and consider what is distinctive about political life.

CHAPTER 2

What Is Political Capacity?

The principal foundations that all states have, new ones as well as old
or mixed, are good laws and good arms. And . . . there cannot be
good laws where there are not good arms.

— Niccolo Machiavelli, *The Prince*

Permit me to observe that the use of force alone is but *temporary*. It
may subdue for a moment, but it does not remove the necessity of
subduing again; and a nation is not governed, which is perpetually to
be conquered.

My next objection is its *uncertainty*. Terror is not always the
effect of force, and an armament is not a victory. If you do not
succeed, you are without resource; for, conciliation failing, force remains, but, force failing, no further hope of reconciliation is left.
Power and authority are sometimes bought by kindness, but they can
never be begged as alms by an impoverished and defeated violence.

— Edmund Burke, *On Conciliation with the Colonies*

Power is not strongest when it uses violence, but weakest. It is strongest when it employs the instruments of substitution and counter attrac-
tion, of allurement, of participation rather than of exclusion, of education rather than of annihilation. Rape is not an evidence of irresistible
power in politics or in sex.

— Charles E. Merriam, *Political Power*

Politically speaking, it is insufficient to say that power and violence
are not the same. Power and violence are opposites; where the one
rules absolutely, the other is absent.

— Hannah Arendt, *On Violence*

Before we proceed to the subject of capacity, we need to explicit about
what we mean by politics. The point may seem rudimentary, but there
remains a good deal of confusion over what politics entails. As will
become clear, the manner in which we define what is political has an
immediate bearing on what is involved in political capacity.

The Relational Nature of Political Power

A good place to begin is with Harold Lasswell's famous text *Politics:
Who Gets What, When, and How?* Lasswell's title reminds us that

politics has to do with the allocation and distribution of goods. We can add to this David Easton's (1957) emphasis on the idea that politics involves the *authoritative* allocation of values. Together, these ideas suggest that politics always involves *conflict* over the distribution of valued goods.

Why is conflict so central? Because we are concerned with the distribution of *valued* goods—income, power, prestige, honor, and the like—over which individuals and groups compete. These commodities have no intrinsic value, and in this sense should not be regarded as possessive, under the exclusive control of one actor. Instead, they are inherently *relational*. That is, their significance stems wholly from the context within which they are expressed, and that context requires at least two actors in a dyadic relationship (this of course is the most rudimentary case). Moreover, these commodities cannot be spread around equally and retain their social value. For example, if everyone has the same prestige, the concept itself loses meaning. One group cannot enjoy high prestige without the existence of other groups of lower prestige. The same is true of income, which acquires its meaning from what it generates: the ability of one group or individual to purchase the labor or product of others. If everyone has the same income, even a very "high" one, the social significance of income disappears. Alternatively, personal income has no meaning for that mythical soul stranded alone on an island—the idea of income assumes consequence only within the context of a wider economy, where it provides the ability to purchase goods and services generated by others.

All that I mean to suggest here is that valued goods should not be regarded as simply possessive. The latter term refers to commodities whose meaning is intrinsic, independently of any context. The possession of such commodities by one individual or group has no implications for or relevance to other people. By contrast, valued goods are relational in that they derive their social and political meaning from the context in which they are located. The value of such commodities stems from the fact that they are unequally distributed across individuals and groups.

That social and political inequalities are fundamentally relational rather than possessive is underscored by Edward Bellamy's parable of the "prodigious coach which the masses of humanity were harnessed to and dragged toilsomely along a very hilly and sandy road." Those fortunate passengers atop the coach frequently express commiseration for their brothers and sisters who toil in the harness, especially when the road gets steep.

It must in truth be admitted that the main effect of the spectacle of the misery of the toilers at the rope was to enhance the passengers' sense of the value of their seats upon the coach, and to cause them to hold on to them more desperately than before. If the passengers could only have felt assured that neither they nor their friends would ever fall from the top, it is probable that, beyond contributing to the funds for liniments and bandages, they would have troubled themselves extremely little about those who had dragged the coach. (Bellamy 1887, 12)

In other words, the seats on the top of the coach are not possessive commodities: their value is wholly determined by the presence of those who labor below.

Once we allow that the valued goods central to politics are inherently relational, it becomes apparent why political life involves a "mobilization of bias," to use Schattschneider's (1960) term. One does not have to adopt the extreme position that political conflict is zero-sum to recognize that this conflict necessarily benefits some people or groups at the expense of others. Were this not the case, then we could not say that politics centers on the distribution of valued goods, because those goods would have no value.

The point becomes clearer when we understand that one of the major activities of states is to manipulate the incomes of their citizens. States have a large repertoire of instruments at their disposal to engage in such manipulation that includes taxation, "public" spending, and regulation. If these instruments are used to maintain the status quo, then it is obvious that political conflict benefits those who profit from the status quo at the expense of those who do not. If, on the other hand, the state chooses to alter the status quo by investing in sector A rather than sector B, that choice favors A at the expense of B. For example, the urban-centered policies of most African governments have hurt agricultural interests, and there is every reason to believe that the agricultural sector would have suffered even had its income remained constant in absolute, nominal terms (which is the best-case and highly implausible outcome—see Bates 1981), because of the decline in its purchasing power *relative to* other sectors.[1]

In addition, we see that politics involves the *authoritative* allocation of goods. Another way of stating this is as follows: politics

---

1. This argument is inconsistent with the criterion of Pareto optimality, which asserts that outcomes can be generated that increase the utility of one or more persons without decreasing the utility of others. The problem with this criterion is that it treats utility as possessive rather than relational.

involves the *resolution* of conflict. I do not mean to convey the impression that the conflict is somehow resolved in the best way. But I do mean to suggest that the conflict is managed or contained.[2] Who does the containing?

Obviously, to assert that conflict is managed is to imply a rough distinction between those who manage and those who are managed, where the former are (or attempt to be) the "authorities." In other words, politics involves power differentials. I have already indicated that, like any other valued commodity, power is necessarily relational (rather than possessive) and unequally distributed. But what does power involve?

In addressing this question, the analysis by Bachrach and Baratz (1970, chap. 2) remains very helpful.[3] These writers make a distinction between four basic concepts: power, authority, influence, and force.

For Bachrach and Baratz, power has three fundamental characteristics. First, it necessarily involves some conflict of interest or values between two or more persons or groups (A and B). Second, A exercises power over B to the extent that B complies with A's wishes. Third, B's compliance with A's demands is due to B's fear of the effective sanctions threatened (explicitly or implicitly) by A. Bachrach and Baratz insist that while each of these components is necessary to the exercise of power, a power relationship can only be said to exist when these three conditions are met simultaneously.

Unlike power, an authority relationship does not necessarily involve any conflict of values. In such a relationship, B does comply with what A wants because B regards A's request as reasonable. The source of this compliance does not involve overt conflict—instead, in an authority relationship B *shares* A's values. The example given by Bachrach and Baratz involves soldiers who obey their commanding officers because they view specific orders and the general line of command that gives rise to those orders as reasonable. As I will indicate below, such a relationship involves conditioning.

Influence lies between power and authority. Unlike authority, it involves a conflict of values along with compliance by B with A's wishes. However, the source of influence is not fear of sanctions. Instead, B may comply with A out of some sense of esteem for A, or because A has something that B wants.

---

2. For a similar definition of politics, see Bueno de Mesquita, Newman, and Rabushka 1985, chapter 1.

3. Although intended as a critique of earlier treatments of power like Dahl's (1961), the analysis offered by Bachrach and Baratz is in many ways an extension of such treatments.

The distinctions offered by Bachrach and Baratz are useful because they show why power is necessarily relational. It is impossible for a prisoner in solitary confinement to exercise power over other persons at midnight. At the same time, it is evident that authority and influence are no more than special cases of power.

The idea that authority does not involve conflict, after all, is fundamentally inconsistent with the idea that politics centers on the management of conflict. The key here, I believe, is the distinction between interests and values. That there is no openly expressed conflict of values does not mean there is no conflict of interests. Instead, it simply indicates that B has been conditioned or socialized to *believe* that values, and therefore interests, are shared. As Lukes puts it,

> Is it not the supreme and most insidious exercise of power to prevent people, to whatever degree, from having grievances by shaping their perceptions, cognitions and preferences in such a way that they accept their role in the existing order of things, either because they can see or imagine no alternative to it, or because they see it as natural and unchangeable, or because they value it as divinely ordained and beneficial? To assume that the absence of grievance equals genuine consensus is simply to rule out the possibility of false or manipulated consensus by definitional fiat. (Lukes 1974, 24)

Whether insidious or not, the phenomenon to which Lukes refers does involve the exercise of power. The general point is that the exercise of power does not require the overt presence of conflict.[4]

Consider Bachrach and Baratz's example again, with the assumption that a widespread common interest is to maximize one's longevity. In this setting, a general's command to engage the enemy may clearly be inconsistent with soldiers' best interests even if the general can induce compliance by appeal to shared and internalized values involving such criteria as honor and valor. And for that small minority of soldiers who somehow fail to internalize the appropriate norms, it

---

4. My distinction between interests and values should not be taken as a ringing endorsement of the general idea of false consciousness, as the latter term is generally used. Instead, I am simply suggesting that values are always situationally defined by conditioning and socializing mechanisms that invoke one or more ideologies. And those ideologies involve arbitrary boundaries. Although nationalism is the dominant political ideology of our time, there is no logical reason for individuals to endorse nationalist sentiments more than sentiments deriving from other group memberships. Political socialization is effective to the extent that those involved come to regard interests and values as isomorphic. For a useful discussion of political interests, see Connally 1972.

is useful to recall that no army is without disciplinary procedures, including courts martial.

Similarly, to suggest that in a relationship of influence, compliance is not induced by the fear of sanctions is implicitly to acknowledge a role for conditioning or socialization. And conditioning can involve positive material and moral incentives, carrots rather than sticks. But the lack of an explicit fear of negative sanctions does not preclude a tacit understanding by B that A has the physical ability to inflict them. Obviously, A's task is much less formidable when sanctions are not explicitly invoked, but the distinction between influence and power is difficult to sustain in any realistic application. I conclude that the central phenomenon involved here is power.

This conclusion is consistent with more recent discussions. Consider Crozier and Friedberg:

> [Power] can develop only through *exchange* among the actors involved in a given relation. To the extent that every relation between two parties presupposes exchange and reciprocal adaptation between them, power is indissolubly linked to negotiation: *it is a relation of exchange, therefore of negotiation*, in which at least two persons are involved. (1980, 30–31)

The same authors go on to observe that while power involves reciprocal relations, the reciprocity itself is unbalanced. In other words, power entails dependent rather than interdependent relations.

Bachrach and Baratz's most useful distinction is between power and force. Like power, force involves a conflict of values, and therefore, of interests. Unlike power, force does not induce compliance: the exercise of force is instead an admission that compliance cannot be induced by other noncoercive means. Those who use force are indeed attempting to achieve their goals in the face of noncompliance, as Burke recognized in his discussion of the American colonies. Additionally, force does not always generate compliance because the intended victim (B) may not fear A's sanctions. Why is this the case? Force is not necessarily relational, but it is always possessive. That A has the wherewithal to inflict physical pain on B does not in itself imply that there is a relationship between the two. Hence Merriam's conclusion that rape is not an evidence of power.[5]

---

5. The distinction between power and force parallels the contrast between "infrastructural power" and "despotic power" drawn by Mann (1986). While Mann labels these two forms as independent dimensions of state power, despotic power simply consists of the ability to employ force ("Great despotic power can be 'measured' most vividly in the ability

Bachrach and Baratz conclude that it is the *threat* of sanctions that is critical to power relations: "the actual application of sanctions is an admission of defeat by the would-be wielder of power" (1970, 28). Indeed, resort to force may result in a loss of power by A. For example, B may conclude that the severity of the sanctions was originally overestimated—the paper tiger phenomenon. It follows that, as a would-be wielder of power, A would rather not invoke threatened sanctions.[6] That the threat be available is critical; that the threat be invoked is highly undesirable.[7]

Although these considerations may seem elementary, they have several implications for the question of national political capacity. First, the distinction between power and force is too often blurred. Goodin, for example, asserts that the exercise of power can assume a variety of forms: "You might get a man's money either by taking it forcibly from him or by persuading him to give it to you; you might change a legislative outcome by buying off legislators or by assassinating them or by voting them out of office" (1980, 3). The implicit identities here are baseless, however, since these scenarios do not all involve the exercise of power. Nor does Goodin's subsequent distinction between legitimate and illegitimate power (see also Beetham 1991) salvage the issue.

In an analogous manner, Gurr suggests that rulers have a variety of available choices to advance their claims to authority, ranging from

---

of all these Red Queens to shout 'off with his head' and have their whim gratified without further ado—provided the person is at hand" [1986, 113]). For the reasons already set forth, labeling this phenomenon as a form of power obscures more than it clarifies.

6. Thus, in 1942, Army Chief of Staff George C. Marshall wrote all commanding generals that the growing use of courts martial in the citizen army was unsatisfactory and prima facie evidence of poor discipline: "Reliance on courts-martial to enforce discipline indicates lack of leadership and faulty command." Generals were instructed to use courts martial only when all other avenues had failed (quoted in Berube 1990). Even in that most egregiously exploitative of institutions, slavery, evidence suggests that there were limits on the use of force, and that compliance was more readily engendered by a combination of force *and* positive incentives (see, e.g., Fogel and Engerman 1974, especially chaps. 4 and 6; Tomich 1990, especially chap. 7).

The point is also widely recognized in modern jurisprudence. For example, Hart writes that the law requires "a general habit of obedience," and that "'Sanctions' are therefore required *not as a normal motive for obedience*, but as a guarantee that those who would voluntarily obey shall not be sacrificed to those who would not" (1961, 23, 193; emphasis added). Raz likewise concludes that while coercion is central to any legal system, "its function is not as the standard motive for any act guided by the laws. It is much more complicated and indirect, though no less essential" (1980, 186).

7. I emphasize that I have not attempted to provide a complete analysis of the nature of political power. Instead, I have sought to make the more modest but essential distinction between power and force by emphasizing that the former is relational while the latter is not. For a good sampling of approaches to political power, see the essays in Lukes 1986.

appeals based on sentiments of legitimacy to the use of violence. "In this conception, the use of violence, including terrorism, is one of many policies that may be chosen to establish and maintain state authority" (Gurr 1986a, 46). But the problem with this argument is the same, since the use of physical force is equated with the exercise of political power.[8]

Finally, Jackson and Rosberg imply that power and legitimacy can be divorced: "A Government may possess legitimacy, but have little in the way of an effective apparatus of power; or it may have an imposing power apparatus, but little legitimacy in the eyes of its citizens" (1982a, 7). But this distinction cannot be sustained either. As I shall argue below, because power is relational, its exercise requires a degree of legitimacy, which is why those who wield power devote a good deal of effort to legitimizing their activities and demands.

My emphasis is equally at odds with those who suggest that an approach to power such as the one outlined above is simply a Western approach that has little or no applicability to other cultures. Such is the conclusion proposed by Anderson (1972) from his study of the conception of power in Javanese culture. For instance, in the Javanese tradition, power is said to be concrete as opposed to relational, so that to employ the idea of power is not to raise the question of legitimacy. More recently, Pye has made the similar argument that conceptions of power vary across cultures:

> It is conventional in the West to conceive of "power" as the distinctive attribute of an elite, the stick that superiors hold over the general public, while "legitimacy" is generally thought of as residing in the public as a check on their rulers, and hence legitimacy is seen as flowing upward from the masses. *In Asia, power and legitimacy operate in exactly the opposite manner*. Power usually flows upward in that it depends critically upon the compliance of subordinates and is not produced out of thin air by the commands and posturing of superiors, whereas legitimacy has generally been defined in Asia by those with the highest pretensions of power. (Pye 1985, 320–21; emphasis added)

It is interesting that while both of these writers are urging that the meaning of power is culturally determined, their conclusions about

---

8. Similar considerations apply to the common equation of a state's military capability with its political power in the context of international relations. For a discussion of this problem, see Baldwin 1979.

the *forms* that power assumes are in fundamental conflict. Anderson's argument is that power is relational when conceived in Western terms but possessive in the Javanese setting, while Pye is making the antithetical claim that Asian views of power are more relational than Western notions.

The problem with formulations like these is that they confuse the ideological justification for a political order with the nature of that order. Consider another example. The fact that papal authority is interpreted in terms of spiritual criteria does not obscure the political nature of the Vatican as a temporal institution. Indeed, Pye himself goes on to acknowledge that "there must be reciprocal responses in the creation of both power and legitimacy, for both are two-way streets" (1985, 321). The point is well taken, but by the same token it undermines his own argument about the significance of cultural differences in the interpretation of political power.

That politics involves the exercise of power and authority and given that these are relational has a second implication. Discussions of political development (e.g., Huntington 1968) and of states (e.g., Nordlinger 1981, 1987) often spend a good deal of time on the question of political *autonomy*. But we need to tread carefully here. The term autonomy seems often to be used as if it referred to an all-or-nothing quantity—institutions are either autonomous or they are not. Consider the following:

> The increase of state autonomy is not an unqualified social good. Autonomous state elites can make disastrous mistakes because there is little countervailing power in the society to prevent their political suicide. The development of extreme state autonomy may lead to the loss of touch with the state's social bases. (Dominguez 1987, 69)

Such usages are troublesome because they carry the misleading implication that power is possessive. Domingucz has cast the state as being effectively insulated from its social bases. It is difficult, however, to see how *political* structures can be completely autonomous from broader social forces. Of course, if politics merely involved the application of force, such a problem would not arise. But if we are concerned with the way in which authorities (as embodied, let us say, in the state) exercise *power* over their subordinates, then the question of absolute autonomy is moot.

To be sure, authorities may be able to induce widespread compliance with their preferences, but this does not mean that they are autonomous in some complete sense. Of course, political structures may be relatively distinct and identifiable. Authorities may even be able to generate considerable consensus and order. But the very relational nature of power means that political authority is inextricably intertwined with wider social forces, and it is in this sense that the state is always "part of society" (Migdal 1987, 396). To say that, under the right circumstances, governments may enjoy considerable room for maneuver does mean that they can enjoy a *measure* of autonomy. The bottom line, however, is that this autonomy is always constrained by the relational character of power and authority.[9]

Third, several writers have distinguished "politics as allocation" from "politics as us against the other" (Poggi 1978). They have gone on to suggest that to adopt the former is to endorse a pluralist view of the political universe that is atomized and individualistic and ignores the place of political institutions. In contrast, the us-against-the-other conception is said to direct our attention to more structural factors. For example, Krasner writes approvingly that "statist approaches see politics more as a problem of rule and control than as one of allocation" (1984, 224).

Given the conception of political life that I have adopted, however, it is difficult to see what Poggi's distinction involves. If politics centers on the management of conflict over the distribution of valued goods, then it is ipso facto concerned with both rule and control *and* with allocation. This point was made with great clarity by V. O. Key: "Politics generally comes down, over the long run, to a conflict between those who have and those who have less" (1949, 307). The haves—those with power, prestige, income, and the like—seek to protect their interests against challenge with a variety of tools, including obstruction and obfuscation. Control and allocation are thus inextricably intertwined.

It follows from this that the "much maligned concept of the common good or the national interest" (Krasner 1984, 232) is justly maligned. Nor is there much to recommend a Hegelian view of the state with its "emphasis on the community that pervades and cuts across individual and class interests . . . and [on] the importance of the state as the instrument for preserving the continuity of and formulating and executing community purposes" (Lentner 1984, 370). Such a view is tacitly revealed in Huntington's claim that "the public interest . . . is whatever strengthens governmental institutions. The public

---

9. Because of this, the common distinction between "society-centered" and "state-centered" explanations is difficult to sustain in practice and is therefore unlikely to generate new research programs.

interest is the interest of public institutions" (1968, 25). The problem with concepts like the national or public interest or the national community become clear when we consider "domestic" politics. Since politics involves conflict over the distribution of valued goods such as income, prestige, and power, and since those goods are relational, when some group wins, other groups *necessarily* lose, albeit in varying degrees. There is no national or common interest.[10]

Finally, the distinction between power (relational) and force (possessive) is important because it suggests among other things that the sustained and continued exercise of physical coercion is fundamentally apolitical. By this, I do not mean to suggest that force does not play a part in politics. The *threat* of force is essential, as I have tried to make clear. It is indeed difficult to see how power can be exercised in its absence. Further, if the threat is to be credible, then force will need to be employed from time to time. For example, the threat of incarceration is more likely to deter widespread tax evasion if a subset (at least) of tax evaders is actually punished and the punishment is publicized.

Beyond this, force clearly plays a role in poorly defined situations. Among the more notable of these are postrevolutionary periods where the winners seek to consolidate their position by eliminating their opponents. Civil wars that are not preceded by revolutions are another instance, as are the periods ensuing military coups d'etat. A similar phenomenon has sometimes been evident in the phase following decolonization. The distinctive feature of such uses of force is that they occur in situations where political authority is ambiguous. In settings like these, the exercise of force may contribute to a political

---

10. It might be countered that "foreign" politics is different. For example, Krasner suggests that "The destruction of the state by . . . alien conquest is a loss for all citizens because it means the destruction or severe weakening of the individual's social and moral community" (1984, 232). The construction one places on a statement like this hinges critically on what one means by "citizen." However, why the destruction of the Nazi state should be considered a loss for all Germans is far from self-evident. Nor is it clear why the possible dismantling of the current South African regime would represent a loss for all South Africans, or even a loss for *all* of those in the white minority. Discussions couched in terms of the national interest too easily cloud whose particular interests are involved.

The apparently obvious retort to this would be that nuclear annihilation is not in anyone's interest (as is the case with being murdered). But such a retort simply asserts the general undesirability of the use of force. Political conflict occurs when choices between various specific policies designed to prevent such uses of force are considered.

For analyses of the difficulties in sustaining the idea of a public interest in general, see the essays in Friedrich (1962), especially those by Montgomery and Leys, and Theobold (1990, 5-6). For the argument that the idea of a national interest is meaningless in the analysis of foreign policy decision making, including decisions on the initiation and esclation of wars, see Bueno de Mesquita (1981, chaps. 1 and 2) and Bueno de Mesquita and Lalman (1992, especially chap. 9).

resolution. But military solutions do not in and of themselves constitute long-term political solutions. Thus, a primary reliance on force is apolitical, as Machiavelli, Burke, and many others before and since have well understood.

Implications for the Study of Political Capacity

While the basic distinction between power and force is relatively straightforward, it has not informed the analysis of political capacity. Instead, many observers have overemphasized the role of force in contemporary politics despite the fact that representation and the right to self-determination are core elements of the ideological justification of the modern state system. Remembering Max Weber's dictum that the state is that entity which claims a monopoly of the legitimate use of force, but sidestepping his remark that "force is certainly not the normal or the only means of the state" (Weber 1946, 78), many have exaggerated the part of force and minimized the role of legitimacy.[11] This problem is evident in at least two areas.

Decolonization brought with it great hopes of exporting "democracy" world-wide. The reality, of course, was considerably different. Most notably, the military coup d'etat has become commonplace in the politics of the Third World. Since 1945, more heads of state in the Third World have in fact been replaced by coups than by elections. Initially, some writers were favorably disposed to military intervention on the grounds that nonmilitary organizations were weak or nonexistent, that the military was most likely to attract the talent of the new states, that military organization assumed a form conducive to development, and thus that the military was likely to provide relative "stability and control" (Levy 1966; see also Pye 1962). Subsequent writers were less sanguine that military regimes would always be progressive (e.g., Huntington 1968; Nordlinger 1970) but retained the view that military regimes were likely to leave a distinctive impact.

When we remember that a military coup d'etat is a forceful and

---

11. In fact, Watkins concluded twenty-five years ago that the major difficulty with the state nomenclature "is that it places excessive emphasis on the coercive aspects of political life." He continued:

> In the days of absolute monarchy it was not unnatural to think of politics as a one-way relationship of command and obedience between a ruler and his subjects. The interaction between a sovereign people and its government cannot be so simply understood. Although modern governments may act coercively, they lack that ultimate identification with the sovereign state which constituted the peculiar strength of the older monarchies. (Watkins 1968, 156)

As I noted in chapter 1, the idea of popular sovereignty is universally advanced and justified with reference to the doctrine of the right to self-determination in contemporary politics.

typically illegal strike against the state, it becomes clear that conclusions like these about military regimes are predicated on the assumption that by using force, such regimes are able to provide technological solutions to political problems.[12] The empirical evidence, however, indicates that there is little to distinguish the performance of military from nonmilitary governments (e.g., Jackman 1976; Zuk and Thompson 1982). What does this tell us?

I believe it underscores the importance of the distinction between force and power. Successful regimes, military or otherwise, are those that are capable of exercising power, while those that rely primarily on force are likely to be unsuccessful. The political significance of the military in many states is that it provides opportunities (not the only opportunities, to be sure) for those with political ambitions. But there is an important difference between *politicians* in uniform and *soldiers* in mufti. Politicians who can effectively use power will be successful regardless of their origins. In contrast, those who rely primarily on force (the "soldiers") are likely to be politically unsuccessful, whether or not they assumed office through a military coup d'etat.

The distinction applies to authoritarian regimes more generally. For example, in his analysis of the bureaucratic authoritarian regimes of southern Latin America, Stepan writes:

> Since coercion is a particularly important part of the regime's power, the degree of internal institutional cohesion of the repressive apparatus is also a key variable. The Chilean regime was strong in all these respects for almost the entire period between 1973 and 1981. (1985, 320)

But if, as I have suggested, the repeated invocation of force is evidence of a loss of power, then Stepan's first sentence is a non sequitur. Similarly, Dominguez (1987) claims that the combination of strong (or autonomous) states with weak regimes and incumbents in Latin America is paradoxical. Again, the paradox hinges entirely on his definition of state strength, which centers on such factors as the increased repressive capacity of regimes, growing military expenditures and interstate conflict. Had Dominguez allowed that legitimacy is as central to the Weberian idea of the state as is force, there would have been no paradox to report.

---

12. The ability of the military to provide technological solutions was seen as stemming from the hierarchical, disciplined and merit-based nature of military organization. In other words, military organizations were viewed as peculiarly modern. As noted by Randall and Theobold (1985, chap. 3), this is a problematic portrayal of the military, derived from Weber's ideal-typical form of rational-legal bureaucracy, a subject I address in chapter 4.

I do not mean to deny that the threat of force is part of power. Nor do I wish to deny that regimes can maintain themselves for substantial periods by the widespread application of force. But I do mean to insist that they cannot do so indefinitely, and that a massive repressive apparatus is not evidence of *political* power or strength.

Finally, much is often made of the role of violence in the formation of nation-states (e.g., Tilly 1975, 1985, 1990; Cohen, Brown, and Organski 1981; McNeill 1982). The evidence is indeed strong that European states were consolidated by force, and military conquest played an obvious role in the creation of the settler states of North America, Australasia, and elsewhere. Moreover, the boundaries of the newer states of the Third World often reflect geographical borders that were established by military competition among the colonial powers. But it is important that we resist the temptation to conclude that because force played a part in the creation of modern states, it plays the same role in their sustenance. Contemporary nation-states are everywhere confronted by norms that justify broad political participation in the face of which successful regimes are those that can exercise power or authority. The distinctions between force and power are simple ones, but the significance of those distinctions for political life is wide-ranging.

Capacity as the Creation of Legitimate Institutions

Taken as a whole, the preceding considerations suggest that political capacity involves the creation of *institutions* that are surrounded with some aura of *legitimacy*. I address these issues in turn.

As I have noted, the concept of development or capacity has sometimes been attacked on the grounds that it is teleological and value laden. This objection loses much of its force if we think of capacity as the creation of infrastructure. Consider the parallel concept of economic development. While it does entail the creation of wealth and a surplus, most observers maintain that economic development embodies more than this.

For example, a small country may possess vast mineral resources and engage in programs designed to extract those resources. That country, which initially had been poor, consequently comes to enjoy a per capita gross national product that rivals those of the wealthiest states. And this occurs despite the fact that the resources are extracted by capital intensive procedures that provide minimal employment opportunities for the indigenous population. Can we describe the country as experiencing economic development? Not necessarily. The answer to this question hinges critically on the kind of economic infrastructure that has been created. If the new wealth has been invested into areas like education, communications, and others that are typically associated with industrialization, then we might conclude that some kind of economic development is taking place. If, in contrast, the bulk of the wealth is siphoned off into foreign bank accounts, we are led to a different conclusion. Economic development clearly involves more than the accumulation of wealth—it must also include the creation of the infrastructure that, in modern times, has been associated with industrialization.[13]

The point applies with equal vigor to the question of political capacity. Since politics inherently centers on the phenomenon of power relationships, there must be a set of political institutions that provide some structure to those relationships. The exercise of power requires a degree of *continuity* to the relations between the participants, in other words, some history to the relationship. The exercise of power also assumes a degree of *regularity* to the relationship between the participants. These requirements of continuity and regularity can only be fulfilled in the context of an institutional infrastructure. Crozier and Friedberg put the case well when they write that institutions "establish and limit the range of power relationships among the members of an organization and thus define the conditions for negotiation. They are constraints imposed on all participants" (1980, 37). North makes the same point: "The major role of institutions in a society is to reduce uncertainty by establishing a stable (but not necessarily efficient) structure to human interaction" (1990, 6).

Because the exercise of power requires organization, the idea that we can avoid some of the problems commonly associated with the "development" label by focusing instead on political change (Huntington 1971) loses much of its weight (see also Ruttan 1991). Political change can involve anything. Huntington's own description of praetorian polities with its bewildering array of regime changes (see the previous chapter) constitutes a description of change (1968). But this change in itself produces no political organization, and may, indeed, be inimical to the creation of such an outcome. Just as eco-

---

13. None of this is to suggest that there is consensus on the definition of economic development. As is the case with political development, explicit references to economic development are a comparatively recent phenomenon, appearing after the Second World War. Moreover, the evolution of these discussions parallels changes in approaches to political development, and appears to have been motivated by many of the same events and considerations. For an interesting history of approaches to economic development, see Arndt 1987; for commentary on contributions to the field, see the entries in Eatwell, Milgate, and Newman 1989.

nomic development involves more than growth, political capacity necessarily comprises more than simple change. Both economic development and political capacity entail the creation of infrastructure. Huntington's (1968) original contention that institutions are central to political development is thus more promising than his subsequent conversion to change.

But capacity encompasses more than this. Specifically, the institutions must be *legitimate* if they are to provide structure to power relationships as I have defined them. Some may think that to introduce the idea of legitimacy is simply to open up a Pandora's box of ethical considerations, but that is not my intention. I use the term in the following sense. A set of political institutions is legitimate to the extent that most citizens have a predisposition to regard compliance with the officers of those institutions as appropriate and reasonable. Compliance thus becomes a habit.[14] Phrased another way, the issue of legitimacy centers on the following issue: "how do some men come to be credited with the right to rule over others" (Geertz 1972, 325)? This usage is intended to be ethically neutral. Authorities may induce legitimacy through fair means or foul, and the line between persuasion and manipulation is inherently ambiguous.[15] Regardless of the way it is generated, legitimacy remains central to political capacity.

Of course, if politics involved no more than the application of physical force, the issue of legitimacy would be irrelevant. But once we acknowledge that power is central to politics and that power is necessarily relational, it is immediately apparent that institutions can only be successful to the extent that they are generally regarded as legitimate. In other words, a relationship has to exist between those who exercise authority and those who are subject to it, whereby the latter acknowledge that the former are in fact authorities. An analysis of legitimacy is crucial precisely because it directs our attention to the nature of this relationship (see also Lane 1984, 209–10). And if we

---

14. My use of the word *most* is necessarily imprecise. While legitimacy does presuppose "a general habit of obedience," the exact proportion of the relevant population who need to comply before the habit can be described as general is difficult to specify with precision (Hart 1961, 23–24).

15. Contrast this with the opinion that the very idea of legitimacy cannot be employed outside the context of liberal democratic politics, because in most non-Western states "legitimacy is *derived* from a baffling mixture of traditional factors ranging from the hereditary principle, religious sanctions, personal following, charisma, military support, cynical manipulation of power, and above all, being in charge of the instruments of power" (Somjee 1986, 15. The problems with Somjee's view is that many of the items he cites are used to engender consent in the democracies as well. Besides, legitimacy is everywhere derived.

recognize that one element of institutional success involves the long-term stability of those institutions, then legitimacy is necessary to stability.

It is important that the issues here not be blurred. In *Political Order*, Huntington (1968) appeared to take stability and order as the primary goal of political development, and as I pointed out in chapter 1, this emphasis was widely criticized (e.g., Hopkins 1972; O'Brien 1972; Kesselman 1973). More recently, Huntington's analysis has been cast as epitomizing a relatively authoritarian "strong government school" of development studies (Randall and Theobold 1985). To the extent that the appearance of stability and order were themselves taken as evidence of legitimacy, these criticisms have some justification.[16] By emphasizing the centrality of political infrastructure to development, I am also underscoring the importance of stability and order. Continuity is critical to political life, which means that stability constitutes a problem that has to be solved before other social and economic issues can even begin to be addressed politically (Roth 1968). However, I am adding the extra proviso that institutions must be legitimate *before* they can be regarded as stable.

On the other hand, the critique of Huntington had populist origins, suggesting among other things that his approach was reprehensible because it excludes the view from the bottom; that is, the interests of those who are excluded from political life. A related criticism is that Huntington shunned any form of class analysis (see, e.g., Smith 1985). One has to be careful here to avoid the alternative trap of equating political capacity with democratic development. I have emphasized the centrality of legitimacy to political life, but legitimacy cannot be equated with democracy. Legitimacy rests on perceptions, which are everywhere subject to persuasion and manipulation. Citizens may be socialized or indoctrinated to accept political institutions. Even if we can sustain distinctions between persuasion and manipulation or between socialization and indoctrination (which, along with Lindblom [1982], I very much doubt), legitimacy rests not on how acceptance is generated but on the more fundamental issue of *whether* it is generated at all.

---

16. It is important to remember that other early development studies were more explicitly concerned with legitimacy. Thus, Deutsch (1961, 502) emphasized that an unresponsive government "will be reduced to ruling by force where it can no longer rule by display, example, and persuasion." Similarly, Almond and Powell (1966, 25–27) stressed the significance of "support inputs" (including goods and services, obedience, and deference) to political systems, concluding that without these essential resources, no political system can meet its goals.

As will become evident throughout this book, my treatment of institutional infrastructure and legitimacy has much in common with approaches like Stepan's:

Institutionalization implies that a regime has consolidated the new political patterns of succession, control and participation; has managed to establish a viable pattern of economic accumulation; has forged extensive constituencies for its rule; and has created a significant degree of Gramscian "hegemonic acceptance" in civil society. It also implies that the majority of the weighty political actors in the polity are pursuing strategies to further their positions within the new institutional framework, rather then directing their energies to resisting, eroding, or terminating that framework. (1978, 292)

The key issue here is national political capacity.

I emphasize finally that capacity is a matter of *degree*. The point would be innocuous were it not for the fact that students of comparative politics are prone to taxonomies, and classificatory skills are regarded as close to godliness. For example, much ink was wasted in the not so distant past on the distinction in the modernization literature between "traditional" and "modern" (e.g., Gusfield 1967). The debate addressed a number of issues, but the central question was: What distinguishes modern from traditional societies? More specifically, where exactly do we draw the line between the two? But surely the idea of modernization can be useful without the delineation of mutually exclusive categories. For example, modernization has been defined as a positive function of "the ratio of inanimate to animate sources of power" (Levy 1966, 35). Such a definition avoids the problems of classification by identifying a continuum. Modernization becomes a matter of degree, and refers to a concrete phenomenon. And the political consequences of modernization, thus defined, may be positive or negative.

The proposition that political capacity is a matter of degree would seem elementary were it not for the common belief among comparativists that concept formation necessarily involves qualitative taxonomies (e.g., Kalleberg 1966; Sartori 1970). This belief has a long history, going back at least to the attempts of Aristotle to classify different kinds of states. In its more recent forms, the belief forms a basis of criticism. For example, Janos finds development studies wanting in part because "no consensus has emerged as to whether [communist states] are 'developing,' 'developed,' or a class of societies that should be treated totally in its own terms" (1986, 66). As I have suggested elsewhere (Jackman 1985), however, the emphasis on qualitative taxonomies is misplaced. That it continues to be expressed has had a debilitating effect on the study of comparative politics.

When political development is cast as a continuous phenomenon that identifies the degree of national political capacity, it is evident that the term does not postulate some end goal or desirable form of government. Instead, the term refers to the extent to which there are national institutions that provide the requisite structure for political life. When viewed in this way, it is clear that capacity is not an all-or-nothing phenomenon. Indeed, casting capacity as a matter of degree also helps emphasize the point that political institutions are everywhere likely to be fragile, a point already underscored by the relational nature of political power.

A Brief Comparison with Earlier Approaches

To cast political capacity as the creation of legitimate institutions is obviously only a beginning. Even so, it is instructive to contrast my approach with earlier ones. Since the comparisons that one could make here are potentially endless, I confine my attention to the two well-known and representative statements by Pye (1966) and by Huntington (1968), respectively.

Pye concluded that there were, as of the mid-1960s, at least ten different commonly used definitions of development. Specifically, political development was defined (1) as the political prerequisite of economic development; (2) as the politics typical of industrial societies; (3) as political modernization; (4) as the operation of a nation-state; (5) as administrative and legal development; (6) as mass mobilization and participation; (7) as the building of democracy; (8) as stability and orderly change; (9) as mobilization and power; and (10) as one aspect of a multidimensional process of social change. While allowing that many of these definitions overlap with each other, one has to conclude that this is a diverse catalog indeed.

From it, Pye (1966, 45–48) extracted a "development syndrome" comprised of three basic elements (the same syndrome was proposed by Coleman 1971). First, he concluded that "equality" is central to development. The idea of equality is complex, but in Pye's usage it includes an emphasis on mass participation, on universalistic and impersonal laws, and on political recruitment based on achieved rather than ascriptive characteristics. Second, the development syndrome stresses national political "capacity," which refers to the scope and size of government, the effectiveness of government and the "rationality" and "secular orientation" of public administration. The last part of the syndrome is "differentiation and specialization" of structures. Although attempts have been made to apply these criteria in empirical studies of development (e.g., Abernethy 1969), it is evident that the syndrome they are said to define is quite heterogeneous. The stress on equality derives from the modernization literature, but it blurs the distinction between political institutions and broader social patterns alleged to apply to mass populations. Some might object to the concern with differentiation of structures on the grounds that this simply introduces a conservative functionalist bias into the analysis. Although it does have functionalist origins, my objection to the inclusion of this factor as part of development is that the idea of differentiation (or specialization) has no clear empirical referent and is therefore unlikely to be fruitful in research.

The only way that my approach ties in with Pye's is that I also stress the importance of political capacity. My usage of this term is, however, much more limited than his. I restrict the concept of capacity to refer to the issue of the political effectiveness of national institutions. Questions of the rationality of administration (as the term is used by Pye and others) and even the issue of government size have no self-evident connection to political capacity conceived in generic terms.[17]

In contrast to Pye's analysis, Huntington's four criteria for political development focus directly on institutions and explicitly exclude societal modernization (1968, 12–24), as represented in Pye's "equality" component. Specifically, Huntington contends that political development requires institutions that can adapt to their environments. It further involves relatively complex institutions. Third, institutions must be autonomous from broader social forces in the sense that they have some life of their own that is independent of those forces. Finally, institutions must be coherent.

Because this is a more restrictive definition, it is an improvement over Pye's approach. But it can be further improved (in part) by an additional constraint. As Huntington notes, adaptability is evidenced by longevity. If the implications of this line of thought are pursued (see chap. 4 below), it becomes clear that institutions that are relatively adaptable are likely to be more complex, to enjoy some mea-

17. Again, Pye's use of the term rationality is derived from Weber's distinction between rational-legal and traditional bases of authority. For the reasons advanced below in chapter 4, this is not a productive distinction.

sure of autonomy, and even to display a degree of coherence. Hence, if we take the notion of institutional adaptability seriously, Huntington's other three criteria are essentially redundant.

Note in addition that the idea of institutional adaptability is very similar to Pye's concept of political capacity, because adaptability goes hand in hand with effectiveness. Since my casting of political development as the creation of legitimate national institutions also incorporates the issue of effectiveness and capacity, it is obvious that my approach derives from elements of the earlier literature. However, it is equally apparent that I place explicit and equal weight on the question of legitimacy.

While my approach remains rather general, it represents (in contrast to previous discussions) an attempt at a minimalist definition. This reflects my view that a major shortcoming of many of the earlier studies is that development was cast in terms that were too broad. As is evident from Pye's summary, political development was typically regarded as an immense umbrella that covered anything that might conceivably be related to political, social, and economic changes that seemed associated with processes like industrialization and decolonization. The danger with such an all-encompassing approach is that the concept is reduced to an analytically blunt tool. I doubt that political capacity can be reduced to a single unidimensional concept. But if the issue is to be made more tractable, we need a minimalist and more sharply delimited approach.

CHAPTER 3

Recent Analyses of the State
and Political Capacity

L'etat c'est moi

—Louis XIV

I have argued that national political capacity hinges on the creation of legitimate institutions. On the face of it, this approach would seem to have much in common with recent analyses of the nation-state, especially those that address the issue of state strength. Indeed, I suggested in chapter 1 that such analyses have brought us back to many of the questions addressed by the earlier literature on development. I now consider the contribution of recent writing on the state to our understanding of political capacity.

To begin, I have already emphasized the distinction between the nation-state as a legal entity and the question of state strength. The legal definition stresses two criteria: that the state consist of a defined territory, and that it be independent or sovereign in the sense that it has the right "to enter into relations with other states" (Brownlie 1979, 73–76). This offers us a juridical definition of the state (Jackson and Rosberg 1982a) that identifies the unit of analysis with which we are concerned. These juridical attributes are possessed uniformly by most modern states.

There is, of course, some variance in juridical statehood because sovereignty involves recognition by the international community and that recognition is not universal in the modern state system. For example, although they were charter members of the United Nations, the former Byelorussian and Ukrainian Soviet Socialist Republics (now Belarus and Ukraine) were not in practice regarded as even potentially independent and sovereign by the broader international community until the end of 1991. The sovereignty of client states like South Vietnam in the 1960s and 1970s or Afghanistan in the 1980s is also questionable, to say the least. On the other side of the coin, the 1971 loss of its membership in the United Nations increased the ambiguity surrounding Taiwan's juridical statehood, although that country still maintains extensive diplomatic relations. Similarly, the Republic of South Africa was denied the right to participate in the General Assembly in 1974, but retained de jure membership in the United Nations itself.[1] These cases remind us that juridical statehood is not without its uncertainties; not all states uniformly possess the requisite properties. But the broader point is that these exceptions, while important in their own right, constitute a tiny handful of the total. The vast majority of states clearly and unequivocally meet the criteria for juridical statehood.

In contrast, the question of state strength bears on the issue of political effectiveness and capacity. To raise this question is immediately to imply that some states are more effective than others. Thus, where considerations of the juridical state identify a relatively constant factor (in the context of the contemporary nation-state system), considerations of state strength isolate one or more variables.

Two basic approaches to the issue of state strength are evident in the literature. The first of these essentially equates strength with size, so that stronger states are those that control more resources. The second approach avoids the issue of size and appears to conceive of state strength as the capability to make independent or autonomous policy decisions. I address each of these general approaches in turn.

State Strength as Government Size

The idea that state strength is associated with the size of the state has been widespread for some time. A straightforward and explicit articulation is to be found in Carnoy's book titled *The State and Political Theory*:

> This is a book about politics. It is a book about the increasing importance of politics in shaping social change in today's world. The primary problem of advanced capitalist societies, after two centuries of economic growth, is no longer the adequacy of resources or their "efficient" allocation for maximum output. The way that output is produced, the definition of what constitutes output, what is produced, and who decides development policy are the significant "economic" problems today. These problems are settled as much in the political arena as in production. There is another reason for the importance of politics: as econ-

---

1. Interestingly, Switzerland has never sought membership, but maintains a permanent observer to the United Nations. Membership in that organization is therefore not the criterion for juridical statehood in the contemporary state system.

omies throughout the world have developed, *the public sector—
what we call here the state—has grown increasingly important in
every society, from advanced industrial to Third World primary-
good exporter, and in every aspect of society*—not just politics,
but in economics (production, finance, distribution), in ideology
(schooling, the media), and in law enforcement (police, military). Why this occurs, and how the *growing state* is shaped, has
become for social scientists a crucial issue—perhaps the crucial
issue—of our times. The state appears to hold the key to economic development, to social security, to individual liberty, and,
through increasing weapons "sophistication," to life and death
itself. (1984, 3; emphasis added)

In this formulation, the state is defined as the public sector, and
state strength or capacity is directly equated with government size.
The broader the range of resources over which government exerts
control, the stronger the state. Moreover, the resources involved are
economic, since government size is defined in terms of the public
sector. The larger the public sector, the stronger the state. What exactly is the public sector? Occasionally it is taken to refer to the
number of government employees, but more generally it is defined in
budgetary terms to refer either to government revenues or to government expenditures. The public sector, then, consists of the ratio of
government consumption to all consumption. As this ratio increases,
so too does the size of the public sector, and hence, the strength of
the state.

On one level, this approach has much to recommend it. As I have
already suggested, politics centers on conflict over the distribution of
valued goods, which involves economic goods more than anything
else. Besides, public policy fundamentally involves the manipulation
of citizens' incomes. Carnoy is surely correct in his insistence that
what may appear to be simply "production" issues that can be resolved according to economic criteria are more properly cast as cen
tral issues in the political arena. In this setting, the specification of
state strength as the size of the public sector has a good deal of
intuitive appeal.

At the same time, Carnoy's approach conceals an interesting
problem. Specifically, his suggestion that politics is assuming an "increasing importance" in the contemporary world presupposes that, in
the not so distant past, politics was somehow less important. In other
words, his approach implies that although issues relating to production and consumption are now properly regarded as political, there

was a period (unspecified when) in which such issues were reasonably construed as economic, and in which questions of allocation were indeed cast as market decisions and resolved on grounds of "efficiency." Hence the "increasing importance of politics."

Now it is true that the nation-state is a modern form that presupposes some degree of technology for its existence, even as a juridical entity. Indeed, anthropologists have drawn our attention to the phenomenon of "stateless" societies that seem to have existed where technology was primitive (e.g., Southall 1968; Mair 1977). But this does not mean that politics was irrelevant to those societies. In a similar vein, the fact that, almost everywhere, national public sectors have grown impressively in the past few decades does not mean that politics has somehow become more important in the same period. It simply indicates that governments have become more effective in extracting economic resources. Although the institutional infrastructures have obviously changed, politics was as relevant to France under Louis XIV as it is to France today. And the many differences between modern Greece and the Greek city-states of antiquity do not include a difference in the level of political activity. Politics has always played a central role.

While Carnoy has provided the most cogent rationale for conceiving of state strength in terms of public-sector size, the conception itself is not uncommon. Indeed, it predates the current interest in state strength. Although the fact often goes unacknowledged, public-sector size has been taken to reflect an important element of national capacity by scholars in the political development tradition like Deutsch (1961), Almond and Powell (1966, 193), Rustow (1967, 289), and Eckstein (1982). In 1970, de Schweinitz proposed the concept of gross political product, which, in the aggregate was "similar, if not equal, to the economists' government expenditures on goods and services" (1970, 526). Similarly, von Beyme has defined state strength in terms of government size, where the state is seen as the "political-administrative system" (1985, 12), while Harris (1986, 145–49) seems to equate the state with the public sector.[2]

Paralleling this usage, it has often been argued that industrialization has been critical to the emergence of modern states because of its impact on their fiscal capacity. Ardant, for example, asserts that industrial strength "influenced the power of states by way of its incidence on their finances, or more exactly, on their fiscal capability. The

---

2. Harris actually describes the use of the term *state* as an "error," but adds that he uses the term "in order to simplify issues" (1986, 148).

fiscal system was the 'transformer' of the economic infrastructure into political structure" (1975, 220). This conclusion reminds us that, like the nation-state, the public sector is a modern form.

Given this, it is not surprising that state strength has also been envisaged in terms of the size of the public sector in a variety of systematic studies of income inequality, economic growth, and related problems (see, e.g., Rubinson 1976, 1977; Rubinson and Quinlan 1977; Weede 1980; Weede and Tiefenbach 1981; Moon and Dixon 1985; Rouyer 1987). The rationale for this specification is very similar to Carnoy's. For example, according to Rubinson,

> Political control, or state strength, refers to the degree to which a state dominates the activities within its population. Since force is an unstable means of control, strong states are those which have transformed force into a stable set of authority relations which give rights of the regulation and control of activities of its population to the state. Thus, the mark of a strong state is not the size of its army or the centralization of power in the hands of an oligarchy, but the degree to which the state apparatus has come to expropriate to itself the rights to control action, among the most important of which are the rights to regulate and control economic activity. (1976, 641–42)

Rubinson's contention that force does not constitute a stable basis for state strength is completely consistent with the argument I developed in chapter 2. Of more interest is his equation of state strength with the capacity of governments to regulate and control economic activity. And it is this equation that leads him subsequently to the operational definition of state strength as the value of government revenues as a percentage of gross domestic product. Given the obvious (if imperfect) connection between government revenues and consumption, this means that state strength is defined to increase with the size of the public sector.

In contrast to Carnoy, Rubinson's formulation does not imply that politics has somehow become more important as public sectors have grown. Instead, it simply suggests that government capacity has increased with technological change, so that the modern state has the potential for a more enhanced ability to exercise political control than did its predecessors. Nonetheless, there are two major problems with this conception. First, if we allow that public-sector size could offer a reasonable reflection of state strength, then there is a practical difficulty of major proportions in choosing among the available measures.

Second, and more fundamentally, it turns out that the task of distinguishing the "public" from the "private" sectors is even more formidable. Let us consider these problems in turn.

Comparing Different Measures of Public-Sector Size

National governments spend much of their time addressing budgetary issues, and a variety of budgetary statistics is readily available for most countries. Most notably, the United Nations Statistical Office produces an annual yearbook of national accounts statistics, and the work of this office is supplemented by other organizations like the World Bank (e.g., World Bank 1983). Drawing on series like these, the last version of the *World Handbook of Political and Social Indicators* devoted a complete chapter to "The size of government and the allocation of resources" (Taylor and Jodice 1983, 1: chap. 1), reporting different estimates of the share of total gross domestic product consumed by government (along with government expenditures in selected areas such as educational and military spending). The *World Handbook* takes figures on public-sector size as reflecting the size of government, and these are also the kinds of figures that are often taken as indicators of state strength or political capacity.

Budgets are, of course, political documents, and it is widely recognized that different accounting schemes hinder crossnational comparisons (see, e.g., Taylor and Jodice 1983, 1:1–4). This has been particularly true for comparisons between centrally planned and other economies. As a result, the United Nations and other organizations have devoted considerable effort to generating a common system of national accounts to facilitate comparisons across countries, and there is evidence that this effort has enhanced the comparability of national accounts. On the face of it, this would seem to justify the use of figures on public-sector size to measure state strength and also to justify the common practice of using the various available sets of estimates of public-sector size as interchangeable.

Unfortunately, the various estimates are not as interchangeable as one might think. To illustrate the problems involved here, I compare three well-known but different sets of estimates. The first involves figures on general government consumption published by the World Bank (1987, table 5); the second comprises apparently comparable estimates by Summers and Heston (1988); while the third consists of calculations of central government expenditures by the United States Arms Control and Disarmament Agency (1990).

The World Bank defines general government consumption as follows:

All current expenditure for purchases of goods and services by government bodies: that is, central, regional, and local governments; separately operated social security funds; and international authorities that exercise tax or governmental expenditure functions within the national territory. It excludes outlays of public nonfinancial enterprises and public financial institutions. The current expenditure of general government covers outlays for compensation of employees, purchases of goods (excluding the acquisition of land and depreciable assets) and services from other sectors of the economy, military equipment, and other purchases from abroad. Capital expenditures on national defense (except for civil defense) is treated as consumption, whereas all expenditure on capital formation (including civil defense) is included in gross domestic investment. (World Bank 1983, 1:xi)

A similar definition underlies the estimates reported by Summers and Heston (1988). The major difference between the latter estimates and those provided by the World Bank is that Summers and Heston's calculations use market price levels rather than international exchanges rates to compute gross domestic product and its component shares.[3] In contrast, the estimates of government size provided by the USACDA refer to the expenditures of central government. All three series report the share of total gross domestic product consumed by government expenditures.

Since series like these are often taken as essentially interchangeable measures of government size, one would expect them to be highly correlated with each other. As the simple correlations in table 3.1 suggest, however, this expectation is belied by the evidence, even with the centrally planned economies excluded (neither the World Bank nor Summers and Heston report figures for the latter). To be sure, the three correlations are all positive, but the hypothesis of interchangeability between the three measures requires more than

---

3. The Summers and Heston figures are available in machine-readable form, and come from a project sponsored by the United Nations Statistical Office and the World Bank (for further details, see Kravis, Heston, and Summers 1982; Summers and Heston 1988). While using market prices rather than international exchange rates to compute gross domestic product should generate different estimates of GDP itself, there is no reason to believe that it should lead to different estimates of the *share* of GDP consumed by different sectors within national economies. For discussion of a slightly revised data set, see Summers and Heston 1991.

TABLE 3.1. Simple Pairwise Correlations among Three Different Measures of Public-Sector Size, 1985

World Bank Government Expenditure	1.0	100	106
Summers/Heston Government Expenditure	.66	1.0	103
USACDA Government Expenditure	.71	.38	1.0
	World Bank	Summers/Heston	USACDA

Note: Entries below the main diagonal are the correlation coefficients; entries above the diagonal reflect the number of cases on which they are based.

this. Given that these are aggregate indicators of apparently the same concept, the striking feature of these correlations is their modest size. The figures in table 3.1 are, of course, only illustrative. However, they offer a representative illustration of the problem in the sense that expanding the coverage to include other series on government consumption and other years would not lead us to a different conclusion. It is also true that a matrix of simple correlations hardly constitutes a fully specified measurement model. On the other hand, the figures at hand do not promise to provide the basis for a fruitful effort to develop such a model.

The idea that these indicators of government size are interchangeable becomes even more difficult to sustain when we consider the relation between economic development and public-sector size. Over one hundred years ago, Adolf Wagner propounded his famous "law" that the public economy expands in direct relation to the growth of the national economy, a proposition that has received a good deal of attention since (see, e.g., Pryor 1968; Chenery and Syrquin 1975). Minimally, this argument implies a positive association between the level of economic development and each of the three indicators of government size.

Again, the evidence is inconclusive. As table 3.2 shows, the relation between level of economic development and the World Bank series on government consumption is positive but weak; the Summers and Heston series is *negatively* associated with level of development (again weakly); the USACDA series is positively related to development. Even the last association is modest: economic development accounts for less than 18 percent of the variance in central government

TABLE 3.2. Simple Correlations between Three Different Measures of Public-Sector Size and per Capita GDP, 1985 (N in parentheses)

World Bank Government Expenditure	+.26	(104)
Summers/Heston Government Expenditure	−.27	(108)
USACDA Government Expenditure	+.42	(115)
	log GDP per capita	

expenditures. In other words, radically different results are obtained with each of the measures of public-sector size, so that these cannot be taken as equivalent measures of state strength or political development.[4]

These results are discouraging to those who believe that state strength is readily measured by public-sector size and that the available measures of the latter behave in a similar manner. Further, it is important to note that the figures in tables 3.1 and 3.2 were calculated with centrally planned economies excluded. This means that the small correlations are not attenuated by different approaches to the admittedly difficult problem of trying to assess the size of the public sector in those states where "private" economic activity is supposed to have been minimal.

An alternative approach to measuring political capacity which builds on the notion of the public sector has been suggested by Organski and Kugler (1980, chap. 2). These writers argue that capacity rests on performance in penetrating and in extracting resources from society. They then go on to propose that the ability to collect taxes is the essential ingredient of capacity. However, they contend that the commonly used measure, the ratio of collected revenues to total product, is inadequate because it ignores the unequal distribution of economic resources across countries that impinge on their ability to collect taxes. Since government revenues have an obvious relation to government consumption, Organski and Kugler's argument applies equally to the use of series such as those employed in tables 3.1 and 3.2 as indicators of state strength.

These writers therefore propose that before tax ratios can be employed to measure political capacity, they need to be adjusted for national differences in the ability to collect revenues. Organski and Kugler suggest three specific adjustments. First, since taxes are more readily collected on exports, the share of the gross national product derived from exports should be controlled. Second, because taxes are more difficult to collect from agriculture (especially subsistence agriculture), the share of total output originating in agriculture also needs to be taken into account. Finally, since mineral wealth reflects luck more than productivity, and given that mineral production is administratively easier to tax, these writers adjust for the fraction of total product due to mining activities.

4. Economic development is measured using the logarithm of the estimates of real GDP per capita for 1985 reported by Summers and Heston (1988). Again, the correlations in table 3.2 reflect the simplest of specifications. In contrast, Chenery and Syrquin (1975) regressed government size on the logarithm of per capita GNP and its square and on the logarithm of population size and its square. Expanded formulations like theirs provide no evidence that contradicts the patterns shown in table 3.2.

To obtain figures on the ability of nations to collect taxes, Organski and Kugler take the predicted scores from the regression of tax ratios on these three factors. The measure of political capacity is then constructed by comparing the observed tax ratio with the predicted tax ratio:

$$\text{Political development} = \frac{\text{Observed tax ratio}}{\text{Predicted tax ratio}}.$$

When this ratio is around unity, governments are said to be collecting revenues at the level one would expect, given their ability to do so. Deviation from unity, however, is taken to be the clear result of *political* factors. Scores greater than one reflect enhanced political development. On the other hand,

> in the cases where a country is found to perform below expectations, the slippage must be attributed to the incapacity of the structure of the political system to do the job . . . . In [developing countries], it is reasonable to argue that the needs of the societies are so great that the governmental elites must be presumed to tax to the limits of political capacity. (Organski and Kugler 1980, 81)

Organski and Kugler's approach represents a clear refinement over analyses that employ unadjusted government expenditure *or* consumption data.[5] And their strategy may well be relevant in the substantive context within which it was originally generated, namely, an analysis of the impact of national differences in capability on the outcomes of international wars. Whether the method can be employed to identify political capacity more generally is, however, less clear. For reasons that I have already detailed, the military capacity of a nation-state in foreign policy is not isomorphic with its internal political capacity. There are two more specific problems.

First, as Organski and Kugler themselves acknowledge, it is not self-evident that the measure can be applied to industrial states. They illustrate this by pointing out that the higher rate of taxation in Sweden than in the United States does not reflect a difference in development. It reveals instead a difference in taste, or, more precisely, a difference

---

5. For elaborations of this general approach, see Organski et al. 1984 and Snider 1987. The tax ratios are used as the measure of domestic state power in Cohen, Brown, and Organski (1981). A parallel formulation that also emphasizes the capacity of governments to extract economic resources but which highlights the political costs of so doing can be found in Lamborn (1983).

in national policy. Used as a measure of national *political* capacity, the point applies with equal weight to countries of the Third World, since it is difficult to presume that governments tax to the limit simply because their citizens have pressing needs. If, as I argued in chapter 2, politics centers on conflict over the distribution of valued goods, then it is hard to argue that the mere presence of "pressing needs" among elements of the national citizenry serves as a general motivator of public policy. Besides, because valued goods are always distributed unequally within countries, the existence of groups who claim to have pressing needs is not unique to poor countries.[6] However, the equation of national differences in policy with variations in state strength is in fact common to much of the recent literature, and I shall return to this issue later in the chapter.

Second, whether we focus on government revenues or expenditures (adjusted or otherwise) as an indicator of state strength, we are confronted with the problem of demarcating the boundaries of the public sector. This problem is in fact overwhelming. As a result, attempts to resolve the practical problems with budgetary data that I have identified may be irrelevant to the analysis of state strength. That is, there may be no best budgetary series to reflect national variations in political development. What distinguishes the public and private sectors?

In Search of the Public Sector

On the face of it, the distinction between the public and private sectors appears easy to sustain. For example, we could count nonmarket consumption as public, and market (or profit-oriented) consumption as private. This, indeed, is the kind of contrast that underlies the definition of public consumption used by the World Bank and other agencies. Further, while it may be more difficult to apply this standard to the so-called nonmarket economies (a rapidly disappearing species) or to those with a substantial subsistence sector, the distinction would appear, minimally, to be readily applicable to the advanced capitalist economies.

The problem occurs when we try to contemplate what these economies would look like without government. This is a difficult question to answer, given the obvious pervasiveness of government. Of course, one can evaluate the impact of particular public policies on

---

6. That governments tax to the limit is more fruitfully explained in terms of a predatory account of rulers as revenue maximizers constrained primarily by the costs of extraction (Ardant 1975; Levi 1988).

specified economic outcomes. But since there are no national economies without governments, there is no easy baseline against which we can estimate the total effects of government on an economy *as a whole*.[7]

Further, all government policies have ripple effects (some intentional, others not) that permeate the private sector. These are called ripple effects because they refer to the impacts of public policies on market behavior. They thus blur our ability to make an unambiguous distinction between market and nonmarket activity. And the total size of these effects is impossible to gauge because we lack a clear counterfactual baseline. Consider the following examples.

By all accounts, government consumption is much higher in Sweden than in Japan. Estimates of the exact difference vary, of course, but figures reported by the Organization for Economic Cooperation and Development for the late 1970s indicate that in Sweden, government spent about 60 percent of GDP, while the corresponding figure for Japan was 30 percent, only marginally different from the lowest-scoring country in the comparison—Spain (Cameron 1982, 49). But this does not mean that the Swedish state was twice as strong as the Japanese state. Indeed, it is difficult to know just what it reflects, apart from differences in national policy.

The often-remarked economic "miracle" that has occurred in Japan since the early 1950s is, in fact, the product of an extraordinarily high level of government intervention in the economy. This intervention has been managed by such agencies as the Ministry of Finance, the Ministry of International Trade and Industry (MITI), and the Bank of Japan. Government involvement has been extensive, and has centered on long-term (rather than short-run) planning. Thus, policies of import controls have been designed to restrict the flow of manufactured goods into Japan, and these policies have been much more far-reaching in Japan than in other advanced countries. The Bank of Japan, in which the government has majority ownership, is generally regarded as the most centralized in the world and is almost the exclusive source of the monetary and credit supply. The bank also has close ties to the Ministry of Finance.

Beyond this, through licensing and other mechanisms, the government has had a major hand in deciding which industrial sectors

---

7. For an interesting discussion of this point within the context of evaluating the overall effects of government economic policy in the United States, see Page 1983. One could, of course, cast the problem in terms of performing a counterfactual thought experiment along the lines discussed by Fearon (1991). The obstacle here remains the same: it is in principle difficult to conceive of national economies without governments.

should be encouraged and which should not. Indeed, the control extends down to decisions about which particular industries and firms *within* sectors should be encouraged. For example, authorization from MITI has been required for the construction of any new dock, any new petroleum refinery, or even any new ship over a certain size. Until 1974, all technology agreements were screened on an individual basis by MITI to ensure that only essential technology was imported and also that when it was imported, it was restricted to those corporations best able to take advantage of it. Similarly, all foreign capital entering Japan has been subject to close government regulation (for good discussions of Japanese economic policy, see Pempel 1978; Johnson 1982a).

It is true, of course, that Japanese industrial policy has been developed in cooperation with major corporate interests. But the history of this policy is fundamentally inconsistent with the idea that the Japanese state lacks capacity. All of the evidence points firmly in the opposite direction, that the public and private sectors are inextricably intertwined. Hence the often-heard reference to Japan, Inc. Despite the comparatively small size of the public sector suggested by the figures, the Japanese state appears to have considerable capacity. Nor does it seem reasonable to conclude that this state has only half the capacity of a state like Sweden.[8] Instead, it is hard to conceive of a state with more national political capacity than Japan.

The problems associated with trying to isolate the extent of the public sector are not unique to the Japanese case. By Cameron's (1982) account, the public sector in the United States is very similar in magnitude to that of Japan. Despite this, it is difficult to distinguish private from public consumption in the United States. For example, like other market economies, the United States promotes subsidies for agriculture that impinge directly on what and how much is grown. As in all other economies, taxation policies provide strong incentives for some forms of economic activity and equally strong disincentives for other types of "market" behavior.

The above indicates that the distinction between public and private consumption is difficult to preserve *even when we restrict our concern to those economies where the distinction should be most readily sustained*—that is, the industrial economies of the West. The problems multiply almost exponentially when we broaden the focus to

---

8. The problem remains even if we ignore the absolute size of the numbers on public-sector size reported by Cameron (1982) and focus instead on their simple rank order. That is, it is hard to think of a strong argument that Sweden has more political capacity than Japan in *any* meaningful sense.

include the economies of the Third World and the so-called nonmarket economies.

In contrast to the industrial states, the states of sub-Saharan Africa are generally regarded as weak. This view has a number of origins, including the recency of decolonization and the persistence of personal rule (see, e.g., Jackson and Rosberg 1982a, 1982b). But even in this context, the size of the public sector provides few clues about the degree of political capacity. Despite their manifest weaknesses, African governments have shown some ability to manipulate economic policy, and the difficulty of separating public from private consumption is as profound on the African subcontinent as it is elsewhere.

An important study by Bates (1981) documents the way in which the market has become a major political arena in many African states whose economies (and therefore principal exports) are overwhelmingly agrarian. In this arena, governments use regulatory and fiscal policy to manipulate the behavior of agricultural producers, generally in ways that are inconsistent with the material interests of those producers (peasants and small farmers). Most notably, despite the importance of agricultural production, African governments have often sought to move resources from that sector to more urbanized areas in an attempt to industrialize and build political support and exert control in urban centers. These resources are generated through regulation of private producers by means of monopsonies in the form of marketing boards to which farmers must sell their crops for export.[9] Although originally intended to accumulate funds for farmers as protection against price fluctuations in world markets, the marketing boards have increasingly been used by governments to tax farmers by paying them lower prices for their crops than international market conditions would warrant. The marketing boards have thus created the resources that have been moved to nonagricultural sectors.[10]

Bates's analysis is noteworthy because it underscores the looseness of the public/private distinction. Just as public subsidies influence private economic behavior in the advanced economies, for example, public regulation and spending bears on market activities in

---

9. Just as a monopoly refers to exclusive control over the sale of a product (goods or services) in a given market, a monopsony refers to the exclusive control over the purchase of a product in a given market. Because they eliminate competition, both allow price-fixing.

10. It is true, of course, that peasants and farmers have attempted to employ the marketplace as a mechanism of defense. For example, they have switched crops, retreated into subsistence in the parallel economy, and engaged in smuggling. But as Bates (1981, 87) points out, this is not a triumph for them because these alternatives are second best and involve economic losses. For further discussion on these issues, see Chazan 1988 (124–31).

poorer dual economies. But Bates's study takes us further than this by documenting the ways in which the so-called private sector—that is, the market—can itself become both a central political arena within which conflict takes place and a mechanism employed to assert political control. Consequently, the size of the public sector becomes an untenable index of political capacity. Even if we were able to distinguish unambiguously between private and public consumption (or production), Bates has documented that politics is not restricted to the public sector.

Parallel difficulties are encountered when we consider the nonmarket or centrally planned economies. As I have already indicated, part of the problem with making east-west comparisons of public-sector size has stemmed from different national accounting systems. Indeed, because of these differences, some sources (e.g., World Bank 1987; Summers and Heston 1988) do not report figures for the nonmarket economies. The problem, of course, is that the meaning of private consumption (or of the market) is inherently ambiguous in economies where the market has been officially relegated to a minor role.

Careful estimates using the best available data indicate that government budgets in the centrally planned economies have been of a similar size to those in the market economies of comparable wealth (Pryor 1968; Bahry 1983). But the next inferential leap is more difficult, because the degree to which government budgets have reflected public-sector size in nonmarket economies is unclear given the ambiguous status of private consumption in such economies. In turn, the bearing of either national budgets or the public sector on the issue of national political capacity in the centrally planned economies is even more murky.

In sum, the idea that state strength corresponds even remotely to the size of the public sector is difficult to justify whatever the type of economic system. Rubinson argued that the mark of a strong state is its ability to control activity, most notably in its capacity "to regulate and control economic activity" (1976, 642). Approaches like Carnoy's (1984) are predicated on a similar rationale. However, the evidence indicates that such ability is not a simple function of public-sector size. Along with the ambiguity of the distinction between public and private consumption, this suggests that little can be gained by refining the fiscal measures considered earlier in this chapter as indicators of national political capacity.[11]

---

11. Occasionally, public-sector size is taken as a measure of "socialism" (e.g., Brunk, Caldeira, and Lewis-Beck 1987). The problems with such a specification parallel the difficulties I have just discussed with the equation of public-sector size and state strength.

State Strength as State Autonomy

A desirable feature of the studies that rely on government size to evaluate state strength is that they do employ explicit criteria to define state strength. But they do not represent the only approach to state strength. The principal alternative to which I now turn also emphasizes the question of national political autonomy, but without primary reliance on government size.[12]

Current interest in the autonomy of the state can be traced back to the views originating with Karl Marx and, especially, Max Weber. In general terms, both Marx and Weber cast the nation-state as the structure of government and administration, but beyond this, they diverged sharply. The Marxist tradition is ambiguous about the role of the state, most notably on the question of its autonomy from broader economic and social forces. Although the state is seen as a distinctive structure, it is an epiphenomenal one—that is, it is essentially a superstructure that serves to rationalize more fundamental forces stemming from class relations based on the means of production. Hence the state's autonomy is necessarily limited.[13]

In sharp contrast to Marx, Weber asserted that political life does have an independence of its own, so that the state cannot somehow be reduced to an extrapolitical phenomenon. Indeed, much of Weber's scholarship can be seen as a debate with and reconstruction of the Marxist legacy (Zeitlin 1990). As I indicated in chapter 1, Weber saw the state as a territorially-defined, established political and bureaucratic order that enjoys a monopoly of the legitimate use of force. And it is the conviction that this political and bureaucratic order is autonomous from wider social and economic forces that is at the heart of Weber's analysis. This conviction was part of his effort to undermine

---

12. While these alternative analyses do not rely primarily on government size to define states, they do refer to government size sporadically. Indeed, Skocpol seems to attribute the revival of interest in the state directly to large public sectors in the West: "*Now that debates about large public sectors have taken political center stage* in all of the capitalist democracies, . . . a paradigmatic shift seems to be underway in the macroscopic social sciences, a shift that involves a fundamental rethinking of the role of states in relation to economies and societies" (1985, 7; emphasis added).

13. Marx's own writing on the state is scattered and incomplete, reflecting in part his view that it is basically a superstructure. For a Marxist treatment of the state, see Miliband 1969. Some Marxists have attempted to modify the argument to allow a greater degree of independence to the state (see, e.g., the discussion of "relative autonomy" in Poulantzas 1978). The problem with such modifications is that if state autonomy is only relative, then the state remains fundamentally epiphenomenal; if state autonomy is more complete, then the revision becomes a Weberian one, and the Marxist element of the analysis loses much of its force. Reformulations like this bring to mind Parkin's wry comment: "Inside every neo-Marxist there seems to be a Weberian struggling to get out" (1979, 25).

the economic determinism which he regarded as endemic to Marxist analyses (his analysis of the role of Protestantism in the rise of capitalism, with its stress on the causal importance of cultural forces, was another part of this same effort).

Given Weber's emphasis on the independent role of the political, it is hardly surprising that his general conception of the state has been central to much of the recent statist literature, as well as to the earlier development studies. I do not mean to suggest that more recent studies have adopted Weber's approach wholesale. Contemporary studies avoid, among other things, his emphasis on the bureaucracy as a rational order, an encouraging tendency given the looseness with which Weber treated the concept of rationality. What they retain is the more fundamental notion that politics is important. As Bright and Harding put it,

> The state remains an autonomous, irreducible set of institutions, but the view of the state as an internally rationalized bureaucracy immune to popular influences or governed by self-generated rules gives way to a view of the state as *the arena of routinized political competition* in which class, status, and political conflicts, representing both elite and popular interests, are played out. (1984, 3–4; emphasis added)

As far as it goes, this approach is unexceptionable. The problem, however, is that it does not go very far. Instead, the state refers simply to the arena within which political conflict takes place. As Easton has observed, where the term *state* "is merely a substitute for government or political authorities or political elite, no great harm is done" (1981, 317). By the same token, as he goes on to note, such usage is hardly distinctive.

The emphasis of contemporary statist literature on the centrality of the state is merely an argument that politics is important. Thus, the introduction to a set of essays on the role of the state in development argues that the distinctiveness of current state-centered analyses stems from their attempt "to restore the significance of the autonomy of the political to their respective analyses of development issues" (Kohli 1986, 17).

Leaving to one side the issue of whether politics can meaningfully be described as completely autonomous from other structures (see my discussion in chap. 2), the suggestion that political life plays an important role is one that should find ready acceptance among students of politics. Indeed, many of these students will feel that despite the new bottle, they have been served a familiar old wine. In this sense, Weber's influence has been monumental. Some statist studies, of course, attempt to be more specific than this. When they do, however, they rapidly encounter formidable problems of reification whereby the state is cast as a unitary actor concerned with imposing its own will and protecting its own interests, which are not isomorphic with other political interests. It is, however, difficult when considering domestic politics to conceive of a national political arena as a unitary actor.[14] As a result, such efforts run into immediate difficulties. For example, an analysis by Korpi attaches great significance to the state. Specifically, he argues that within industrialized societies, the state has played a major role in redistributing wealth and other material goods. However, his treatment of the issues simply illustrates the problems involved. Consider the following:

> The state can be conceived of as a set of institutional structures which have emerged in the struggles between classes and interest groups in a society. The crucial aspect of this set of institutions is that they determine the ways in which decision-making on behalf of the whole society can legitimately be made and enforced. The state must not, however, be seen as an actor in itself, or as a pure instrument to be used by whichever group that has it under its control. While the institutional structures and the state can be used to affect, e.g., distributive processes in the society, these structures also affect the way in which power resources can be mobilized and are, in turn, affected by the use of power resources. (Korpi 1983, 19)

This treatment raises at least two major issues. First, Korpi insists that the state not be reified—that is, not "seen as an actor in itself, or as a pure instrument." If the state is not an actor, however, then it simply cannot be engaged in a process of "tripartite societal bargaining between the state, labour, and capital" (Korpi 1983, 25), because any such engagement reifies it. Second, although Korpi appears to imply that the state consists of more than the incumbent government and its administration, he also suggests that it can be under the control of one or more social groups. But this suggestion renders any distinction between the government and the state untenable. Indeed, Korpi's

---

14. Viewing the state as a unitary actor often does make sense in the analysis of foreign policy (for a perceptive analysis of this issue, see Bueno de Mesquita, Siverson, and Woller 1992). However, my concern is with domestic politics.

analysis would have been more tractable had he substituted the term government for the term state throughout.[15]

The same problem is evident in other studies. One inquiry into the role of nation-states in the international economy begins by noting the behavior of three different national governments (Ikenberry 1986a). Two paragraphs later the term *state* is substituted for government, and the state is cast as a strategic actor both domestically and internationally. The author's conception of the state follows Weber's, although he adds the provisos that states are organizations that are staffed by officials, and that they are organizations that, all other things equal, would like to survive. Ikenberry continues:

> The use of the terms "state organization" and "state elite" to define the logical properties of the state is not an inconsistency: the latter term is used metonymically to refer to the former. Beyond that, it is useful to talk about an elite when exploring propositions about the state empirically. Also, because this essay concerns state strategy—or the self-conscious choice of policy by the state—the analyst must ultimately confront the fact that decisions are made by individuals. Nonetheless, those choices flow from the organizational position of the state within larger national and international structures. (Ikenberry 1986a, 55)

What does this tell us about the state? Basically, we learn that the state cannot be defined directly. Instead, it can only be delineated metonymically—that is, one attribute or adjunct of the state (namely, the group of individuals who staff it) is substituted for the broader concept itself, so that when Ikenberry employs the term state, what he really means is the state elite (i.e., public officials). Further, his suggestion that this is a particularly useful and perhaps necessary strategy when contemplating the state empirically implies that, conceived in broader terms, the state has no clear and distinctive empirical referent. While this approach might appear to avoid the unitary actor problem by recognizing that individuals make decisions, the fact that Ikenberry resorted to metonymy constitutes a telling criticism of the approach, because it means that the state has been defined solely in terms of *one* of its components. Again, the state is no more than its public officials and the government.[16] It is perfectly reasonable to argue that national

---

15. For a more complete discussion of Korpi's analysis, see Jackman 1986.

16. Ikenberry and his colleagues employ a similar definition of the state in subsequent work. See, for example, Mastanduno, Lake, and Ikenberry 1989, where the state is defined as "politicians and administrators in the executive branch of government."

governments can act, subject to domestic and international constraints, but the statist terminology adds nothing to the analysis. A similar problem plagues another study of bargaining between the Mexican state and transnational corporations (Bennett and Sharpe 1979). Although this purports to be a statist analysis, the terms *government* and *state* are used interchangeably throughout (yet another example of this usage is provided by Haggard 1986). Toward the end of the study, constraints on the exercise of state power are considered:

> When an actor in a power conflict is a collectivity rather than a single person, there may be organizational constraints on the utilization of potential power. For *internal* reasons, the actor may not be able to draw on all of the potential power that is theoretically available to it. With a complex entity like the state, such internal constraints may stem from the lack of the organizational coordination that is necessary to wield its potential power to full effectiveness. (Bennett and Sharpe 1979, 83–84)

The lack of coordination is then traced to competition between ministries of the national government, competition within ministries, and a failure of the president to provide clear guidance and support to national policy.

Finally, consider Nordlinger's approach, which is said to constitute a "modified Weberian definition:"

> The state refers to those *individuals* who occupy offices that authorize them, and them alone, to make and apply decisions that are binding upon any and all parts of a territorially circumscribed population. The state is made up of, *and limited to*, those individuals who are endowed with societywide decision-making powers. (Nordlinger 1987, 362; emphasis added)

Nordlinger lays great emphasis on the state as a set of individuals, in order to avoid problems of reification and to acknowledge the fact that only individuals act. At the same time, he rules invalid those conceptions of the state that emphasize either administrative and coercive systems or public institutions. But if this is the case, then it becomes quite unclear why we should take the state seriously as an important analytic entity.

The only reasonable conclusion to be drawn from studies like these is that the nation-state constitutes the national political arena within which conflict takes place, but there is a vast difference between an arena and an actor. Attempts to treat the two as synonymous in treatments of domestic politics necessarily introduce a major problem of reification that is impossible to resolve. The current fascination with state-centered analyses represents no more than an attempt to reintroduce a label that has no clear empirical referents.

It is important to remember that state-centered analyses are hardly novel. Such analyses were, indeed, at the heart of political analysis until the 1950s. That the earlier analyses foundered was due both to their excessive formalism and to their failure to identify what the state is. For example, Sabine complained sixty years ago that the term was poorly defined in general. He noted specifically that "the fact that the word state usually emphasizes political organization makes it especially difficult to draw a clear line between state and government" (1934, 329). I am not the first to suggest that more recent efforts suffer the same problem and should therefore be abandoned. Consider Easton's conclusion:

> If it is time for Marxism to inter the state as a concept, no less must be said about its use by non-Marxists. In recent years, the state has slipped back into the vocabulary of conventional social science, unobtrusively. The very casualness of its reception is particularly disturbing, if only because we have thereby skirted the meticulous scrutiny of new terms now becoming customary in social science. Unfortunately, perhaps because of its long tradition in political science, we are prone to take for granted that we know what the concept of the state means. In fact, the very history of the term throughout the ages, a history that led to its abandonment in the last quarter of a century, has testified to its obscure meaning and to its operational difficulties. My analysis of Poulantzas's explicit usage in his complex theoretical enterprise would seem to confirm the lessons of history. (Easton 1981, 321)

Easton's critique of current statist writing is detailed and powerful. It is puzzling that subsequent analyses have neither acknowledged nor addressed the problems he has raised.[17]

Finally, some contemporary analysts attempt to go beyond a general discussion of the state to consider problems of state strength. In one such formulation, Krasner (1978) argues that the American state

---

17. For example, no mention is made of Easton's paper or its specific criticisms by Krasner (1984), or by the contributors to Benjamin and Elkin (1985). Even Skocpol (1985) makes no reference to the argument even though she thanks Easton for his assistance.

is domestically weak, when compared, say, with the modern Japanese state, and that this weakness has consequences for the conduct and content of the national and international economic policy of the United States. However, it is difficult to gauge exactly what is involved in this claim. Although at one level Krasner appears to be offering a distinctively statist interpretation, his essay uses the terms *state* and *political system* interchangeably, which suggests again that he sees little practical difference between the state and the government.

As used by Krasner, state strength seems to refer to the degree of consensus among those who count in politics on domestic policy goals. In Japan, this consensus appears more complete for a variety of reasons, but most notably because certain interests (especially those of labor) have been excluded from the agenda (Pempel 1978). The American state, by contrast, is said to be weaker because there is much less consensus on domestic goals, which constrains the ability of political leaders to mobilize resources and implement policy. Phrased differently, Krasner is suggesting that the American state is weaker because more people and groups need to be accommodated.[18]

In a broader formulation, Katzenstein reaches the parallel conclusion that the state is likely to be stronger in the late industrializers (e.g., Japan) than in the early industrializers (e.g., Britain and the United States) because the state has assumed a different character in these two types:

> Among early industrializers political parties were instruments of political mobilization from the bottom; a progressive coalition focused on political participation rather than bureaucratic penetration. Among late industrializers political parties were instruments of political implementation from the top; an absolutist coalition concentrated its efforts on bureaucratic penetration rather than political participation. (Katzenstein 1978, 332)

The laissez-faire, weak-state tradition of the early industrializers is attributed to their emphasis on participation, while the concern with penetration in the late industrializers generated a more interventionist

---

18. In addition, the conclusion that the American state is weak rests on analyses that restrict their attention to political institutions at the federal level. Even on its own terms, this is a questionable conclusion, but note further that it ignores political structures below the federal level, which, among other things, control most police functions in the United States. As Lentner has correctly pointed out, writers like Krasner "are confusing the problem of national concentration versus federalism with the strength or weakness of the state" (1984, 373).

tradition. The result is that the latter display more consensus over national policy *and* distinctive policies that place more emphasis on long-term goals and accumulation. Conversely, the early industrializers exhibit less consensus on policy goals and a heavier emphasis on short-term policy and consumption. Thus, state strength is manifested in public policy.

More recently, Katzenstein has modified the argument to suggest that state capacity has at least two dimensions. First, the state can be seen as an actor, and his comparison of Austria and Switzerland suggests that in this regard the Austrian state has more capacity because it is larger (in terms of public spending and the size of the national bureaucracy). However, the state can also be seen as part of a "policy network," in which case there is a "far-reaching interpenetration of state and society" in both Austria and Switzerland (Katzenstein 1985, 236).[19] Katzenstein concludes that each of these viewpoints "offers an important half-truth about Austria and Switzerland" (1985, 248), by which he seems to imply that they collectively constitute a whole truth.

A more defensible conclusion is that public-sector size tells us little about political capacity for the reasons advanced earlier in this chapter, and that Katzenstein's newer formulation simply reasserts that state strength is somehow manifested in public policy. Even so, this remains an imprecise definition of state strength with no obvious implications for measurement. I believe that this imprecision is an unavoidable outcome of the fact that the state itself means no more than the national political arena. Loose definitions of the term *state* necessarily lead to vagueness when one subsequently attempts to provide some meaning to the idea of state strength.

Some believe that loose working definitions of the state are more useful than more specific approaches, and proceed to claim that the latter are necessarily artificial and superficial. Thus, Evans and his colleagues conclude that state capabilities are not in any real sense fixed, but vary from issue to issue and from one period to another in a complex dialectic fraught with contradictions or paradoxes:

> [The evidence] points us resolutely away from any temptation to characterize states simply as strong or weak, or even stronger and weaker according to some generalized continuum . . . . Possibilities for state interventions of given types cannot be derived

---

19. A similar distinction is apparently involved in the "irony" of state strength discussed in Ikenberry (1986b).

from some overall level of generalized capacity or "state strength." More finely-tuned analyses must probe actual state organizations in relation to one another, in relation to past policy initiatives, and in relation to the domestic and transnational contexts of state activity. (Evans, Rueschemeyer, and Skocpol 1985, 352–53)

This argument implies that a general definition of national political capacity is to be avoided because any such attempt is bound to be counterproductive. It further implies that to adopt a more rigorous conception is to preclude the possibility that state strength varies over time, but this implication is quite misleading.

The prescription offered by Evans and his colleagues is a prescription for historicism. Essentially, they are suggesting that little of a general nature can be said about the capabilities of nation-states. Instead, state strength is situationally determined and in a constant state of flux, so that more is to be gained by examining specific contexts and avoiding the urge to generalize.[20] As I indicated in chapter 1, I believe this is an unnecessarily restrictive prescription on methodological grounds. But it is also important to understand that, substantively, there is more than a little touch of irony here.

In his survey, Krasner concludes that contemporary writing on the state represents a paradigm shift away from the behavioralism said to be rampant in the 1960s. To illustrate the point, he compares Dahl's pluralist study of power in New Haven (1961) with the newer literature on state power. What can we learn from this comparison? According to Krasner, the pluralist approach is excessively individualistic and atomistic. In contrast to more recent treatments of state power, "Institutional imperatives and constraints, including general political beliefs, do not play a significant role in Dahl's formulation" (Krasner 1984, 227). Apparently, there is more than one way of reading Dahl.

The basic conclusion of *Who Governs?* was, after all, that it is difficult to make general statements about power or to identify a clear power elite. Instead, argued Dahl and his associates (e.g., Polsby 1980), it is critical to examine specific issues in varying contexts and historical settings before advancing more widespread claims about the

---

20. In a minor variant on this theme, Mitchell acknowledges that the state is difficult to define but goes on to suggest that little is to be gained by sharper definitions. Instead of seeking "explanations in the form of generalizable statements" (1991, 91), he proposes that the state "should be examined not as an actual structure, but as the powerful, metaphysical effect of practices that make such structures appear to exist" (1991, 94). The research implications of Mitchell's argument are obscure. Nor are these implications clarified in his response to commentaries especially by Bendix and Sparrow (see Bendix, et al. 1992).

exercise of power. Once this is done, it becomes clear that the exercise of power is situationally determined, and that the power of different actors is contingent on the policy issue and historical conditions at hand. Thus, Dahl concluded by referring to the "complex processes of symbiosis and change that constitute the relations of leaders and citizens" (Dahl 1961, 325), and that thereby constrain the exercise of power.

Contrast this with the more recent conclusion that "issues of 'state strength' . . . can be fruitfully broached only via thoroughly dialectical analyses that allow for non-zero-sum processes and complex interactions between state and society" (Evans, Rueschemeyer, and Skocpol 1985, 355). The novelty of the prescription offered by the new statism is more apparent than real. Indeed, that prescription has a longer history than its proponents acknowledge.

Implications

The foregoing indicates that contemporary writing on the state is of limited use in the analysis of political capacity. First, those studies that have employed the size of the public sector as a criterion for state strength suffer from serious practical and conceptual problems. Most important, it is never clear how the public and private sectors are to be distinguished. But these analyses do have the clear virtue of explicitness and represent a serious attempt to identify what state strength means in some general sense.

In contrast, the alternative approach denies both the feasibility and the desirability of a general definition of state strength. Beyond suggesting that the nation-state consists of the national political arena, however, this alternative is unacceptably vague. When applied to the issue of national political capacity, it leads to problems of reification that are overwhelming to all but the likes of Louis XIV and Jean-Bedel Bokassa. But the basic difficulty with this approach remains its ambiguity. The failure to provide a clear definition of the state is reminiscent of difficulties encountered in an earlier literature that attempted to distinguish the political community from the regime, and both of these from political authorities (Easton 1965). And the problems inherent in efforts to discuss the question of state autonomy parallel earlier endeavors to discriminate between the "political system" and the wider "environment." In those instances where it has attempted to be more concrete, the statist approach seems to represent little more than a relabeling of earlier arguments. Almond's judgment is telling: "It is difficult to see what new insight, what new research

programs will have been stimulated by 'Bringing the State Back In'"
(1987, 477). On a more methodological level, much current writing
on the state appears to constitute a denial that generalization is possible or even desirable.

I believe we can go further than this. In the international arena, it
is clear that some states are more powerful than others because they
possess more resources including population and industrial capacity.
The question of domestic political capability would seem amenable to
a similar treatment, even if the criteria for capability are somewhat
different. On the face of it, most industrialized countries are also
relatively developed in political terms, although, as cases like Weimar
Germany and, to a lesser extent, the French Fourth Republic remind
us, institutional collapse is not unknown in wealthier countries. In
contrast, national political capability in Lebanon since 1975 has hov-
ered between minimal and nonexistent, and there are several other
cases where the possibility of coups, revolutions, and other upheavals
underscore the fragility of national political institutions. The question
is how can we evaluate the degree of that fragility?

CHAPTER 4

Institutions and Political Capacity

Nothing is more difficult to handle, more doubtful of success, nor
more dangerous to manage, than to put oneself at the head of introducing new orders.

—Niccolo Machiavelli, *The Prince*

Like prophecies, revolutions restart time, and the distance between
l'An I and l'An X is greater than any other decade in history. After
that, or a little bit more, things seem to slow down, not because less
happens but because less happens for the first time.

—Clifford Geertz, "The Judging of Nations"

To this point I have emphasized the centrality of institutions to political capacity. I turn now to the question of what it is about institutions
that impinges on capacity. The goal is to identify a generic type of
political capacity, although in view of the recency of the modern state,
the kinds of politics involved are peculiar to this century. This means
that although capacity is concerned with the degree of government
rather than its form, we cannot entirely escape questions of form as
these relate to the basic unit of analysis—what Jackson and Rosberg
(1982a) have labeled the juridical state. If it is agreed, however, that
the subject is a generic type of national political capacity (with the
understanding that the focus is on twentieth-century politics), then
whether institutions are modeled on a liberal ideal of political democracy, an authoritarian model, or some religious precept is beside the
point. The latter distinctions only illustrate the variety of forms that
modern national political institutions may take or attempt to emulate,
but they have no intrinsic bearing on the effectiveness of those institutions.

The proposition that degree of government is the relevant quantity is hardly novel. After all, studies like Almond and Coleman
(1960) and Huntington (1968) also sought to identify a general form
of national political development that could, in principle, be applied
to all modern states. But the emphasis on governmental effectiveness

73

implies that the question of political capacity is initially best broached as a problem in creating viable organizations.

Max Weber on Organization

In the classic treatment of this subject, Max Weber (1947) argued that *rules* are central to organizations, or, in his terminology, social "orders." More specifically, while organizations involve regularities of behavior or "a uniformity of social action," they consist of more than this. Organizations consist of regularities embedded in a set of rules. And the organization is effective to the extent that actors regard those rules as desirable. When most actors consider the rules to be desirable, Weber concluded, the social order can be characterized as legitimate.

Weber further suggested that the legitimacy of an organization can be maintained in two ways. The first of these involves convention and the second, law:

> A system of order will be called *convention* so far as its validity is externally guaranteed by the probability that deviation from it within a given social group will result in a relatively general and practically significant reaction of disapproval. Such an order will be called *law* when conformity with it is upheld by the probability that deviant action will be met by physical or psychic sanctions aimed to compel conformity or to punish disobedience, and applied by a group of men especially empowered to carry out this function. (Weber 1947, 127)

Weber's discussion is particularly pertinent to the question of political capacity. As I argued in chapter 2, political power differs from force because it is relational. While power is ultimately maintained by at least an implicit threat of force, the application of force may involve a power loss. Power is more readily exercised when it is widely regarded as legitimate. In this setting, laws that include sanctions for noncompliance ultimately hold organizations together, but those laws are more effective if they are regarded by subjects as reasonable "conventions." Political organization, then, involves the internalization of rules as conventions, with the proviso that those conventions are backed up by a body of law.

It is thus evident that the question of national political capacity refers to the degree to which there is an accepted national legal order.

Weber's discussion is also germane to the issue that this raises, namely, what is the process by which a legal order comes to be accepted? As is well-known, he identified three kinds of authority: rational-legal authority; traditional authority; and charismatic authority. Let us consider the three in turn.

Rational-legal authority consists of a body of generalized rules. These rules are universal and impersonal, in that they apply to all relevant persons (citizens of nation-states, in the present context). Such authority is typically enveloped in a bureaucratic structure with an organized administrative staff. And these structures are one of the hallmarks of contemporary industrial states.

Traditional authority derives less from a series of formalized explicit rules and more from attachment to the value of tradition itself. Authority is held to be binding because it has "always" been so regarded. Rules are not necessarily impersonal or universal in their application, and indeed, Weber described traditional authority as the "most primitive case" (1947, 131).

Although there are differences between traditional and rational-legal forms of authority, for our purposes it is more important to note that they share one fundamental trait: neither can be created, generated, or imposed rapidly. By its very nature, traditional authority is a form that evolves over a long period, one of at least sufficient length that those subject to it believe that it has "always" existed. But it is equally important to recognize that rational-legal authority also takes time to evolve, even though it is a modern phenomenon as described by Weber. Assuming for the moment (rather heroically) that this form of authority is currently manifested in the so-called industrial democracies, it is clear that the constitutional orders of these states were not created overnight.[1] Instead, they are the product of a lengthy and typically bumpy evolution during which the scope of the political sphere was broadened in two ways. First, citizen rights were made increasingly universal: though this process often involved concessions grudgingly made, it did expand the size of what Deutsch (1961) termed the "politically relevant strata." Second, the scope of government was simultaneously expanded, in terms of both economic and

---

1. The assumption is heroic because Weber's usage of the term rational, when applied to bureaucracies, emphasizes that administration is impersonal and evenhanded. Such a conception is restrictive because it assumes that modern bureaucracies are neutral in an apolitical sense. Power relations within the organization tend to be ignored, as do conflicts of interests between the organization as a whole, its members, and those whom it serves. As a result, Rudolph and Rudolph (1979) conclude that Weber's ideal-typical contrast between bureaucratic and traditional forms of authority cannot be sustained empirically.

social policy. For our purposes, the evolution implied by Weber's discussion of rational-legal and traditional forms of authority is important because it underscores the issue of the *timing* of development. *Charismatic authority* takes a quite different form. In Weber's view, the bearer of charisma is an individual leader, one surrounded by a coterie of followers or disciples. This person is a revolutionary leader whose claims to authority are necessarily in conflict with the institutionalized status quo:

> Charismatic authority repudiates the past, and is in this sense a specifically revolutionary force. It recognizes no appropriation of positions of power by virtue of the possession of property, either on the basis of a chief or of socially privileged groups. The only basis of legitimacy for it is personal charisma, so long as it is proved; that is, as long as it receives recognition and is able to satisfy the followers or disciples. But this lasts only as long as the belief in its charismatic inspiration remains. (Weber 1947, 362)

Because it is a revolutionary force, Weber saw charismatic authority as the major basis for political change. The successful charismatic movement is one that is able to undermine the legitimacy of the existing order, whether that legitimacy was based on rational-legal or traditional criteria.[2]

Weber's own discussion is peppered with numerous historical instances, ranging from the Chinese monarchy to the founder of Mormonism, Joseph Smith. More recent political history provides us with many other examples. Consider revolutionary figures such as Vladimir I. Lenin in Russia, Mao Ze-dong in China, Fidel Castro in Cuba, and the Ayatollah Khomeini in Iran. The list rapidly grows if we expand the net to include nationalist figures who were active in decolonization. Notable charismatic leaders here would include Mohandas Gandhi of India, Ho Chi Minh of Vietnam, Gamal Abdel Nasser of Egypt, Kwame Nkrumah of Ghana, Jomo Kenyatta of Kenya, and Julius Nyerere of Tanzania.

Weber's discussion of charismatic authority is thus important because it draws attention to the way that political orders change or are overthrown. This focus is of manifest relevance to the question of political capacity, because political orders do disintegrate, as is evi-

---

2. For useful discussions of both Weber's approach to charisma and more recent treatments of charismatic leadership and authority, see Eisenstadt 1968, Theobold 1978, and Parkin 1982.

denced by the major revolutions of this century, the collapse of European imperial power, and the dissolution of the former Soviet Union. But Weber's concept of charismatic authority has further implications. Much attention has focused in the past three decades on the problems of the "new" states. It is one thing to overthrow the existing order, but quite another to replace it with a new one. For Weber, charisma is *personal*, in a way that is "specifically foreign to everyday routine structures" (1947, 363). This, indeed, is why it is a revolutionary force. But once the old order has been toppled, charismatic authority itself has to be "routinized" if the movement is to be successful, and this process involves a fundamental transformation. Indeed, charisma would seem to provide no more than a transitory basis for authority:

> In its pure form charismatic authority may be said to exist only in the process of originating. It cannot remain stable, but becomes either traditionalized or rationalized, or a combination of both. (Weber 1947, 364)

That it is a transitory form implies that charismatic authority is an unsettling phenomenon that contains the seeds of self-destruction.

This fact is clear as charismatic leaders attempt to consolidate their position, but it is nowhere more apparent than when leaders retire or "disappear," and the disciples are confronted with the problem of succession. What motivates the members of the new movement to seek to consolidate their position in a new social order? Weber's answer is simple. First, the disciples (e.g., the members of revolutionary or nationalist cadres) have both an "ideal" and a "material" interest in the continuation of their community. Second, they have an even stronger interest in continuing their "relationship," that is, in consolidating the new order of which they are a part:

> Not only this, but they have an interest in continuing [the new order] in such a way that both from an ideal and a material point of view, their own status is put on a *stable everyday basis*. This means, above all, making it possible to participate in normal family relationships or at least to enjoy a secure social position in place of the kind of discipleship which is cut off from ordinary worldly connexions, notably in the family and in economic relationships. (Weber 1947, 364; emphasis added)

In other words, members of the new movement seek to routinize and thereby transform the nature of charismatic authority because they are fundamentally driven by office-seeking considerations, and by a "striving for security" (1947, 370). The argument was later expanded and elaborated by Michels in his famous iron law of oligarchy (1958, 1927), and it is no accident that Michels was once a student of Weber's (see, e.g., Mommsen 1989, chap. 6).

I have indicated that the process of routinization begins with the removal of the old order. However, it becomes critical with the retirement of the charismatic leader, because with that retirement, any remaining vestiges of personal authority are removed, so that the disciples cannot rely on such authority to advance their goals. If, by that stage, the movement has been unsuccessful in routinizing a new order, it fails. This, of course, is not to imply that routinization is completed with a successful transfer of leadership. But it is to insist that succession is pivotal to consolidation because "in it, the character of the leader himself and of his claim to legitimacy is altered" (Weber 1947, 371).

How is succession achieved? Weber argued that it could take a variety of forms, but that the most important were (*a*) where the successor was designated, either by the original leader or by his followers, and (*b*) where hereditary charisma formed the basis of change. In the light of its history since 1945 and the role of the Nehru-Gandhi dynasty in postindependence Indian politics, it is of at least passing interest to note that Weber regarded the classic case of hereditary charisma to be India.

But we should not become sidetracked here. Several scholars have concluded that Weber's discussion of charismatic leadership is ambiguous (e.g., Friedrich 1961; Blau 1963; Ratnam 1964), and indeed there is some basis for this charge.[3] For example, Weber's use of papal succession as an instance of the "designation of a successor by the charismatic followers of the leader" (1947, 371) could be taken to mean that popes continued to rely on charisma as a source of authority. In this vein, more recent writers have sometimes appeared to suggest that charisma can often serve as a continuing basis of power (e.g., Anderson 1972; Willner 1984).

Such suggestions obscure Weber's more fundamental point that charisma can only serve as a transitory basis for power by challengers to the established order. Once the old order is displaced, the chal-

---

3. Weber's analysis has many ambiguities, stemming in part from its fragmentary and incomplete nature, and in part from Weber's penchant for qualifying details.

lengers have to turn to the task of routinizing their own authority. True, that goal is more easily attained when there is a charismatic figure who can provide a personal framework within which his or her operatives can work, but this only masks the temporary nature of charismatic authority. That it has always been in the Vatican's interests (and therefore part of its official ideology) to have papal authority viewed as charismatic does not negate the essential fact that papal authority is highly routinized. Similarly, the prominence until recently of one family in modern Indian politics does not obscure the continuity and routinization of political institutions in that country.

Weber's emphasis on the importance of leadership succession has a direct and obvious bearing on the question of political development or institutionalization. This is clear when one considers the process of consolidation and institution building after revolutions. It is equally clear when one contemplates political events in the new states after decolonization. And the concern with the problem of succession is evident in the attempts of analysts to evaluate the prospects of success for new institutional orders. For example, will the Cuban state persist in its current form after Castro? It is clear that the Yugoslav federation ultimately failed to survive Tito. What are the long-term prospects for the current regime in Iran after Khomeini? Will political arrangements in Tanzania survive Nyerere?

On a more general level, Weber's discussion of charismatic authority redirects our attention to the *timing* of development. I have already suggested that the one basic property shared by his concepts of traditional and rational-legal authority is that they are forms that require considerable time to create. This implies that the chronological age of national political institutions may be one major yardstick of their effectiveness. In a parallel manner, the concept of charismatic authority draws notice to the problem of leadership succession and institution building in new orders, an issue that is particularly germane given the sheer number of new nation-states. This also brings us back to the timing-of-development issue conceived in terms of the generational age of institutions.

All of this underscores the proposition that organizational age has two components: chronological age and generational age. Weber's analysis remains the classic statement on these issues, and it has had a far-reaching impact on contemporary scholarship dealing with the "liability of newness" for organizations (Stinchcombe 1965). What are the implications of that scholarship for the analysis of political capacity?

The Chronological Age of Organizations

In a major statement, Starbuck defined organizational development as "change in an organization's age" (1965, 451). Equating development with chronological age is predicated on the assumption that the probability that the organization will survive increases with its age, an assumption of which the available empirical evidence is generally supportive. For example, business corporations in the United States that are fifty years old constitute only 2 percent of those initially created. Similarly, federal agencies that have survived to the age of fifty in the United States comprise just 4 percent of those originally established (Starbuck 1983). Such patterns are perfectly consistent with the idea that there is indeed a liability of newness, coupled with a corresponding advantage of age.[4]

I do not mean to suggest that there is some magical age beyond which organizations become immortal. Indeed, Starbuck reports that 30 percent of those corporations that do survive to the age of fifty years disappear in the subsequent decade; the corresponding figure for federal agencies in the United States is 26 percent (Starbuck 1983). The liability of newness argument asserts more modestly that the *probability* of survival increases with age. In other words, the odds of death are reduced (but hardly eliminated) for older organizations. This reminds us that development is always a matter of degree, so that organizations always retain a measure of fragility.

Starbuck's explanation of this empirical regularity is couched in terms of adaptive behavior (1965). Successful organizations are those that have in the past demonstrated an ability to adapt to their wider environment, and that can therefore be expected to continue to be relatively adaptable in the future. Age is the critical ingredient here simply because adaptation involves formalization and learning, both of which require time.[5]

---

4. Empirical evidence for the negative relation between age and organizational mortality is extensive. For a sampling of the relevant work, see Carroll 1983; Carroll and Delacroix 1982; Freeman, Carroll, and Hannan 1983; Hannan and Freeman 1984, 1989; Singh, Tucker, and House 1986; Baum and Oliver 1991; and Levinthal 1991. A minor variant on this theme casts the liability as one of adolescence rather than of newness, such that organizations enjoy a brief honeymoon upon their founding, after which organizational mortality rates peak and then decline (see, e.g., Bruderl and Schussler 1990; Fichman and Levinthal 1991). In an interesting empirical study of national political leaders, Bienen and van de Walle (1991) show that individual leaders' odds of survival increase with the length of their tenure in office. While their emphasis on time parallels mine, they are particularly concerned with individual leaders, as opposed to political regimes and the institutions they embody.

5. Thus, Ake (1974) to the contrary, a focus on the age (longevity) of institutions does not confuse stability with an absence of political change. Instead, the liability of

Patterns of formalization are readily understood. With time, general patterns of behavior are stabilized, roles come to be defined and assumed by individuals and groups, and "standard operating procedures" emerge. That age is central to this process is self-evident—for example, the very idea of a *standard* operating procedure presupposes a modicum of organizational continuity. Starbuck argues that formalization should increase with age because it is a learning or adaptive process, "though no doubt the earliest manifestations of formalization are the most striking ones" (1965, 478).

We should avoid the conclusion that this process implies that the organization is becoming more "rational." Instead, formalization simply refers to the creation or emergence of *routines*. As Starbuck notes,

> Young organizations have little experience in distinguishing important problems from unimportant ones, and few mechanisms for dealing with routine problems routinely . . . . Older organizations have learned to ignore unimportant problems, and have accumulated mechanisms for attending to routine problems. (1965, 481)

In other words, assuming that the environment is relatively stable, with age comes a collective memory (Walsh and Ungson 1991). This provides the organization with a repertoire of routines that constitute its "skills" (Nelson and Winter 1982, 124). Routines are essential to day-to-day operation of the organization, and also to the management of new problems. Without routines, it is difficult to identify problems as "new." Further, innovations can themselves be seen, in large part, of "new combinations of existing routines" (Nelson and Winter 1982, 130). The routines that come with age are therefore essential if the organization is to fulfill its goals.

What are those goals? On one level, this question is difficult to answer because, in general terms, organizations have a huge variety of stated goals and perhaps an equal number of implicit purposes. Moreover, the way we address this question would seem to depend on the level at which we ask it. For example, different sectors *within* organizations may also have unique goals (on this general subject, see Perrow 1968; Simon 1976, chap. 12).

The question becomes more tractable if we consider it at another level. The variety of manifest goals that organizations proclaim are all

newness argument implies that older institutions are more likely to survive precisely because of their demonstrated track record in adapting to and dealing with age.

predicated on the assumption of *survival*. In principle, business firms may exist to make profits, interest groups may express the political interests of their members, and other groups may profess even more lofty goals. But in no case can an organization be at all effective unless it tends to the more fundamental issue of ensuring its continued existence.[6]

There is reason to believe that the prominence of survival as a goal increases with organizational age, so that older organizations are more flexible. Simon has suggested that some people are attracted to organizations because they find the stated goals congenial, while others are attracted by the nature of the organization itself.

> The individual who is loyal to the *objectives* of the organization will resist modification of those objectives, and may even refuse to continue his participation if they are changed too radically. The individual who is loyal to the *organization* will support opportunistic changes in its objectives that are calculated to promote its survival and growth. (Simon 1976, 118)

It should be self-evident that nascent organizations tend to be populated by people of the first type, but Starbuck (1965, 473–77) offers three reasons for expecting that, with time, those of the second type will come to play a dominant role. First, with age, structures emerge so that individuals and groups within the organization are associated with particular roles. Second, those people in key roles spend a good deal of effort promoting the value of loyalty to the organization itself. Finally, those most committed to the organization's survival are also the people most likely to populate central positions in policy determination and administration, from which they can exert considerable influence over the agenda.

In light of this, older organizations escape the liability of newness and are more likely to continue surviving. Whether we describe their behavior as flexible or opportunistic is largely irrelevant. The more important point is that those in critical positions have incentives to engage in tactics to maximize institutional longevity. Of equal interest are the Weberian roots of this argument. Recall that Weber saw charismatic authority as no more than a transitory form that needs

---

6. In the most dramatic instances, the goals of an organization may become obsolete, and it identifies new goals to survive. The classic case of this phenomenon in the United States occurred with the transformation of the National Foundation for Infantile Paralysis into the National Foundation, which sponsors the March of Dimes. The transformation was an outcome of the success of Salk polio vaccine (sponsored by the foundation) in eradicating infantile paralysis (Sills 1957). Other cases of transformation (some successful and others not) are discussed in Aldrich (1979, chap. 8) and Perrow (1986, 159–64).

to be routinized if it is to lead to more enduring authority relationships. He further argued that the members of charismatic movements
are motivated toward routinization by their *material* interest in preserving the new order that they helped create.[7]

As I have emphasized, the proposition that the odds of organizational survival increase with age is predicated on the assumption that,
with time, organizations become more adaptable to their environments. The process further assumes that, over time, those members in
key positions within the organization become increasingly committed
to and motivated by the question of its survival. Although it has been
applied in a variety of settings, such a view seems particularly relevant to political organizations.

When we consider business firms, the criteria for effective performance are unambiguous. Such firms are primarily concerned with
maximizing their profitability—their survival, in fact, is contingent
on this. Profitability is a quantity to which we can readily attach
numbers (ignoring for the moment distinctions like that between long-
term and short-run performance). In contrast, political organizations
are not profit making, which means that their performance cannot be
evaluated using straightforward economic criteria. Instead, they deal
with goods whose meaning is inherently uncertain, so their performance is necessarily judged against social and political criteria. Political organizations employ ambiguous technologies in a context where
information about cause and effect relationships is poor to nonexistent
(see, e.g., Edelman 1964; Thompson 1967; March and Olsen 1976).
The clarity of performance standards is therefore low.

In such a setting, where accomplishment is judged in uncertain
social and political terms, survival is particularly likely to figure
prominently as *the* organizational goal precisely because of its clarity.
This point has been made with great clarity in Schlesinger's (1991)
analysis of competitive party behavior. But it is equally applicable in
other political contexts. For example, Bates's appraisal of agricultural
policies in Africa is predicated on the assumption that in general,
"policies are designed to secure advantages for particular interests, to
appease powerful political forces, and to enhance the capacity of
political regimes to remain in power (1981, 5–6). More recently,
Ames (1987) has shown that patterns of public spending in Latin
America can only be understood in terms of the pressures for survival
among chief political executives, and that these pressures affect civilian and military administrations alike. Politics, then, centers on calcu-

---

7. Again, the parallels between this argument and the description of organizational
behavior offered by Michels is striking.

lating (under conditions of considerable uncertainty) those policy mixes most likely to attract supporters and ensure the political tenure of existing administrations.

The case for the preeminence of survival as the dominant goal seems irresistible. After all, as another analyst of Third World politics observes,

> No agenda is worth anything if its sponsor has not lasted through the hazards of politics. Political survival becomes the prerequisite for achieving any significant long-term social change. It becomes the central issue occupying the attention of state leaders. Programs for social change may still be the basis for public rhetoric and even for policy statements and legislation, but at the apex of the state the politics of survival denudes state agencies of their capabilities to see those programs through. (Migdal 1987, 418)

Migdal's emphasis on the importance of survival goals is well placed, but his further suggestion that the politics of survival is testimony to diminished political capacity is less convincing. That key elements in the organization become increasingly concerned with issues of survival as routinization takes place is an indication of political life, not evidence of the substitution of opportunism for principle. Indeed, maintenance and continuation assume their prominence as criteria for effectiveness in political organizations precisely because no clear alternative performance criteria are available.

I noted earlier that Starbuck defined organizational development in terms of chronological age (1965). A useful measure of national political capacity needs to incorporate more than this, of course, but the perspective I have just considered indicates that chronological age is a key component of political capacity.[8] This point was recognized in the earlier literature on political development, with its emphasis on the *new* states. Shils, for example, attached considerable significance to the recency of the sovereignty of the new states, and argued that, despite their manifest problems, the older Third World states had some political and bureaucratic traditions on which they could draw (1963). By contrast, the new states lacked even this. Jackson and

---

8. Contrast this with Olson's (1982) argument that chronological age reflects institutional sclerosis, so that older states are likely to experience diminished economic and political performance. Olson's view is predicated on the assumption that the passage of time simply allows for the formation of distributional coalitions or cartels that inhibit innovation and growth. However, as Rogowski (1988, 301–10) has shown, the available evidence is not consistent with this argument.

Rosberg have pursued the same line of thought in their discussion of the general weakness of states in sub-Saharan Africa (1982a). And Weiner has emphasized the point that, compared with African states, those of Asia and the Middle East "have a long precolonial history of well-established bureaucratic institutions . . . . Contemporary Asian states may be no less autocratic than those of Africa, but they are typically more effective" (1987, 41). In view of the recency of decolonization in sub-Saharan Africa, such conceptions are also fully consistent with my emphasis on chronological age.

The Generational Age of Organizations

In addition to chronological age, we need to consider the issue of generational age. The latter term refers to the number of individuals who have occupied top leadership positions in the political order. At one extreme, the leader is the same individual who was associated with the creation of that political order and who is often seen as personifying it. At the other extreme, patterns of leadership succession are highly routinized and the political order has experienced and survived several successions. This means that it has an identity of its own that is largely independent of the individuals who comprise its current leadership. Chronological and generational age are related to each other. A set of institutions that is young on the first count is usually young on the second count as well. Nonetheless, there are useful distinctions here that bear particularly on the question of national political capacity.

Most notably, issues of chronological age refer to institutions. When applied to modern nation-states, for example, these concerns direct our attention to phenomena like the age of the national constitutional form or of the national bureaucracy. By way of contrast, the idea of generational age centers on individual leaders rather than on institutions. It is an idea that points us to the kinds of issues raised by Weber's discussion of the routinization of charismatic authority, where we want to determine whether the basis of political authority in a given setting is primarily personal or institutional. The question is important because with early-generation leaders (especially those in the first generation) it is always difficult to know whether political authority has a nonpersonal basis. This forms another aspect of the liability of newness, and it helps to account for the attention generally paid to the phenomenon of leadership succession in discussions of the long-term viability of political institutions.

Consider Mao Ze-dong, one of the major political figures of this century. His leadership role in the revolutionary movement before 1949 was so pervasive (accompanied as it was by events like the Long March) that he came to symbolize the new order produced by the Chinese Revolution after 1949. Such was the extent of his influence that toward the end of his life a good deal of political analysis addressed the question: What would China be like *after* Mao? The significance of this question derived wholly from the apparent centrality of his *personal* leadership in postrevolutionary China. For example, the Maoist cult seemed to suggest that his personality was an inherent part of the new political order, that the two were inseparable. The issue then was what would happen with the removal of his apparently dominant personality?

Modern political history is, of course, replete with instances of this general phenomenon. Generally, the first heads of state after decolonization were already well established as political leaders of the nationalist movement that had preceded decolonization. They were widely recognized for their role in the struggle for independence, and in many cases (e.g., Nkrumah of Ghana and Kenyatta of Kenya) had been imprisoned by the colonial powers for their efforts. As a result of their visibility in the politics of decolonization, they also came to be personally identified with the new state that emerged.

These are all cases of personal leadership in new political orders. Their relevance to the question of national political capacity stems from the fact that new political orders are, by definition, fluid and inchoate. In such settings, the major task at hand for political leaders is to consolidate their position, a process that involves, among other things, the cooptation or elimination of potential rivals. Because of the fluidity of new political orders, such efforts at consolidation are risky and the probability of failure is high. To be sure, in the short run, the records of Mao Ze-dong and Kenyatta would seem to represent successes. But in the even shorter run, Nkrumah was obviously a failure.

The idea that generational age is an important component of national political capacity is predicated on the difficulty of institutionalizing new political orders. It takes as axiomatic Weber's observation that charismatic authority is a personal form that is necessarily fragile and no more than transitory. It thus assumes that the first order of business for charismatic leaders and their followers is to routinize their authority, but recognizes that this is a formidable task.

My use of the concept of charisma is political, however, and differs in this sense from other contemporary treatments. The common usage of the term is more faithful to the letter of Weber's argument, but not to its spirit. As I have already indicated, that argument has often been criticized for its ambiguity (e.g., Friedrich 1961; Blau 1963; Ratnam 1964), and the criticism is not without justification. Specifically, Weber's discussion does include the suggestion that charisma has psychological and social sources, and, further, that the former are more important than the latter. Moreover, part of his purpose was to contrast charisma and rationality as bases for legitimacy.

In recognition of this, charismatic authority has generally been cast in psychological terms and seen as fundamentally irrational. For example, Dekmejian and Wyszomirski (1972) argue that the exercise of charisma involves the interaction between a leader and followers that requires a situation of "acute social crisis," an "exemplary personage," and "value transformation." At one level this may appear reasonable, but consider what these terms are said to involve. Crisis situations are defined as follows:

> A pathological response of society arising from the breakdown of the existing mechanisms of conflict resolution. In such times, irrational, schizophrenia-like disorientations occur creating a deep sense of psychological dependence and heightened expectation. At the political level, a crisis in legitimacy engulfs the system, its leaders, ideology and institutions. The prevailing milieu of mass alienation, social atomization, and identity crisis renders the populace vulnerable to mass appeals. (Dekmejian and Wyszomirski 1972, 195)

What is a charismatic leader?

> He is . . . a revolutionary inclined to take major risks. Being a product of his own crisis-torn environment, he is an acutely alienated individual. Usually his alienation can be traced back to an unstable family life and his failures and sufferings experienced in society, i.e., inability to gain upward mobility, imprisonment, identity crisis   factors that propel him toward revolutionary action. In this sense he is a "marginal" who draws himself to other "alienates" or "marginals" who eventually become the core of his movement dedicated to enlarge his *Gemeinde* or "congregation" to include the alienated masses. (1972, 196)

Charismatic authority is exercised where such a leader is able to exploit a crisis situation:

> One of the most distinguishing characteristics of charismatic authority . . . is to be found in the highly spiritual relationship that

develops between the leader and his followers. Based on a "bridge" of leader-inspired values, the charismatic relationship places the leader "in communion" with his *Gemeinde*, in a state of intense spiritual union. In this context, the charismatic performs certain psychological functions, one of the most significant being his role as "agent for the identification of alter-ego with a transcendent state." Furthermore, he accords his faithful a feeling of comfort, consolation, and sense of belonging. (1972, 197)

The most striking feature of Dekmejian and Wyszomirski's treatment lies in their insistence that charismatic authority is fundamentally irrational and mystical. The charismatic leader is cast as a messianic figure. Of course, such an emphasis is perfectly consistent with Weber's analysis—indeed, it forms a critical ingredient in modern analyses of the phenomenon.

For example, Willner defines charismatic leadership as a relationship between a leader and set of followers which has the following properties:

1. The leader is perceived by the followers as somehow superhuman.
2. The followers blindly believe the leader's statements.
3. The followers unconditionally comply with the leaders directives for action.
4. The followers give the leader unqualified emotional commitment. (Willner 1984, 8)

Again, the emphases on superhuman qualities, on blind followers whose allegiance is unconditional, and on emotional commitment all underscore the alleged irrationality of the phenomenon.

Casting the problem this way is counterproductive, however, and diverts attention from what is distinctive about charismatic authority. The principal difficulty is that introducing irrationality into the analysis obscures the essentially political nature of charismatic leadership in a way that the term becomes little more than a pejorative adjective. Instead of casting charismatic figures as mystics, it is more useful to conceive of them as people who have the political skills to convince their followers of their own distinctive and indispensable talent for leadership in the creation of a new order. Moreover, while it is important that all "disciples" receive the message, it is not necessary that all potential followers be so convinced.

That an emphasis on the psychology and irrationality of charisma is too restrictive is clear from Willner's own analysis. For example, she concludes that Castro, Gandhi, Hitler, Mussolini, Franklin Roosevelt, and Sukarno are correctly seen as charismatic. In contrast, we are told that figures like Ataturk, Lenin, Mao, Magasaysay, Nasser, Nkrumah, and Peron can only be regarded as "probable charismatics" or "quasi-charismatics" because they were insufficiently mystical. Consider the discussion of Lenin:

> The posthumous myth of Lenin's charisma is so firmly established that there is a tendency to overlook the fact that in 1917–18 he had his way over the objections of his closest followers not because of their absolute belief in his judgment but through the force of his will and his logic and by his threats to withdraw. Similarly often forgotten is that during this period his support from the Petrograd populace waxed and waned. (Willner 1984, 39)

The problem, of course, is that there is every reason to believe that the allegedly superhuman leaders were subject to exactly the same sort of pressures—certainly, Willner provides no convincing substantiation for an alternative conclusion. Nor should we expect to find such evidence. For example, Gandhi, whom she does classify as charismatic, withdrew from the Indian National Congress in 1934 precisely because it refused to adopt in its entirety his program following the London Conference on India. To repeat, charismatic authority is a political commodity, not a psychological or an irrational phenomenon.

Although Weber's consideration of the psychology of charisma does much to obscure the fact, his fundamental point was that charisma can only be a transitory basis for political authority in times of political upheaval—of which Russia in 1917-18 is a prime example. In such times, charismatic leaders can be a potent personal symbol of a new order and personally help to define it in revolutionary terms. Such definitions are pivotal because they impose some pattern to the otherwise structureless political situation, a pattern that is symbolized by the leaders' personae. Because periods of political upheaval involve constantly shifting coalitions with rival contenders for power, charismatic leaders are those people with the *political* skills to maintain their position. These skills include the ability to convince others by force of will and logic and by political maneuvers that include threatening to withdraw. In fact, that the threat of withdrawal is successful (as Willner claims it was with Lenin) itself constitutes acknowledgment by his associates (i.e., followers) of his *personal* indispensability. It is this recognition that is at the heart of charismatic leadership, and absolutely no gain is achieved by portraying it in irrational or mystical terms.

In a similar vein, Dekmejian and Wyszomirski's suggestion that the charismatic figure is a marginal alienate profoundly troubled by experiences like imprisonment for political activities fundamentally misses the point. There is abundant evidence that many nationalist leaders were able to derive considerable political profit from their imprisonment at the hands of colonial governments. Imprisonment enhanced their political stature by converting them into martyrs who personified the goals of anticolonial movements.[9] In this sense, incarceration should not be seen as a psychologically damaging experience: instead, it was a force that helped *create* the political charisma of the figures involved.

Applied to the analysis of political capacity, charismatic authority is distinctive because it is a personal form and because it is most likely in the fluid political situation surrounding the emergence of a new order. The big question is always whether charismatic authority can be institutionalized. That is, can charismatic leaders use their presence which personifies and symbolizes the new order as a framework within which new political organization can be created? As Machiavelli and many others have recognized, the task is a formidable one. Moreover, the degree to which charismatic authority has been routinized is difficult to gauge in the abstract. It is only at the moment when leadership is transferred from one individual to the next that we can begin to get some sense of how routinized the new political order has become, or whether it has evolved into a more mundane system of personal rule. This accounts for the widespread interest in leadership succession (see, e.g., Burling 1974; Calvert 1987).

Even if charismatic authority has been effectively used to create new organization, the first leadership succession is likely to be rocky. But, following a success-breeds-success mechanism, the process by which leadership is transferred from one individual to another should become increasingly predictable over time. In other words, although the first succession is likely to be somewhat traumatic, the process becomes progressively straightforward with routinization. Jackson and Rosberg argue that this outcome is more likely (but far from guaranteed) where the state as a juridical unit is older (as in the cases of Russia and China after their revolutions of this century), because

---

9. Perhaps the best-known instance of this phenomenon was Gandhi, whose approach to nonviolent resistance was predicated on the assumption that martyrdom is not without its political benefits. Similarly, the experience of being a prison graduate helped create leaders like Kenyatta, Nkrumah, and most recently Nelson Mandela.

under those circumstances there is more of an existing political tradition at the national level (1982b, 21-22). In contrast, succession is likely to continue to be problematic where the state as a legal entity is newer, as is the case in much of sub-Saharan Africa.

When the process of leadership transfer is not effectively routinized, then it is clear that charismatic authority has not been used to create substantial political institutions. Under these circumstances, the most likely outcome is a chain of personal or patrimonial leaders (Zolberg 1966; Roth 1968; Jackson and Rosberg 1982b, 1984b). Personal rule suffers from all the problems of charismatic rule and more, because patrimonial rulers seldom display anything resembling a charismatic gift and rarely proclaim a distinctive political mission. Indeed, as Theobold has noted, such rule is characterized by "a shifting series of tasks and powers commissioned and granted on an ad hoc basis by the ruler/chief. In the absence of clear-cut spheres of competence and regular fixed salaries, *there can be no unequivocal division between incumbent and office*" (1982, 555; emphasis added). Cases in point include the "faceless" officers of many military juntas, or the Duvaliers (father and son) in Haiti.

Of course, all political leadership requires personal political skill, whether or not the context is routinized. Patrimonial leadership is distinctive, however. In Third World politics, it typically involves patron-client relations in a phenomenon commonly labeled "clientelism," where leaders are bound together in patterns of mutual assistance and support with associates, followers, and even rivals (on this general subject, see the essays in Schmidt et al. 1977). At one level, these configurations might appear to resemble patterns of coalition formation common to all political life and may not seem particularly distinctive. But any such resemblance is more apparent than real:

> Individual patron-client linkages are contingent upon the persons in a relationship and ordinarily cannot outlast them—unlike institutions. While systems of patron-client ties can survive beyond the lives or fortunes of the persons bound up in them—as do institutions—they are different from political institutions insofar as they are much affected by the power and fortunes of individuals. A change of ruler . . . can alter greatly both an existing clientelist pattern and the political fortunes of those entangled in it. (Jackson and Rosberg 1982b, 40)

Personal leadership is thus inherently unstable because it is ultimately dependent on persons rather than on institutions. Any institutions that do appear to be in place are weak because they have been "captured" and subordinated by leaders (Pye 1985, 23). The striking feature of personal rule is that upon the transfer of leadership, the clock marking the generational age of organizations is restarted (or at least set back considerably) because there are no institutional mechanisms to provide a framework for succession. Instead, leadership transfer is extraconstitutional, often revealed by a military coup d'etat, but sometimes evidenced in other ways (witness "Baby Doc's" accession to the Haitian presidency upon the death of his father in 1971).

All of this underscores the centrality to political capacity of the generational age of national institutions. At least since Max Weber, much emphasis has been placed on the proposition that institutions require routines if they are to be even minimally effective. Because of its stress on personal factors, charismatic authority is fundamentally antithetical to the idea of routines. As a result, it is most prominent in attempts to create new orders, but such authority is inherently transitory. When charismatic authority evolves into patrimonial leadership, the routines that do emerge retain a personal basis. The significance of generational age stems from the fact that this is a feature that redirects our attention toward the routinization of the leadership succession process and the centrality of institutionalization to political capacity.

Implications

Throughout this chapter I have emphasized the ways in which age impinges on the capacity of national political institutions. My discussion has drawn heavily on Max Weber's treatment of organizations in general and underscores the magnitude of the liability of newness— there is good reason to believe that the creation of new orders is every bit as difficult as Machiavelli argued. My emphasis is consistent with the repeated references in studies of political development to the "new" states. While those states are less new now than they were thirty years ago, their *relative* youth remains one of their most salient political characteristics.

I have considered two elements of institutional age—chronological and generational. The two are, of course, interrelated, and some might be tempted to conclude that we should concentrate primarily on the former and ignore the latter. Much is to be lost by that strategy, however. Along with their intrinsic interest, matters centering on generational age and succession processes are important in helping determine the point at which we should start the clock in our efforts to measure even the chronological age of institutions. I return to this question in chapter 6.

Finally, the question of institutional age is not one to be treated in straightforward linear terms. That is, meaningful comparisons across countries cannot be made on the basis of simple counts of political age because development is not a linear function of age. It seems more plausible instead to suggest that the liability of newness is most pronounced in the first years or decades, and that it becomes less significant with age. As a result, the difference in development between a pair of countries with institutions that are one-hundred and two-hundred years old, respectively, should be much less noteworthy than the difference between two countries that are, in turn, fifteen and thirty years old. This nonlinearity stems directly from the adaptive nature of organizational formalization. While it is reasonable to propose that routinization increases with age, it is also important to remember that "the earliest manifestations of formalization are the most striking ones" (Starbuck 1965, 478). As Geertz (1977) suggested, the first few years are the decisive ones. After the first decade or so of a new order, the pace of change slows down and new routines start to emerge.

CHAPTER 5

Legitimacy and Political Capacity

The ultimate power of the Law is the coercive power of the State. It is the characteristic of civilized communities that direct physical coercion (with some limitations) is the prerogative of the State, and the Law is a set of rules according to which the State exercises this prerogative in dealing with its own citizens. But the Law . . . is almost powerless when it is not supported by public sentiment. . . . Law, therefore, as an effective force, depends upon opinion and sentiment even more than upon the powers of the police.

—Bertrand Russell, *Power*

Enforcement . . . is practical only when it is directed against a relatively few and sustained by the compliance of the many, usually at least a majority, and the active support of at least a substantial group.

—Karl Deutsch, "The Crisis of the State"

In chapter 4, I argued that organizational age is a central element of institutionalization. But this is only half of the picture. I turn now to the other key element, which centers on the legitimacy of national political organizations. Legitimacy is fundamental to political life because it reflects the degree to which those who seek to rule (i.e., to exercise power) are accepted by the ruled. It thus identifies the nature of the relationship between rulers and ruled.

Because age itself impinges directly on legitimacy, the two elements are intertwined. Even in Weber's original formulation, for example, traditional organizations gain their authority from the perception that they have always been there. In broad terms, then, traditional institutions are accepted as legitimate precisely because of their age: the people subject to them accede to the authority of those institutions because they cannot conceive of a viable alternative. With age comes habit.

More recent studies have pursued a similar point. For example, an analysis of the liability of newness among voluntary organizations concludes that new organizations are more fragile in good measure because they lack legitimacy, conceived as recognition by other organizations (Singh, Tucker, and House 1986). Defined in such terms, this argument can be applied to the legitimacy of nation-states as juridical units (Jackson and Rosberg 1982a). That is, nation-states are legal entities of a wider state system, most members of which have an ongoing interest in preserving the system as it exists and from which they benefit. Because of this, most states are legitimate in the sense that their sovereignty is internationally recognized, which is reflected in their membership in various international and transnational organizations.

The bearing of age alone on legitimacy becomes less clear when the discussion is broadened so that states are conceived as political units with varying degrees of domestic capacity. Revolutions offer the most dramatic reminder that old orders can collapse, but institutional disintegration is not uncommon even in the absence of full-scale revolution. The possibility of such an outcome is, of course, anticipated in analyses of the liability of newness. Those analyses do not, after all, claim that age assures immortality. Instead, they conclude more modestly (and more accurately) that the *probability* of organizational collapse decreases with age, but this probability never approaches zero (e.g., Starbuck 1965, 1983).

Since age reduces but does not eliminate organizational fragility, we need to expand our conception of national political capacity. Such an expansion entails explicit attention to the other ingredient of capacity—legitimacy. My purpose in this chapter is to argue that the analysis of political capacity cannot be divorced from issues of political legitimacy.

The Meaning of Legitimacy

Few terms in the vocabulary of politics cause more trouble than the word *legitimacy*, and for obvious reasons. Legitimacy is universally held to be desirable. Legitimate regimes are those that can successfully assert their own authenticity, legality, and validity, and it is not surprising that regimes everywhere devote a great deal of effort to promoting their own claims to legitimacy. Conversely, it is difficult to conceive of a more devastating political declaration than a triumphant claim by its challengers that a regime is illegitimate, because it is on the basis of such a declaration that challengers are able to replace the existing regime with their own.

It is this linkage of legitimacy with political values and ideology that blunts the analytical force of the word in everyday language. In the contemporary world, moreover, the concept of legitimacy is often employed to identify the *type* of regime in place. With the spread of nationalist ideology and its doctrine of the "right" to national self-determination, imperial rule lost any claim to authenticity that it had once enjoyed. At times, the legitimacy of political orders is said to inhere in the process by which officials achieve power. In the West, regimes are often judged by their basis in "popular consent" (as manifested in elections), defined with reference to democratic principles, so that the refusal of any government to employ the electoral test is itself taken as evidence against its legitimacy. Outside the West, many other legitimating tactics of a political nature are available (see, e.g., the discussions in Lane 1984; Nelson 1984; Rigby 1984; White 1986). At other times, it is asserted that the legitimacy of political orders can only be judged by policy outcomes. Thus, those regimes that generate more economic growth or eliminate poverty and illiteracy are sometimes seen as more legitimate than others regardless of the means by which they achieved power (e.g., Epstein 1984; White 1986). Still others claim legitimacy on the basis of "tradition."[1] Since all regimes seek recognition of their authenticity, it is evident that distinctive kinds of values are invoked as justification by different types of political orders.

This underscores the analytical limitations of the term legitimacy as it is commonly used. The idea of national political capacity refers to the degree of government, independent of its type. To the extent that the idea of legitimacy is bound up with contrasts between types of governments (such as the distinction between democratic and authoritarian governments), the bearing of legitimacy on political development is clouded.

At the same time, everyday usage of the term does remind us that legitimacy necessarily involves norms and values. It is a phenomenon that is generated or manufactured by regimes through ideological appeals to symbols such as nationalism, equality, and democracy. These appeals are designed to engender consent among the governed so that the latter acquiesce to the political order. The form of these efforts varies greatly and depends on the context in which they occur, but the general point is that the appeals themselves are central to

---

1. These traditions need not be ancient. For example, Lane (1984) discusses the use of ritual as a legitimating force in the former Soviet Union. This ritual involved traditions originating with the revolution of 1917. In fact, many traditions have been self-consciously created, often by invoking heroes and martyrs from political movements. On this general issue, see the collection of essays titled *The Invention of Tradition* (Hobsbawm and Ranger 1983), which includes analyses that range from the "customs" of the Scottish Highlands to those of colonial Africa. Of course, manufactured traditions must be believable if they are to be effective, which means that they must have some basis in external reality (van den Berghe 1983).

political life. In Geertz's words, governments everywhere are involved in "providing an answer to that most immediate of political questions: who are you that I should obey you?" (1977, 251). Successful regimes are those that can, by whatever means, promulgate a general sense that they are duly constituted and therefore have the right to rule.

The idea that legitimacy is manufactured by the use of symbols implies that legitimation is an ongoing process. An analogy has often been made between this process and the theater, where the relationship between rulers and the ruled is compared with the link between actors and their audience (see, e.g., Nettl 1967, chap. 9).[2] The metaphor is useful because it reminds us that the legitimacy of a regime is not a quantity that can simply be created, set in place, and left to operate by itself as a purely self-regulating mechanism. Instead, legitimation is a matter to which those in power need to return and address themselves continuously.

The analogy is also helpful because it underscores the centrality of legitimacy to political capacity. In chapter 2, I distinguished power from force and argued that the exercise of power is relational and can only occur within a context where those subject to power regard its claims and demands as reasonable, that is, as legitimate. Since politics centers on the use of power rather than on force, legitimacy is fundamental to the political capacity or development of nation-states. Consent and compliance are the decisive ingredients here. Deutsch expressed the issue clearly:

> Every state ordinarily must issue commands. Whatever the form of such commands—laws, decrees, court decisions or administrative regulations—most of them must appear as binding to most people at least for most of the time, if the state is to endure. That is to say, they must be obeyed to that very large extent and they must be expected to be so obeyed. The limits of the effective domain of the state are thus the limits of its probability of finding popular obedience, both in regard to the territory where its writ runs with effect, and to the set of persons who are likely to obey it. (Deutsch 1981, 341–42)

A regime is thus legitimate to the extent that it can induce a measure of compliance from most people without resort to the use of physical force. The compliance need not be total, but it does need to be extensive. Despite common claims to the contrary (e.g., Eckstein

---

2. As Nettl points out, this analogy is an old one, appearing in the writing of Adam Smith, among other places.

1971, 50–65; Scott 1985, chap. 8; Beetham 1991), legitimacy need not involve an active belief in the justice of the political order in any absolute terms. Indeed, such an outcome seems highly implausible given that politics everywhere involves conflict over the distribution of valued goods. Legitimacy instead simply requires a degree of acquiescence, an acceptance of the political order as generally reasonable, *given the known or feasible alternatives*.

This approach to legitimacy has an obvious parallel with Gramsci's (1971) discussion of hegemony. Unlike domination, which involves physical coercion by the state, hegemony requires persuasion and manipulation to generate consent. While the former, with its use of force, may be common to political crises, hegemony is the "normal" mechanism by which compliance is induced (Williams 1960, 591). Moreover, compliance is likely to be passive rather than active:

> [Consent] emerges not so much because the masses profoundly regard the social order as an expression of their aspirations as because they lack the conceptual tools, the "clear theoretical consciousness," which would enable them effectively to comprehend and act on their discontent. (Femia 1975, 33)

Hegemony is thus successful to the extent that it generates acquiescence by compressing the range of conceivable alternatives.[3]

A variety of symbols is used in the process of legitimation, but in the context of *national* political capacity, the expression of nationalist sentiments is perhaps most common. The goal is to engender a widespread sense of affiliation with the institutions of the nation-state that is as strong as, and preferably stronger than, popular ties with other groups. Phrased differently, the purpose of legitimation is to create an identification with the nation-state and its institutions.

Ethnicity and the Legitimacy of Nation-States

I have already emphasized that the contemporary nation-state is a comparatively recent form. Because of this, along with the fact that it is a form protected by international law and custom, there is often a

---

3. Contrast this with the argument that legitimacy necessarily involves *active* judgments that the political order is *morally* fit so that compliance based on either cost-benefit calculations or just plain habit does not evidence legitimacy (Eckstein 1971, 50–52). This view is unnecessarily stringent. Acceptance based on habit would seem most desirable from a regime's perspective. Further, the fact that legal systems everywhere rely ultimately on the threat of sanctions coupled with the conflict endemic to politics suggests that cost-benefit calculations are central to the question of legitimacy. Acquiescence generated by physical repression is, of course, another matter.

tendency to regard national affiliations as more objective, reasonable, and modern (rational, in Weber's terms) than others, most notably in comparison with ethnic affiliations. However, nationalism is simply one form of ethnic identification. Both involve groups with fluid boundaries and levels of awareness, and one is no more arbitrary or traditional than the other. The legitimacy of national political institutions is in good measure an ongoing problem because of the fluidity of national boundaries, with the result that all nation-states are, in varying degrees, "multiethnic."

Even in well-established states, ethnic boundaries are often ambiguous. This fact is obvious in the case of such multilingual states as Belgium and Switzerland, while in the former Soviet Union, the "Russification" of ethnic groups was an ongoing political issue (Silver 1974) that ultimately became explosive. Although it may be less obvious, the issue persists in other cases. For example, Italian unification is of comparatively recent origin but Italy, as currently constituted, does not incorporate all Europeans of Italian language. In Canada and Spain, it remains unclear that national unification has been achieved. And the persisting appeal of ethnic political movements in otherwise apparently homogeneous "nations" like Great Britain underscores the softness of national identifications. Indeed, such movements constitute a direct attack on the legitimacy of national political institutions.

The problem is more visible in the newer states. Despite the 1947 partition of the Indian subcontinent along religious lines, the subsequent ethnically based division of Pakistan, and federalism in India, ethnic conflict is an ongoing phenomenon in the area. Events in the Punjab and Sri Lanka are simply among the more visible manifestations of this friction. Even with the secession of Singapore from the Malayan federation, ethnic considerations continue to play a prominent role in Malaysian politics. Although it might appear to offer a radically different kind of case, ethnicity is an important political factor in Iraq, where it is manifested in competition between the Shiite and Sunni branches of Islam. Perhaps the most conspicuous cases in contemporary politics are to be found in the states of sub-Saharan Africa, where state boundaries are relatively arbitrary in the sense that they reflect the outcome of military and economic competition between European colonial interests in the last century, without particular regard to ethnic boundaries (on these patterns, see Rabushka and Shepsle 1972; Young 1976, especially chap. 3; Young 1988, 37–48; Jackson and Rosberg 1984a; Hobsbawm 1990, 171).

In many studies of political development, these issues were addressed under the rubric of "national integration." But it is important to understand that ethnicity is central to the question of national political capacity generally, and legitimacy in particular, because (as I suggested above) nationalism is but one form of ethnic awareness. The word *ethnicity* itself is derived from the Greek *ethnos* and refers to a group sharing a common descent. As Horowitz points out, the idea of an ethnic unit is somewhat elastic, but it refers minimally to a social unit whose members *believe* it to be distinctive and that recruits members primarily through kinship. "So conceived, ethnicity easily embraces groups differentiated by color, language, and religion; it covers 'tribes,' 'races,' 'nationalities,' and castes" (Horowitz 1985, 53). Whatever their form, ethnic groups share one important element: all are based on "primordial" sentiments (Geertz 1963) that reflect those givens of life which provide identity to individuals.[4]

But nationalism is no more than one form of ethnicity. Well before nationalist doctrines acquired their contemporary political significance, John Stuart Mill addressed the problem in *Considerations on Representative Government*.

> A portion of mankind may be said to constitute a Nationality if they are united among themselves by common sympathies which do not exist between them and any others . . . . This feeling of nationality may have been generated by various causes. Sometimes it is the effect of identity of race and descent. Community of language, and community of religion, greatly contribute to it. Geographical limits are one of its causes. But the strongest of all is *identity of political antecedents*; the possession of a national history, and consequent community of recollections; collective pride and humiliation, pleasure and regret, connected with the same incidents in the past. (1861, chap. 16;. emphasis added)

Almost sixty years ago, Sabine defined a *nation* in the following similar terms:

> Nation refers to a unity of culture: a feeling of loyalty for a common land; common language and literature; identity of history and common heroes; and common religion. Most distinctive

---

4. "By a primordial attachment is meant one that stems from the 'givens'—or, more precisely, as culture is inevitably involved in such matters, the assumed 'givens'—of social existence: immediate contiguity and kin connection mainly, but beyond them the givenness that stems from being born into a particular religious community, speaking a particular language, or even a dialect of a language, and following particular social practices" (Geertz

of all perhaps is an aspiration to political self-determination. (1934, 329)

Emerson's conclusion echoes these themes:

> The simplest statement that can be made about a nation is that it is a body of people who feel that they are a nation; and it may be that when all the fine-spun analysis is concluded this will be the ultimate statement as well . . . . In the many definitions of the nation . . . four elements which insistently recur as essential to the creation of a common sense of destiny are territory, language, a common historical tradition, and the intricate interconnections of state and nation. (1960, 102–4)

Of particular interest here is the proposition that values and norms are as central to nationalism as they are to ethnicity. Further, like ethnicity, nationalism entails the invocation of a common historical and political *tradition*. The only difference between ethnic and nationalist groups is that the former do not profess a preference for political self-determination. Van den Berghe summarizes the distinctions clearly:

> A *state* is a political entity wherein a group of people claim authority over others who are neither kin nor spouses, and over the territory occupied by them. An *ethny* [ethnic group] is a group of people who claim common descent and share a common language and culture . . . . A *nation* is a politically conscious ethny, claiming statehood rights on the basis of common ethnicity. (Van den Berghe 1983, 222; see also Gellner 1983)

It follows that nationalist sentiments are neither less primordial nor less traditional than ethnic sentiments. By the same token, ethnicity is no less modern than nationalism.[5]

1963, 109). In other words, primordial attachments reflect cultural traditions. This, however, does not mean that they are immutable, for "traditions" are themselves often created, as I indicated earlier in this chapter. For different discussions of the ways in which "primordial" identities are often created and re-created, see van den Berghe 1983; Smith 1987; and Newman 1991.

　　5. In fact, Connor (1972, 1987) contends that since all contemporary states are multinational, the term nation-state makes little sense. Thus, in some usages certain nations (e.g., the "Arab nation") are said to transcend state boundaries while others (e.g., the "Scottish nation") are taken to refer to distinct groups within states. In light of this, Connor prefers the phrase "ethnonationalism." Although his argument is perfectly reasonable on substantive grounds, the neologism is awkward. I prefer the more conventional language, which takes the nation-state to refer to sovereign states, juridically defined (see, e.g., Young

In the context of nation-states, the process of legitimation therefore involves the creation and inculcation among the general population of a new primordial identity that replaces or at least outweighs older primordial identities, such that the nation becomes the "terminal community" with which people identify (Emerson 1960, 96). This process of amalgamation was at the heart of earlier studies of national integration, which took as their problem the creation of "a sense of territorial nationality which overshadows—or eliminates— subordinate parochial loyalties" (Weiner 1965). In other words, the process represents an attempt to create a myth that symbolizes an identifiable collectivity, a new tradition, or an "imagined community," to use Anderson's felicitous phrase (1991).[6] The obvious contradiction involved here is exacerbated in at least three distinct but overlapping ways.

First, it is difficult to underestimate the significance of the primordial nature of ethnic ties. While the exact boundaries of an ethnic group may be fluid and subject to varying interpretations, ethnicity itself is inextricably bound up with people's fundamental sense of being, of personal identity (see, e.g., Smith 1987). As a result, attempts to amalgamate identities across groups are confronted with a formidable obstacle. The tension between ethnicity and the "nation," while not unique to the newer states, occurs in that context with singular force. Geertz identified the problem clearly thirty years ago:

This tension takes a particularly severe and chronic form in the new states, both because of the great extent to which their peoples' sense of self remains bound up in the gross actualities of blood, race, language, locality, religion, or tradition, and because of the steadily accelerating importance in this century of the sovereign state as a positive instrument for the realization of collective aims. Multiethnic, usually multilinguistic, and sometimes multiracial, the populations of the new states tend to regard the immediate, concrete, and to them inherently meaningful sorting implicit in such "natural" diversity as the substantial content

---

1976, chap. 3; Smith 1986). Ethnic groups, in my usage, lack a sovereign state. Given that most states are multiethnic, and since national loyalties are no less primordial than ethnic loyalties, this usage means that national identity is likely to be problematic everywhere. At the same time, the severity of the problem varies considerably from one setting to another.

6. My emphasis on the importance of symbols is not meant to trivialize the process of legitimation. Given the complexities and ambiguities inherent to political life generally, symbols and myths always perform a vital simplifying role (Edelman 1964). In the context of ethnic and national attachments, which reflect feelings of personal identity, their role is of particular importance (see, e.g., Armstrong 1982; Smith 1987).

of their individuality. To subordinate these specific and familiar identifications in favor of a generalized commitment to an overarching and somewhat alien civil order is to risk a loss of definition as an autonomous person, either through absorption into a culturally undifferentiated mass or, what is even worse, through domination by some other rival ethnic, racial, or linguistic community that is able to imbue that order with the temper of its own personality. (Geertz 1963, 108–9)

Second, as I noted in chapter 1, the anticolonial movements that came to prominence after the Second World War were based on a combination of nationalist and democratic ideology that attached great weight to the idea of representativeness. This ideology provided the political justification for decolonization, manifested in the doctrine of the "national" right to "self-determination." Such a doctrine was essential to the success of the decolonization movement, and provided a basis for mobilizing large numbers of people in opposition to the appropriate colonial power and in support of movements that sought to centralize political authority behind an indigenous nationalist banner. It thereby helped engender the us-versus-them sentiments that form the basis of any primordial groups (Armstrong 1982) and, in so doing, fostered one element of the sense of national history associated with such groups.

Although the mobilization of nationalist sentiments was vital to the overthrow of colonialism itself, it also opened something of a Pandora's box for Third World governments in the *post*independence era. While those governments must have found this result perverse, it was altogether to be expected. As one analyst phrased it,

In the new nations, political leaders now in power have only recently been in the business of challenging colonial authority and weakening men's obedience to political rule. To some extent, when popular enthusiasm and revolutionary ardor began to wane these political leaders inherit an instability of regime and authority that is partly of their own making. (Apter 1963, 81)

Apter's observation reminds us that once large numbers of people have been ideologically mobilized on the basis of the doctrine of the national right to self-determination, it is often difficult to demobilize them. Instead, the same doctrine is likely to be used by groups *within* states to justify resistance to the regime. And recall that nationalist movements were rarely more than loose ethnic and class coalitions (see, e.g., Clapham 1985, chap. 2), and therefore initially fragile. The problem is particularly severe where ethnic groups are physically segregated from each other (as they are most notably in multilingual states), because those groups can then more convincingly threaten to secede. In such cases, ethnic segregation raises the specter of balkanization, a specter present in most civil wars (consider the cases of Pakistan or Nigeria), and a term whose currency has been resuscitated by events in the former Yugoslavia.

But segregation does not create the problem—it simply exacerbates it. Nor is this an issue unique to the new states, even though it has been manifested most visibly in them. The anticolonial movement created a demonstration effect that has touched and given political justification to ethnic sentiments everywhere, ranging from the Huks in the Philippines to the often-discussed "ethnic revival" in Western Europe to the former Soviet empire.

Third, *social* mobilization has been as important to ethnic politics as political mobilization. Following Deutsch (1961), I take the former term to define the changes that come with industrialization and the introduction of technology. Particularly relevant here are changes in patterns of communication and the mass media. Social mobilization is important because it increases contact between groups and makes them more aware of the existence of each other. This, in turn, increases the odds that ethnic groups within states will come to view themselves as being in mutual competition. As Deutsch originally argued,

> Rapid social mobilization . . . may tend to strain or destroy the unity of states whose population is already divided into several groups with different languages or cultures or basic ways of life . . . . It may tend to inhibit, or at least to make more difficult, the merging of states or political units whose populations or ruling personnel differ substantially in regard to any of these matters. (1961, 501)

Social mobilization may indeed help to *create* ethnic awareness and ethnic groups themselves (see, e.g., Melson and Wolpe 1970; Milne 1981, chap. 5; Nielsen 1985). And in the years since Deutsch wrote, the pace of such mobilization has grown exponentially with the diffusion of the electronic media, which provide the capability for rapid and graphic communication of political messages without requiring a literate population of recipients. Given this setting, we should expect an enhanced role for ethnic politics.

I do not mean to suggest that ethnicity is the sole basis for conflict within nation-states. Some of the major revolutions of this century were plainly driven by other considerations. But the fact that nationalism is no more than one form of ethnicity, distinctive only in that it seeks recognition as the terminal community embodied within the state, helps to explain the prominence of ethnic conflict in recent political history. It also reminds us that the national identity central to the legitimation of national political institutions is no more than a particular case of an ethnic identity. The contradictions involved in creating and legitimizing traditions (that is, in inculcating values) based on alternative ascriptive and primordial sentiments obviously make that a hazardous process.

At one level, this returns us to the liability of newness because traditions take time to evolve. And, indeed, the older states are advantaged by the national political traditions on which they can draw even though the legitimacy of their institutions is far from guaranteed. Such traditions become "political monuments" (de Schweinitz 1970, 535), symbolized by factors like language and military history that provide a clear, ongoing national identity that is distinct from other subnational ethnic identities.[7]

By the same token, it is misleading to conceive of the "older" states as more modern in political terms. To the extent that they are collectively wealthier, they do, of course, enjoy a technological advantage over other states. But the national traditions on which their political legitimacy draws are not intrinsically modern. Instead, they simply provide the basis for a national sense of community that is part of the general family of identifications based on ethnic considerations (Smith 1987, 1988).[8]

For the newer states, a sense of a corporate past has to be forged. In many cases, the decolonization movement itself provided part of

7. And occasional military operations have a pronounced rally-around-the-flag impact on public opinion that reinforces these traditions. The military expeditions by Great Britain and the United States in the Falkland Islands and Grenada, respectively, are simply among the more recent examples of this phenomenon. Adam Smith was aware of the pattern over two centuries ago:

In great empires, the people who live in the capital, and in the provinces remote from the scene of action, feel, many of them, scarce any inconveniency from the war; but enjoy, at their ease, the amusement of reading in the newspapers the exploits of their own fleets and armies . . . . They are commonly dissatisfied with the return of peace, which puts an end to their amusement, and a thousand visionary hopes of conquest and national glory, from a longer continuance of the war. (Smith [1789] 1976, 2:455–56)

8. It is thus ultimately impossible to sustain the distinction between the primordial politics associated with "modernizing" societies from the "civil" politics said to be characteristic of "modern" societies (for an example of this distinction, see Geertz 1963).

the requisite history by creating visible "indigenous" political leaders and organizations that, after independence, formed the basis of a nationalist, single-party system. Perhaps more importantly, the decolonization movement was instrumental in identifying a common external threat. An external threat, of course, intensifies the us-versus-them feeling characteristic of ethnic groups and incipient states that are typically defined by principles of exclusion and distinctiveness from other groups (Armstrong 1982, chap. 1). Such factors are essential in helping establish what Apter (1963) termed a national "political religion" that legitimizes the state by symbolizing the political order as a corporate entity, by distinguishing "good" from "evil," and by identifying incumbent leaders as good and associating them with the political order as a whole.

After independence, external threats provide a continuing basis for the legitimation of nation-states by identifying a corporate enemy. This is clear from the experience of states like Israel in which military service combined with a clearly identifiable external challenge have helped integrate a culturally diverse population. Similar processes have been evident in Castro's Cuba and the Sandinistas' Nicaragua, where military pressure from the United States has been used domestically in an effort to legitimize particular regimes. More generally, the specter of neocolonialism is repeatedly invoked to legitimize the purposes of national political leaders. Some have indeed argued that many older Third World states are less legitimate than they might otherwise be precisely because of the lack of a recent colonial past and the absence of major military threats. Thus, Scott concluded that "the external threats of invasion and the memories of imperialism [are] the strongest catalysts in encouraging disparate interests to cooperate and integrate within the political process . . . . It is the lack of this incentive, if nothing else, that sets Latin America apart from much of the rest of the world" (Scott 1963, 83).

Implications for the Analysis of Political Legitimacy

Of course, not all challenges to the legitimacy of political orders have an ethnic basis. But ethnic challenges constitute a distinctive and ongoing issue for modern nation-states, most of which remain multi-ethnic.[9] Casting nationalism as one form of ethnicity serves to highlight critical components of political legitimacy.

---

9. Van den Berghe points out that "only some 10 percent of the world's 150-odd states are nations by the criterion of 90 percent or more of their population speaking the same language" (1983, 221).

First, legitimacy is never an all-or-nothing matter. This follows from the fact that all states have the capacity to employ violence against their subjects and most exercise this capacity in varying degrees. Even were this not the case, no political order can profess complete legitimacy. All regimes strive instead for a *working* consensus on procedures, a consensus they seek to engender among politically relevant groups. But national boundaries, like ethnic boundaries, are fluid. While the modern doctrine of the right to "self-determination" is inclusive in its emphasis, the size of politically relevant groups varies over time and from one state to another and the substantive interests of those groups are often in conflict. The process of legitimation is, therefore, ongoing.

It is not productive to view regimes as illegitimate in any absolute sense. It is more useful to conceive of legitimacy in continuous terms, where political orders are overthrown or replaced when their loss of legitimacy exceeds a critical point and when there exists a viable contending alternative. The location of this critical threshold varies from one setting to another—consider the twentieth-century revolutions in Russia, China, and Iran, or the falls of Marcos in the Philippines, of Duvalier in Haiti, and of the military governments in Greece and Argentina, or repeated military coups in sub-Saharan Africa. Legitimacy is consequently always in flux.

Second, the linkage between nationalism and ethnicity reminds us that legitimacy always involves values. Specifically, the degree to which national political orders are viewed as authentic hinges on the extent to which they are accepted and the extent to which the relevant population identifies with them. Since regimes can adopt a variety of tactics to legitimize themselves, the form or content of these values is likely to vary considerably from one setting to another. As a result, the legitimacy of a political order cannot be judged according to the form of that order—"democratic," "socialist," or "nationalist."

Legitimacy must instead be evaluated according to the political actions of regimes, whatever their ideological orientation. In particular, have they generated compliance or a framework within which political life can take place? Since politics involves the exercise of power or authority, legitimacy increases with the ability of regimes to make problems go away peacefully. Thus, the legitimacy of regimes must be judged according to their ability to resolve conflict (*a*) without employing physical force on their opponents (actual or potential), and (*b*) without mobilizing physical opposition or resistance by those opponents. I discuss these two components in turn.

The "Official" Use of Physical Force

I have emphasized throughout that all national political orders have the capacity to employ coercion in pursuit of their goals. The idea is, of course, an old one. But I have also stressed that a continued reliance on physical force is fundamentally apolitical and represents a loss of power. It follows that the persistent use of force by authorities has high political costs. Beyond some point, such behavior signifies that those "authorities" are no longer recognized as such, in which sense their status as "officials" is also called into question.[10]

Since the exercise of power or authority requires a degree of compliance on the part of those subject to it, the resort by regimes to force in the domestic arena can be taken as prima facie evidence of a loss of legitimacy. Because legitimacy is a matter of degree, this loss need not be total, but it remains a loss nonetheless. The retreat to physical force reflects the fact that compliance cannot be politically induced by less costly means (see also Mason and Krane 1989). That the sustained employment of official violence entails costs is evidenced by the efforts of regimes everywhere to conceal such behaviors.[11]

In the last section, I noted the variety of ways in which regimes go about engendering a sense that they are duly constituted. This variety reflects differing ideological orientations, among other things. It is impossible to develop common criteria for evaluating the procedure by which consent is manufactured, because there is no single procedure. But it is important that we not become sidetracked on the question of how consent is generated. When cast as a matter of political performance, the more fundamental question is *whether* consent and compliance have been effectively manufactured at all. My emphasis on the use of physical force by regimes is an attempt to address this issue.

Physical coercion or repression by the state takes many forms. In terms of their severity, the less extreme of these actions include physical restrictions on the political activities of individuals and groups intended to inhibit political mobilization by challengers to the regime or the political order as a whole. The banning of political rallies, the

---

10. Remember that, in common usage, the noun *official* incorporates the concept of authority and trust. Hence the quotation marks.

11. Recognition of the costs of repression does not imply that repression "is not generally used without good cause" (Eckstein 1971, 57). Whether nor not there is cause for repression has no bearing on the question at hand.

arrest and imprisonment of political activists, and the banning of political parties are typical actions of this genre. Although these are relatively mild forms of state sanctions, they remain applications of physical force. Their use constitutes either an admission that compliance cannot be politically induced by bargaining or by an attempt to redefine the situation prior to further efforts at bargaining.

The severity of official coercion can be increased in two different ways. First, the regime may continue to employ the same general tactics but, instead of using them sporadically, begin to apply them more systematically and continuously. The banning of political parties would change from a short-term to a permanent injunction. Similarly, short-term detentions of individual opponents may be escalated into longer-term incarcerations, often involving declarations of martial law. These efforts are intended to increase the costs of noncompliance with and opposition to the state through sustained intimidation.

Second, the regime may step up the level of violence by inflicting higher levels of physical harm on those who challenge it. Instead of being incarcerated, opponents thus begin to disappear permanently, and without trace. The number of political executions increases. Rather than simply proscribing political rallies and arresting those who ignore the ban, the state begins to employ deadly force against its opponents. Such use of deadly force may be intermittent, but often escalates into an ongoing pattern of regime behavior. Even when intermittent, however, this use of violence is a clear attempt to increase the costs of challenging the political order.[12]

Most discussions of such use of force employ labels such as "repression" or "state terror" to describe the phenomenon (e.g., Gurr 1986a, 1986b). These treatments are often concerned with questions of human rights, conceived primarily in liberal Western terms (for interesting approaches and bibliography, see, e.g., Donnelly 1984; Howard and Donnelly 1986). My usage is different. Instead of viewing the problem in human-rights terms, I take the use of physical force by the state as one element of national political power or capacity. Since all states possess the instruments for physical coercion, the less they actually employ those instruments, the greater their *political*

---

12. From the above, it is evident that I distinguish in principle between the use of physical violence by the state and law enforcement, even though the latter also includes force. Those accused of transgressing civil and criminal law do not generally question the validity of that law but claim instead that they were not themselves guilty of a transgression. In contrast, those accused of and punished for political offenses typically question the validity of state laws and policies or the procedures by which those laws are implemented.

capacity. This difference in emphasis reflects my argument that besides the obvious problems repression creates for its recipients, the repeated use of physical coercion by the state constitutes a major political difficulty for incumbents who seek to exercise power.

Some have disputed this argument. Consider the alternative advanced by Bourdieu:

> Gentle hidden exploitation is the form taken . . . whenever overt, brutal exploitation is impossible . . . . Gentle exploitation is much more costly . . . . [because it involves] the endless reconversion of economic capital into symbolic capital. (1977, 192–95)

Drawing on this and other analyses, Scott concludes that "the euphemization of economic power is necessary both where direct physical coercion is not possible and where the pure indirect domination of the capitalist market is not yet sufficient to ensure appropriation by itself" (1985, 307). Thus, the use of physical force ("overt, brutal exploitation") is cast as a more effective mode of control than the exercise of political power ("gentle hidden exploitation").

The problem with formulations like these is that they contain an incomplete accounting of the costs associated with the two strategies (and they altogether neglect the benefits those strategies may generate). Specifically, power is seen as more costly because it requires ongoing efforts as legitimation, the "endless reconversion of economic capital into symbolic capital." True, this does involve costs, but it also generates benefits in the form of compliance and perhaps even active support. Entirely overlooked in the argument is that the use of physical force also entails economic and other costs that may be much higher in terms of disruptions to production. It also entails benefits that can be considerably lower. For example, force may not induce compliance, and is unlikely to engender active support.

Although predicated on somewhat different calculations, a similar argument is clear in the Tillys' well-known view of violence by both states and challengers as an inextricable part of struggles for

---

While the boundary between ordinary law enforcement and political coercion by the state is sometimes blurred (especially in revolutionary and other fluid political contexts), my concern is with the use of physical force by the state that is intended to resolve political issues. Offsetting this ambiguity, I reiterate that legitimacy is always a matter of degree, and few states avoid coercion altogether.

power. Casting these struggles as an essential ingredient of a political process, they conclude that "repression works." More specifically,

> The business of governments is to maximize their positions with respect to rivals and to maintain the structures of power prevailing within their own domains. Agents of government therefore face a different set of calculations from challengers. They have access to concentrated repressive forces. Despite hopeful liberal mythology to the contrary, furthermore, violent repression works. It works in the short run. It works even better in the long run: as far as we can tell, it is not true that a population beset by consistent tyranny eventually becomes so frustrated that it will do anything to throw off the yoke; in fact, repressed populations demobilize, work through the approved channels of collective action, and seek noncollective means of accomplishing their ends. Repression works in the sense that the imposition of violent penalties—damage or seizure of persons or objects—to collective action diminishes its frequency and intensity. In general, then, the choice of the violent path is much more effective for governments than for challengers. (Tilly, Tilly, and Tilly 1975, 285)

But this perspective blurs several key issues.

First, the same authors go on to assert that collective protest against governments by challengers also works in many cases. It is more likely to be successful, they contend, when its goals are limited and concrete, but success is not uncommon even where the goals of challengers are broader. Further, they believe that this is a general pattern, not one unique to the history of Europe in the last century and a half. Stated in this form, however, the argument attempts to have it both ways, in which case the meaning of the claim that violence "works" is unclear. True, repression does raise the costs for challengers, but is it an effective tactic in general? The Tillys also suggest a nonlinear relation between repression and collective violence, where the latter is most pronounced at moderately high but not extreme levels of repression. Such a proposal is consistent with earlier analyses (e.g., Gurr 1968), but again, this does not demonstrate the effectiveness of repression, especially in the long term.

A second general problem with the Tillys' conclusion is that it depicts governments as if they were unitary actors: the government (and its agents) is cast as one actor warding off its challengers from below. But the most common challenges to governments do not emanate from below. Instead, governments are more fruitfully seen as coalitions of interests, including the military, and all coalitions are fragile. Violence by agents of the state is seldom directed solely against challengers from below, but also includes violence against other elements of the coalition. In light of this, the use of violence divides civilian from military interests and amplifies factions even within military interests themselves. The fragility of government coalitions increases directly with the clarity of these divisions. As is apparent from most military coups, the use or threat of violence within government coalitions often breaks up those coalitions and is thus inherently destabilizing. Once we recognize that governments (or states) are not unitary actors, it becomes quite unclear why repression can in principle be judged an effective tactic for them to pursue in the long term.

Third, repressive governments are often personal governments, as that term is used by Jackson and Rosberg (1982b) and Hutchcroft (1991). Cases in point include Haiti under the Duvaliers, Spain under Franco, Uganda under Amin, and the Philippines under Marcos. To the extent that they are personal, they are likely to be unstable for the reasons advanced in chapter 4. Of course, the outcome of this instability may simply be that one ruthless regime is succeeded by another with equally brutal proclivities. But that does not mean that repression worked for the first government, as many former heads of state and their associates have discovered for themselves.

Of course, the argument advanced by the Tillys does contain an element of truth. It is true that all governments possess at least some ability to repress, and repression certainly increases the costs to political challengers. Further, it is apparent from cases like the Stalinist purges in the Soviet Union that severe repression can demobilize potential challengers for prolonged periods. But this is a far cry from claiming that repression *works* in some sense to generate either legitimacy or political capacity. Instead of adopting such a position, it is more fruitful to understand the costs of repressive tactics for those regimes that rely on them. Even before Gorbachev, the Soviet regime was employing repressive tactics at a reduced level, and there is evidence that it had also turned increasingly to a variety of positive (symbolic and material) inducements in its efforts to maximize its internal political support (see, e.g., Lane 1984; Rigby 1984; White 1986; Silver 1987; Bahry and Silver 1987).

When the costs of repression are acknowledged, it becomes clear that a strategy of repression is inimical to political legitimacy. I recognize that few governments entirely abandon the use of physical coercion to pursue political goals (although some employ it with much more frequency than others). But this is simply another way of stating that legitimacy is always a matter of degree and should never be construed as an all-or-nothing matter.

Challenges to the Political Order

The other side of the legitimacy coin involves the kinds of challenges that are mounted against the political order. Since, as I have emphasized, politics centers on conflict over the distribution of valued goods, it follows that all regimes face opposition from both within and without. The critical question has to do with the *nature* of that opposition.

While challenges can be examined from a variety of perspectives, the essential distinction for our purposes is between those that are conveyed through "normal" channels and those that are not. There is nothing mystical about normal channels beyond the proposition that they are central to the question of political capacity. Specifically, if those channels do contain most political demands, then they can be regarded as reasonably effective and legitimate institutions. Naturally, there is an important qualification to the last statement: it holds only if the regime is not simultaneously engaged in substantial repression of political challengers. If this last condition is met, or at least approximated, then the use of conventional channels to convey political demands indicates that those channels are generally regarded as reasonably authentic.

The alternative form of challenge occurs outside normal political institutions. Indeed, this option can be construed as an "irregular" form of political participation, provided that we remember that such a label refers to the nature but not the frequency of such challenges. As I use the term, it refers to a heterogeneous set of behaviors. In terms of the mildness or severity of the events involved, this set ranges from nonviolent protests against particular policies of the regime (including vigils, marches, and the like) to full-scale revolutions that topple the old order and replace it with a new one. Often, relatively mild forms of protest escalate into more violent forms that include riots, and, on a larger scale, civil wars. Further, the behaviors in the set include but are not restricted to those with a mass base. For example, military coups are challenges even though they typically involve a small number of people and high levels of secrecy. Finally, challenges of this sort are not necessarily illegal, but are irregular because they do not involve normal political channels and because they are distinguished by at least the threat of force on the part of the challengers.

The distinctive feature of these forms of participation is that they are potentially more costly for those who engage in them (see also Eckstein 1980, 158–59). Compared with the process offered by normal channels, challenges of this sort are less structured and therefore less predictable, in terms of both the forms that they take and the kinds of outcome they are likely to generate. Moreover, such activities are likely to run the risk of a response in kind by authorities, often involving repression of the challengers. All of these factors increase the costs of participating in confrontations that assume an irregular form, and these costs rise with the severity or violence of the challenge.

Assuming that challengers prefer to avoid these costs, that they choose otherwise is evidence of two interrelated conditions. First, it implies that they do not believe that normal channels provide a viable mechanism for the pursuit of their own political interests, which speaks directly to the ineffectiveness of those channels. Second, it suggests that they estimate a reasonable chance of deriving higher benefits to offset the increased costs of irregular participation. Evaluations of this sort can have a number of sources. For example, they may stem from a judgment that the status quo is so bad that any alternative is preferable, or from a calculation that the ineffectiveness of normal channels itself constitutes evidence that the regime is vulnerable to their challenge. While the mix of these calculations varies from one setting to another, and although the calculations themselves are surrounded by considerable uncertainty, the important point is that the presence of such evaluations attests immediately to the existence of significant groups who challenge the legitimacy of the political order.

This conception of irregular forms of political challenge follows in a straightforward manner from my discussion of power in Chapter 2. Just as the sustained use of physical force by authorities undermines the political basis of their authority, so too does the use of irregular forms of participation reflect a deterioration in political capacity. This perspective also parallels those discussions of protest that cast the phenomenon as an attempt by relatively powerless groups to create political resources for themselves either by enlisting the support of third parties or by raising the costs to the authorities of ignoring their preferences (e.g., Lipsky 1968; Wilson 1973, chap. 14). According to this argument, recourse to protest itself stands as evidence of the relatively weak political position of the initiators: by definition, more powerful challengers possess sufficient resources that they are able to avoid such tactics and pursue their interests through normal institutional channels.

Running through all of this (and through my discussion of repression in the last section) is the theme that participants in the political arena act rationally in order to gain the maximum possible advantage for themselves at the least possible cost. That is, all participants, whether they are authorities, challengers, or relatively inactive citizens, behave instrumentally to place themselves in the best feasible position. Their calculations are not restricted to economic considerations, but instead incorporate political and social (as well as economic) goods (see, e.g., Wilson 1973, chap. 2). At the same time, this instrumental behavior is constrained by the fact that all participants have imperfect information. This introduces uncertainty into their cost-benefit calculations, which, in turn, means that political decisions will often have unintended consequences.

The assumption of instrumental rationality with imperfect information is widely used to good effect in analyses of conventional forms of political participation like voting and party behavior (see, e.g., Downs 1957; Fiorina 1990; Aldrich 1993). Such analyses are, of course, concerned with a relatively well-defined context in which the rules of the game are comparatively clear. Even in this context, political behavior is limited by the costs associated with uncertainty. The problem is magnified when we turn to challenges that involve irregular forms of participation because these involve much more fluid situations in which the rules of the game are much more poorly defined. The more ambiguous those rules, the greater the uncertainty for all participants. With the decreasing predictability of political life, cost-benefit calculations become more hazardous, and the probability of unanticipated and often perverse outcomes is magnified, even when all participants are behaving rationally.

This is why the costs of unconventional political activity are inherently much higher than they are for routinized forms of political participation, which means that those who engage in such activity must anticipate greater benefits from it. After all, the predictability that comes from routines is preferable to the alternatives, all other things equal. In this sense, the recourse to irregular activity comprises an admission that all other things are not regarded as equal. It is an escalation that reflects a failure of political institutions to channel demands, grievances, and challenges. The existence of such activity thus constitutes prima facie evidence that institutions have lost legitimacy.

While this perspective will strike many as straightforward, it diverges markedly from the prevalent interpretation of political participation in studies of national political development. Scholarship on the subject displays an ambivalence toward the value of political participation generally.[13] Even in the context of established democracies, many have argued that participation is simply one of several conflicting values, all of which cannot be simultaneously maximized. Thus, the often-heard conclusion that high rates of mass participation are not necessarily desirable because they often undermine the ability of governments to act effectively. The ambivalence is compounded further because of disagreement over what stimulates political activity. In particular, it is often suggested that for many people, emotional factors are at least as important as instrumental considerations in accounting for political behavior, where the relevant emotions include anomie and alienation. The idea that even normal forms of mass participation may be governed by irrational emotional factors has led many scholars to question the desirability of high rates of conventional participation (for further discussion on these points, see Jackman 1987).

The ambivalence is even more pronounced when we turn our attention to irregular forms of participation that have often been interpreted as a *social* pathology rather than political behavior, a product of rootlessness rather than of calculation. Thus, Kornhauser (1959) contended in his classic study that such behavior is simply a form of extremism generated by personal isolation from the community. It is a product of an atomization endemic to mass society. As such, it is no more than a simplistic emotional response that serves to discharge aggressive tendencies but that has little political content.

In an influential paper on the destabilizing effects of rapid economic growth, Olson (1963) concluded that growth is a dislocating force. It undermines old ways of doing things so that significant numbers of people believe themselves to be worse off than they had previously been. Those who are newly rootless are precisely the people who are likely to engage in irregular forms of politics: "[they] tend to be distinguished by the relative absence of bonds that tie them to the social order. They tend to lack close attachments to any of the social subgroups that comprise a society" (Olson 1963, 532). The participation of the new declasses is not oriented around a clearly defined political agenda but instead is an emotional and essentially irrational outburst, an almost spontaneous reaction against change.

---

13. Consider the study of political participation in Third World countries by Huntington and Nelson (1976), which is titled *No Easy Choice*.

Huntington's argument about the sources of political decay is an extension of this perspective and includes a similar conception of political participation, which is cast as a simple function of "social frustration" (1968, 55). In the institutionless environment of praetorian societies, mass political involvement is no more than a square-off between primitive social forces that "confront each other nakedly" (1968, 196). The possibility that these social forces might represent individuals and groups consciously seeking to advance their own political interests is given scant attention. Instead, the emphasis is placed on the *chaos* induced by this participation, a chaos that defines the political disorder itself, a chaos that elites have been unable to prevent.

The same view is clear in Johnson's well-known analysis of revolutions. Rapid social change is again the mechanism that undermines the social equilibrium. "Disequilibriated social systems," in turn, are cast as a prerequisite of revolutions, generating "personal tensions" experienced by all. The catalyst is ideology: "Where do ideologies come from? They are created by people who may be motivated by personal psychological needs, life experiences, disequilibrium-induced tensions, or a combination of all these" (Johnson 1982b, 88). The key element in this argument is that those who engage in irregular forms of political activity do so because they have been cut loose from society. They are adrift. The absence of social controls gives rise to the anomic expression of people's needs and anxieties in revolutionary movements.

Most recently, Eckstein (1992) has asserted that many political behaviors, especially those involving rebellion or resistance are not goal oriented. Instead, they entail the minimization of pain, as opposed to the maximization of utility. According to Eckstein, because efforts to minimize pain are based on frustration they cannot be goal oriented. Irregular forms of participation thus lack political purpose.

I am hardly the first to note the Durkheimian origins of this general treatment (see, e.g., Tilly 1978, chap. 2; Kohli 1986; Rule 1988). It is a view which casts irregular forms of participation as pathological activity that tears at the social fabric. This activity is seen more as an expression of irrational and deep-seated psychological drives than as a political challenge. Durkheim had already outlined the argument in *Suicide*:

With increased prosperity desires increase. At the very moment when traditional rules have lost their authority, the richer prize offered these appetites stimulates them and makes them more exigent and impatient of control. The state of de-regulation or anomy is thus further heightened by passions being less disciplined, precisely when they need more disciplining. (1951, 253)[14]

But casting irregular political participation as an undisciplined and almost involuntary response to social change distorts the problem. It leads us to expect more such behavior than actually occurs. After all, there has been an exponential growth in the diffusion of technology in recent years, which has involved precisely the kind of dislocating change addressed in Durkheim's argument. Yet there has been no evidence of the corresponding exponential increase in anomic behaviors (or in challenges to political orders) anticipated by that argument. The anomie interpretation fails because it neglects the potential costs of the tactic for those who employ it. If we cast the issue in a manner that ignores those costs, we are much less likely to understand the conditions under which challengers will feel obliged to act outside of normal channels. This, of course, is an empirical failure.

Beyond this, to view irregular forms of participation largely as an anomic, psychological response is to denigrate their political content. Such a perspective defines these activities as outbursts that may require discipline, but that lack any instrumental component: the idea that they are challenges oriented toward political ends is precluded. Further, because they are outbursts against social and economic change, their incidence is seen as essentially independent of actions by the regime. Any connection between irregular forms of participation and the problem of political legitimacy is thus simply precluded by definitional fiat.

Given these problems, it is more fruitful to regard irregular forms of participation as rationally motivated. This approach recognizes that such behavior is instrumental, it acknowledges the role of uncertainty (and hence of costs), and it underscores the political basis of that behavior (Jackman, 1993).[15] Not surprisingly, the evidence suggests that this conception leads us to a more reliable empirical understand-

---

14 This perspective is consonant with two of Weber's (1947, 115) four types of social action, classified according to their "mode of orientation": (1) a "rational orientation to a system of discrete individual ends"; (2) a "rational orientation to an absolute value" or an ideology; (3) an "affectual orientation, especially emotional, determined by the specific affects and states of feeling of the actor"; and (4) action that is "traditionally oriented, through the habituation of long practice." The Durkheimian argument assumes that all action is of the third or fourth type and is irrational since it is not instrumental. In contrast, the conception of rational behavior I am adopting includes the first two of Weber's types of action.

15. Interesting recent discussions of political violence that view the phenomenon in rational-choice terms include Hechter (1987), Lichbach (1987), Taylor (1988), Mason and Krane (1989), and Moore (1989).

ing of the mechanisms by which challenges are actually mounted (Tilly 1978; Fireman and Gamson 1979; DeNardo 1985; Lichbach 1990) and of the behavior of such "marginal" groups as slum dwellers in the cities of Latin America (Portes 1972) and peasants (Popkin 1979; Tong 1992). By the same token, this conception underscores the linkage between irregular forms of participation and the legitimacy of the political order as a whole.

Implications

In this chapter I have argued that legitimacy is central to political capacity and, in turn, that legitimacy always involves values. It is thus a fluid phenomenon in the sense that the process of legitimation is always ongoing and never complete. This has two major consequences.

First, legitimacy is invariably a matter of degree. In view of this, it is difficult to envision how any political order could be accurately described as completely legitimate in the sense that all those subject to it value it under all circumstances. It is more fruitful instead to judge some regimes as more legitimate than others, recognizing that the degree to which any political order is regarded as authentic is also likely to fluctuate over time. This reminds us that legitimacy, and hence political capacity, is a fragile quantity.

Second, the fragility of legitimacy is underscored by the fact that it rests on values that reflect compliance and consent. Some may be tempted to conclude that the concept is therefore too soft to be of much analytic use. This temptation would seem to be reinforced by the fact that distinctive values are involved in different national contexts and that values are, in any event, difficult to measure. Such conclusions are premature. That values are involved underscores the fragility of the phenomenon. That these values vary from one context to another simply reminds us that legitimacy can be generated in a variety of ways, which means that regimes have wide latitude in the inducements they use to build support. Instead of being led astray by the variety of tactics they are likely to employ, it is more important to judge the success of those tactics, however they are manifested. This directs us to the more fundamental issue of performance. I do not mean to denigrate the issue of how regimes induce legitimacy, but simply to suggest that the more critical issue centers on their effectiveness in this endeavor.

For the reasons set forth in this chapter, performance in generating consent is reflected in two broad ways: the degree to which the regime can govern without resort to physical violence and the degree to which challenges to the regime are processed through normal channels. Given that the subject is *political* capacity, this approach follows directly from the distinction introduced in chapter 2 between power and force, and from my argument that the sustained use of force is fundamentally apolitical. Finally, I placed great weight in that chapter on the proposition that the exercise of power involves *relationships* between rulers and ruled. It follows that any definition of political capacity must explicitly address the behavior of the rulers and the ruled in relation to each other. That is what I have attempted to do in this chapter.

CHAPTER 6

The Measurement of National Political Capacity

It is a capital mistake to theorize in advance of the facts.
—Arthur Conan Doyle, *The Adventure of the Second Stain*

My discussion of organizational age and political legitimacy in the preceding two chapters has been couched in terms that have clear implications for measurement. The task that remains is to address those measurement issues directly. As will become clear in this chapter, the fact that political concepts are designed with measurement in mind does not mean that all possible empirical ambiguity has been resolved. Quite the contrary.

For example, the notion that political orders should be dated from the period of their establishment does not in itself identify that date. In many cases, reasonable people will disagree over the exact date despite the clarity of the measurement *principle* involved. Similarly, asserting the importance of the generational age of the national political leadership sounds relatively straightforward, but the argument leaves unresolved the identity of the real (as opposed to titular) leaders. The problems are amplified when we turn our attention to the measurement of legitimacy. One tactic commonly employed by regimes to maximize their legitimacy is to conceal information about the use of physical force to repress challenges, along with details about the extensiveness of the challenges themselves. For obvious reasons, this tactic hampers the collection of systematic data on legitimacy.

It is important to acknowledge that these are real problems—indeed, they are quite familiar to students of political conflict. However, it is equally important that we not allow ourselves to become paralyzed by these obstacles. The fact that relevant information is sometimes obscured (and typically in an active way) means that measurement may not be as precise as we would like. But this does not imply that efforts to gauge phenomena like political legitimacy should be abandoned. Indeed, to endorse such a conclusion would be tantamount to conceding that the phenomena are inconsequential simply because there are measurement challenges. Since one would expect these difficulties to increase directly with the political sensitivity of the material, this is ultimately an intellectually indefensible position.

Even with inexact measurement, much valuable information is available about the political capacity of modern nation-states. Although it is subject to error, I will suggest in this chapter that such material can usefully be employed to make comparisons across states of institutional capacity and political legitimacy. These comparisons will involve general orders of magnitude for each case, but, as I have emphasized throughout, national political capacity is always a matter of degree.

Institutional Age

I concluded in chapter 4 that age impinges directly on political capacity and that two components of age are critical in this regard. The first refers to the chronological age of institutions, and the second centers on the generational age of leaders. I address these in turn.

The Chronological Age of Institutions

Longevity has often been linked to stability and political performance (e.g., Black 1966; Rustow 1967; Huntington 1968; Eckstein 1971). Even so, different solutions have been proposed to the problem of how to identify the most appropriate start-up date for national institutions. Two prominent treatments help to define the issues.

For Black, the critical period is that time in which there is a "consolidation of modernizing leadership" (1966, chap. 3), by which is meant that time when traditional leaders lose their power in struggles with newer elites. These struggles have three distinctive attributes. First, they include an assertion of a "determination to modernize," often manifested in violent revolution, and emanating either from disaffected elements of the traditional leadership or from those representing new political interests. Second, there is a decisive break with institutions representing agrarian interests in favor of industrial economic forms. Third, there is an expansion of political authority and organization. All three elements of this consolidation take time (at least a generation) and all are conflictual.[1] Further, this is a *political* consolidation that predates economic and social transformation.

---

1. Black placed considerable emphasis on the conflictual nature of these changes. Consider the following: "'Transfer of power' is perhaps too colorless a phrase to describe

TABLE 6.1. Organizational Age of Selected Nation States as Estimated by Black and Rustow

	Consolidating Period (Black)	Independence Year (Rustow)
Argentina	1853–1946	1816
Brazil	1850–1930	1822
China	1905–49	before 1775
Cuba	1898–1959	1901
Egypt	1922–52	1922
France	1789–1848	before 1775
India	1919–47	1947
Indonesia	1922–49	1949
Italy	1805–71	before 1775
Japan	1868–1945	before 1775
Nigeria	1960–	1960
Russia	1861–1917	before 1775
Tanzania	1961–	1961
United Kingdom	1649–1832	before 1775
United States	1776–1865	1776

Sources: Data from Black 1966, 90–94; Rustow 1967, 292–94.

The first column of table 6.1 displays the period in which Black estimates modernizing leadership was consolidated, for selected states. It is clear that this consolidation occurred over a lengthy period in most cases: of those judged to be complete, the process took the longest in the United Kingdom (183 years) and was shortest in Indonesia and India (17 and 28 years, respectively). Among the older states, the process is often associated with revolution (e.g., China, France, and Russia), although in some cases it is coded as beginning with revolution (e.g., France and the United States) while in others it is said to end with revolution (e.g., China and Russia). Among the newer states, a similar pattern obtains around the date of independence from colonial rule: contrast Nigeria and Tanzania (where the process was judged to have just begun with independence) with India and Indonesia (where it is coded as having been completed by the date of independence).

In contrast to Black's identification of a period of modernizing leadership, Rustow (1967) dated nation-states from the time that they achieved independence as sovereign political units. His figures for the same illustrative set of countries are displayed in the second column

these events, for they involved in every country political struggles of the first magnitude. We know now, and many were confident then, that the modernizers would in the end be victorious—but the leaders of the old regimes fought bitterly and often skillfully to maintain their positions" (1966, 71).

of table 6.1. For the newer states, this procedure is straightforward since the date of decolonization is readily identified. Among the older states, the date in which sovereignty was achieved is often more difficult to determine, and Rustow codes twenty-two states as having gained independence before 1775 (including the 5 so listed in table 6.1).

Although it may not be immediately apparent from the cases displayed in this table, the approaches adopted by Black and Rustow have much in common. Indeed, when computed for all 124 countries for which data are available on both measures, the rank-order correlation (Spearman's rho) between the indices developed by Black and Rustow is .79. The size of this correlation is due in part (but not exclusively) to the fact that countries with extreme (high or low) scores on one measure tend to have a similar score on the other. Thus, for most of the countries of sub-Saharan Africa, both measures refer to the date of independence. At the other end of the scale, most industrialized Western countries are coded as old by both analysts. However, there are cases in which the acquisition of political sovereignty predated Black's period of consolidation by a substantial margin. These include, but are not restricted to, states in which there were major political revolutions: consider the figures for China, Japan, and Russia as noted in table 6.1. In other cases, independence preceded the period of consolidation by a smaller margin (e.g., Argentina and Brazil). What are the implications of these differences for the measurement of organizational longevity?

To address this question, I believe we need to return to the distinction between the state as a juridical entity and the state as a political entity (Jackson and Rosberg 1982a). It is evident that, construed as legal units, states have proven in recent years to be very durable (that is, they have generally continued to exist with their boundaries intact), and this is true for even those cases whose lack of political capacity is perhaps their most striking characteristic. Once we conceive of the problem in these terms, it becomes clear that approaches like Rustow's employ a juridical definition, while procedures like that adopted by Black reflect more of an interest in states as political units.

The distinction is important because the durability evidenced by states as legal units has not been matched by a corresponding longevity of constitutional orders. This fact is obvious where there have been major political revolutions, but it is also apparent where such revolutions have not occurred. While most of the states of Latin America, for example, achieved their current sovereign status in the early nineteenth century, many of them have experienced considerable political instability since then, typically in the form of military coups d'etat. While falling short of full-scale revolutions, these coups have generally included the suspension and abrogation of constitutions, whose weakness was already evidenced by the occurrence of the successful coups themselves. In a parallel vein, while it was perfectly reasonable for scholars of sub-Saharan Africa in the middle 1960s to equate date of independence with the beginning of the current constitutional order, the years since have seen much evidence of a similar type of political instability (see, e.g., Jackman 1978; Jackson and Rosberg 1982b; Londregan and Poole 1990), again involving the abrogation of constitutional orders.

Such patterns indicate that the state as a juridical unit recognized in international law should not simply be equated with the state as an entity that demonstrates some political capacity. On the other hand, it is important to understand that the former is a prerequisite of the latter, and that longevity on both dimensions needs to be considered in the evaluation of national political capacity. Specifically, there is good reason to believe that in comparing two states that have both experienced recent major political upheavals, that state which is juridically older has more political capacity (both states would, of course, have less capacity than a third state that had experienced both juridical and constitutional longevity).

As many have noted, the issue for states that are young on both counts is that they are confronted simultaneously with the processes of state building and the creation of political institutions (e.g., Rustow 1967; Linz 1978). In the terms used by Weiner (1965), this involves territorial *and* political integration, and that they are faced concurrently reduces the odds that either process will be successful. The creation of Pakistan in 1947 and events in many countries in sub-Saharan Africa after independence are often taken to illustrate the problem that this generates.

By contrast, issues of territorial integration centering on the state as a juridical unit were encountered and largely (but never completely) resolved in the earlier developers *before* questions of political integration. The decoupling of the two issues increases the probability that they will be resolved. At the same time, the consolidation of the juridical state helps provide a national history, which, I argued in chapter 5, is a key symbolic ingredient in the generation of political legitimacy.

On a more mundane note, with the creation of the juridical state comes the gradual emergence of a bureaucratic order that is likely to persist in some form even in the face of apparently major political transformations. This provides that measure of continuity to the political life of older juridical states that is lacking in their younger counterparts. As a result, the impact of upheavals involving the suspension and replacement of constitutional orders is less severe in older than it is in the youngest juridical states.

Weber made the argument some time ago with his insistence that "once it is fully established, bureaucracy is among those social structures which are the hardest to destroy" (1946, 228). But bureaucracies persist even when they fall short of being "fully" established. Thus, Weber commented that

> with all the changes of masters in France since the time of the First Empire, the power machine has remained essentially the same. Such a machine makes "revolution," in the sense of the forceful creation of entirely new formations of authority, technically more and more impossible . . . . In classic fashion, France has demonstrated how this process has substituted coups d'etat for "revolutions:" all successful transformations in France have amounted to coups d'etat. (1946, 230)

A similar view is represented in Siegfried's description of the "stable instability" of the French Fourth Republic (1956). The label was not intended to identify a paradox, but rather to show that even with the apparent instability of politics as reflected in cabinet turnovers, there remained a considerable underlying continuity in personnel, at both cabinet and civil-service levels. Hence the stability of the instability. Veliz has made the same case with respect to Latin America. Despite chronic instability involving coups and suspensions of constitutions throughout the area, centralist bureaucracies have survived and grown, even in periods in which there was apparent consensus that the role of the state should be minimized. "Perhaps with the arguable exception of Cuba, none of the other bureaucratic establishments of the region has been dismantled in ways that would prove the Weberian thesis wrong" (Veliz 1980, 288).

None of this should be taken to minimize the importance of recent political upheavals and the abrogation of constitutional orders for the capacity of political orders. Instead, I am suggesting that of the states that do undergo such upheavals, the experience is less incapacitating for those that are older in juridical terms. At the same time, such upheavals are consequential for all states. It follows that the measurement of the chronological age of nation-states should have two components that reflect their age in both juridical and constitutional terms.

To gauge the chronological age of juridical states, I employ an updated version of the figures provided by Rustow (1967, 292–93). Adopting his convention, those states that achieved political sovereignty before 1775 are treated as a single group and coded as if 1775 were the year in which they became independent. This procedure is predicated on the view, discussed at the end of chapter 4, that the first few years (or decades) are the most important in evaluating the longevity of institutions. I shall return to this issue below.[2] For those states that became independent between 1776 and 1966 (the last year included in Rustow's survey), I rely generally on Rustow's figures. Temporary interruptions to sovereignty, such as those experienced by several Western European countries during the Second World War, are disregarded. Longer suspensions of sovereignty, as experienced by the Baltic states, are counted. The measure amends Rustow's survey by including the date in which sovereignty was achieved by former colonies in the years from 1967 through the end of 1985.

As many have observed, states conceived in juridical terms have been relatively stable and clearly defined in the modern era. In conjunction with the fact that I am ignoring temporary interruptions to sovereignty, this means that determining the age of such states is unambiguous for most cases. But some troublesome cases do remain. For example, Rustow dates both Germanies and Italy as having been independent prior to 1775. While this is reasonable at one level, unification came much later in both cases and I have adopted the later date. Even my modification does not address the issue raised by the partition of Germany from 1949 to 1990.

This raises the more general matter of how changes in the unit of analysis are best treated. Following normal procedure, I have dated Pakistan's independence at 1947. But with the creation of Bangladesh in 1972, Pakistan's territorial definition underwent a fundamental transformation and the state of Pakistan lost more than half of its population. Similarly, the age of the Vietnamese state is somewhat unclear. One could treat the French colonial period in Indochina and the subsequent military intervention by the United States as temporary interruptions to Vietnamese sovereignty, but that stretches unacceptably the everyday meaning of the adjective "temporary." Alternatively, one could trace the current Vietnamese state back to the North Viet-

---

2. Alternative conventions could, of course, be followed. For reasons that will become clear below, these alternatives do not generate measures that can be distinguished in meaningful empirical terms from the one that I have adopted here.

namese state founded by Ho Chi Minh. This would acknowledge the military victory of the north, but would by the same token overlook the approximate doubling in size and population of that state effective in 1975.

Finally, as I noted at the beginning of chapter 4, juridical statehood implies recognition by at least a large proportion of the international community of states. I therefore ignore the "unilateral declaration of independence" from Britain made in 1965 by the white minority regime in Rhodesia in favor of the recognized state of Zimbabwe created in 1980. The case of Taiwan is more difficult to resolve, given its recognition by a large number of other states in 1949. The difficulty here stems from the withdrawal of that legal recognition that came with the diplomatic dialogue between the People's Republic of China and the United States.

Such instances, with their disputes over territory and sovereignty, remind us that even though juridical states (our units of analysis) have been relatively well delineated in recent years, some definitional uncertainty remains. Moreover, these cases are widely recognized because the disputes that have centered around them have been highly visible. But the problem should not be overstated. For the vast majority of modern nation-states, estimating the year in which sovereignty was achieved is straightforward.

My measure of the age of the current political order—or, to use Jackson and Rosberg's term, the age of the empirical state (1982a)— is the year in which the constitutional form in effect as of the end of 1985 was introduced. The construction of this variable is similar to (and the result updates) figures on the age of the current constitutional form as of 1970, computed earlier by Hudson (Taylor and Hudson 1972). In those cases where no constitutional form has been formally adopted, but where a previous constitution has been explicitly suspended, this measure refers to the date of introduction of the extra-constitutional rules effective at the end of 1985.

As was true with the first variable, identifying that year in which the current rules became effective is uncomplicated in most instances, but some cases require more judgment. After all, procedures and the constitutions in which they are embodied typically evolve through processes of amendment. The problem, then, is to differentiate fundamental changes in the rules governing political life from less substantial amendments, and to date the current arrangement as having begun when the last fundamental change became effective.

The general rule I have adopted distinguishes fundamental changes as those induced either when a new juridical state is created or when the prior set of political rules is overturned and suspended. In the first case, the age of the juridical state is identical (or close) to the age of the empirical state. In the second case, abrogation of constitutional orders is most commonly manifested through successful revolutions or coups d'etat (remember that this latter term refers literally to strikes against the state). The changes are fundamental because they entail relatively abrupt breaks with the past political order, in contrast to the more evolutionary and gradual patterns of change normally associated with amendments to constitutions. The classification rule involved here is clear from the following examples.

The People's Republic of China was established in 1949, and its first constitution was adopted in 1954. In the years since, three new constitutions have been promulgated (in 1975, 1978, and 1983). While these more recent documents have introduced several major changes, none of them can be taken as a fundamental and abrupt break with the past, as was the constitution of 1954. The current (as of 1985) set of political rules for China is therefore dated as beginning in 1954. A new constitution was approved in the Republic of South Africa in 1983. However, the changes it initiated cannot be interpreted as fundamental modifications to the document of 1961. The 1961 document, in turn, reflected minor changes associated with South Africa's departure from the British Commonwealth. I therefore employ 1910 as the date for this case. Finally, the original republican constitution in Yugoslavia under Tito became effective in 1946. Three new constitutions were subsequently introduced (in 1953, 1963, and 1974), but since the fundamental political change was associated with the 1946 document, that date is taken as the relevant date for Yugoslavia, as of 1985.[3]

In contrast, the constitution adopted in Greece in 1975 came after the military juntas that lasted from 1967 to 1974. Since the 1967 coup had included the explicit suspension of the 1952 constitution, the age of the current constitutional form in Greece is set at 1975. For similar reasons, Argentina and Spain are assigned the dates of 1983 and 1978, respectively, on this variable. In 1961, General Park Chung Hee mounted a successful coup d'etat in South Korea. After the end of his regime (which came with his assassination in 1979), a new constitution was adopted in 1980, which serves as the date in which the current political form was adopted in Korea. In June 1985, elements of the Ugandan government staged a successful coup. Although no

---

3. The recent disintegration of Yugoslavia, of course, represents a more fundamental change, so that both the constitutional order and the juridical state in place at the end of 1985 no longer exist.

constitution was formally adopted by the end of that year, 1985 serves as the date when the political rules in effect as of the end of 1985 were established in Uganda (yet a newer set of procedures was introduced early in the following year).

The general rule here, then, distinguishes upheavals according to their origins. Temporary interruptions to sovereignty brought about by external forces or by civil wars are ignored in the calculation of constitutional age. But internally induced, forceful abrogations of the political order are treated as events that reset the clock and thereby mark the beginning of a new political era.

Country values for both measures of the chronological age of nation-states as of December 1985 are reported in the Appendix. I postpone an examination of these two measures to introduce the data on generational age.

The Generational Age of National Political Leadership

I argued earlier that chronological age provides us with only part of the picture, and that the measurement of organizational age should also address the nature of top leadership. The specific issue here is whether leadership is primarily personal and institutions are secondary, or whether institutional procedures have primacy. To evaluate this process, we need to focus on leadership succession, which is especially problematic in newer states for the reasons advanced in chapter 4.

Consider two countries which are of the same or similar current chronological age but different generational ages. In case A (e.g., Cuba), there has been no leadership succession and the founder continues to rule, while case B (e.g., Jamaica) has experienced several relatively orderly transfers of leadership involving a series of individual leaders. The argument is that although each has the same chronological age, case B has more political capacity (or institutional structure) simply because of its *demonstrated* history of successful transfers of leadership. Operationally, this raises three questions: to which period should estimates of the number of leadership transfers refer; which leaders should be included in the calculations; and how should multiple terms of office be counted?

On the first matter, counts of the number of leadership transfers should be made within constitutional eras. If we are concerned with the current constitutional period, the relevant quantity is thus the number of successions since the beginning of that period, as defined in the last section. If we are interested in earlier eras, then we would examine the number of successions within those eras. In other words, we need to exclude leadership transfers associated with extraconstitutional revolutions or coups because these reflect political upheavals and institutional collapses that restart the clock for leadership transfers. After such upheavals, the important issue is whether the individual who toppled the old order was able to establish a new political order. This is the sense in which the succession process must be judged to be relatively orderly before it can be included in estimates of generational age.

The second question is which leaders should be counted? In principle, the answer is straightforward: we should include the single individual who wields the most political power. This criterion directs us toward that individual who is the head of state in many instances, especially where presidential systems are involved. But in many other cases, the head of state is no more than a figurehead. At the end of 1985, for example, President Gromyko as head of state of the Soviet Union was less significant politically than Gorbachev as general secretary of the Communist party, and this pattern has been emulated by many other states. Similarly, prime ministers are more influential than heads of state (presidents or monarchs) in parliamentary systems. It is obvious that the title of the office held by the top political leader varies from one state to another. In gauging the number of leadership transfers, it is therefore important first to distinguish the relevant office and then to identify the individuals who have held that office.

Finally, I have emphasized the number of *individuals* who have held leadership positions rather than the number of terms that the office has been held. Individual leaders who have held the office for more than one term are thus counted once only, whether the terms involved were consecutive or nonconsecutive. Among other things, this procedure reflects the underlying continuity of top political leadership despite cabinet instability in systems like that of postwar Italy.

Country values on the generational age of national leaders are displayed in the Appendix. These figures identify the number of individuals who have held the top political position in each country during its present constitutional era, which refers to the years from the creation of the current constitutional (or extraconstitutional) arrangement through the end of 1985.

Characteristics of the Data on Institutional Age

The values listed by country in the Appendix are summarized in table 6.2, which shows the ranges and means for each of the three mea-

TABLE 6.2. Summary Statistics for Measures of Age of Nation-states as of 1985

	Number of Years Independent by 1985	Number of Years by 1985 since Constitution Adopted	Number of National Leaders since Constitution Adopted
Minimum value	6	1	1
Maximum value	211	199	61
Mean value	83.2	31.3	5.1
Median value	43.0	20.5	2.0
Skewness	0.76	2.49	3.39
N	134	134	133

sures.[4] Two interrelated features of these data are immediately apparent.

First, most nation-states are very young. In almost all instances, of course, juridical age exceeds that of the current constitutional form, but even so, it is youth that is conspicuous. At one level, this is not surprising given the pace of decolonization after the Second World War and the concomitant expansion in the sheer number of sovereign states. But evidence of youth in terms of constitutional age is also striking, even among many of those states that became independent in the last century. Since the measure of the generational age of the top political leadership refers to the current constitutional period, it follows that most states should be young on this count too, and, indeed, they are. While the number of leaders ranges from one to sixty-one, the median value is only 2.0.

Second, for all three indicators, the distribution of country values is heavily skewed right. Thus, the means are all larger than their respective medians, and the measures of skewness are positively signed. This skewness is, of course, consistent with the liability of newness argument, particularly with respect to constitutional age. It also suggests that the differences among low-scoring countries are more interesting than differences among those with higher scores. As I noted at the end of chapter 4, there is good reason to expect that the severity of the liability of newness should decrease with organizational age, since the first few years or leaders are the most critical for

---

4. The two measures of chronological age have been rearranged in table 6.2 and those following to reflect the number of years that had elapsed by the end of 1985 since sovereignty was achieved and the current constitutional arrangement was adopted, respectively. Thus, each country score in the Appendix has been subtracted from 1986. No such modifications are necessary for the measure of generational age, for obvious reasons.

TABLE 6.3.   Median Age of 124 Nation-states as of 1985 by Wealth

	Number of Years Since Independence	Number of Years since Constitution	Number of National Leaders
Low-income economies			
(N = 36)	26	11.0	1.0
Lower middle-income economies			
(N = 36)	43	11.5	1.0
Upper middle-income economies			
(N = 21)	76	16.0	2.0
East European nonmarket economies			
(N = 10)	76	38.0	2.5
Industrial market economies			
(N = 21)	155	112.0	19.0

Note: Countries are grouped by wealth following the classification employed by the World Bank (1987, Annex), except that I have included "high-income oil exporters" (Kuwait, Libya, and Saudi Arabia) with upper middle-income economies.

institutionalization. In conjunction with the distributions of country values evident in the Appendix, this implies that differences between lower values ought to be weighted more heavily than differences between higher-scoring cases. This is most readily achieved by examining the logarithms (rather than the raw scores) of the organizational age of nation-states.[5]

Additional perspective is gained on these data when we inspect differences in organizational age by wealth and geographic region. Table 6.3 displays the median age on all three measures by level of national wealth, where the latter is indexed by the classification of per capita GNP for 1985 employed by the World Bank (1987). For each measure, there is a pronounced monotonic relation between wealth and age. Taking age as the criterion, the Western industrial states as a group have more political capacity than others by a considerable margin. Indeed, the size of that margin increases from the first to the third column of the table, so that the contrast in generational age between industrial states and all others is substantial.

Setting to one side the industrial economies, table 6.4 reports median organizational age by geographic region for Third World countries. The figures on the number of years since independence in

---

5. The logarithmic transformation, of course, substantially discounts the weight of extremely high country scores. This is why I argued earlier in this chapter that different conventions in coding the date of sovereignty for older states have no discernible impact on the empirical results (I adopted 1775 as the earliest date for this variable). By the same token, the distinction between having one or two leaders is more heavily weighted than the distinction between forty and sixty leaders.

TABLE 6.4.   Median Age of One Hundred Nation-states in the Third World as of 1985 by Geographic Region

	Number of Years since Independence	Number of Years since Constitution	Number of National Leaders
Asia ($N = 21$)	39	15.5	2.0
Latin America ($N = 24$)	152	16.5	2.0
Middle East and North Africa ($N = 18$)	39	15.5	1.5
Sub-Saharan Africa ($N = 37$)	26	11.0	1.0

Note: Calculations exclude countries in the East European nonmarket and industrial market economy categories of the last table, along with Greece, Madagascar, Mauritius, Portugal, and Yugoslavia.

the first column reflect patterns of decolonization, where the countries of Latin America as a group became independent first, while those of sub-Saharan Africa were decolonized last (with the average date for African states being 1960). But the figures in the second and third columns of the table indicate that regional contrasts in juridical age do not translate neatly into differences in constitutional or generational age. Although the states of sub-Saharan Africa are somewhat younger in terms of constitutional age than those in the other regions of the Third World, the differences are not pronounced. Further, the last column indicates that there are no systematic regional differences in generational age as reflected by the number of national political leaders in the current constitutional period.

While instructive, the figures in tables 6.3 and 6.4 ignore the systematic association between geographic region and national wealth. Table 6.5 accordingly reports regression estimates for all three measures of political age on wealth and region, where regions are defined as in the last table and wealth is measured by per capita energy consumption rates for 1985.[6] No causal argument is implied by these estimates: instead, they are presented simply as a way of summarizing the data in general terms.

---

6. Data on rates of energy consumption are from the World Bank (1987, 218–19), and are employed to maximize the number of cases. The World Bank does not report estimates of GNP for the nonmarket economies. While Summers and Heston (1988) do report estimates of real GDP for those economies, their coverage of other states is less complete. Energy consumption figures are available for all but two (Chad and Lesotho) of the countries included in table 6.5. For the 108 countries for which estimates of both real GDP and energy consumption rates are available, the simple correlation between the two (using logged scores) is .95.

The figures in the first column of the table indicate that the simple association between juridical age and wealth disappears with region controlled. Instead, juridical age reflects regional differences, with the states of sub-Saharan Africa in the youngest group, those of Asia and the Middle East/North Africa in an intermediate group, and the remainder in the oldest group. In terms of constitutional age, the association with wealth persists, although the coefficients for Latin America and the Middle East/North African states suggest that they are somewhat younger than one would expect on the basis of their wealth. The estimates for generational age are somewhat different. Consistent with the raw figures in table 6.4, there is little regional variation *within* the Third World with wealth controlled, although all Third World states have experienced fewer leadership successions than others.

These patterns are noteworthy because they indicate that organizational age (one key ingredient of political capacity) is not a simple function of economic development, and therefore cannot be reduced to the latter. First, although there is a pronounced zero-order association, the coefficients of determination show that this association is far

TABLE 6.5. Regressions of Age of Nation-states as of 1985 on Wealth and Geographic Region ($N = 122$)

Dependent Variable	Number of Years since Independence	Number of Years since Constitution	Number of National Leaders
Log energy consumption	−.03	.34*	.22*
per capita, 1985	(0.06)	(.08)	(.07)
Asia	−1.06*	−.35	−.96*
	(.23)	(.33)	(.28)
Latin America	.06	−1.04*	−1.07*
	(.21)	(.29)	(.25)
Middle East and North	−1.05*	−1.00*	−1.29*
Africa	(.21)	(.30)	(.25)
Sub-Saharan Africa	−1.67*	−.50	−1.15*
	(.26)	(.37)	(.31)
Constant	5.07*	1.18	.32
	(.48)	(.67)	(.57)
R^2	.53	.45	.53
Restricted R^2 (energy			
consumption only)	.23	.35	.42

Note: For each regression, the dependent variable has been transformed logarithmically. Main table entries are metric regression coefficients, and numbers below them in parentheses are their standard errors. Starred coefficients are more than twice the size of their standard errors. With the exception of Chad and Lesotho (for which energy consumption rates are unavailable), these estimates are based on the same cases as the figures in table 6.3. Thus, the regional effects represent contrasts between the region indicated and non–Third World countries, net of energy consumption rates.

from perfect: the figures in the bottom row of the table range from .23 for juridical age to .42 for generational age. Second, the table reveals that there are notable regional differences in the association. In other words, the argument I have made about the importance of organizational age is not a brief for the proposition that political capacity is an unadorned "unilinear" function of wealth.

That the regional patterns vary according to the specific element of organizational age under consideration has a second implication. The three different components cannot be treated as interchangeable indicators of capacity. Further evidence on this point comes from the correlations among the three components: that between juridical and constitutional age is .27; for juridical and generational age the correlation is .42; the correlation between constitutional and generational age is .79.[7]

The first two of these correlations are quite low, which underscores the distinction between juridical and constitutional age that was also clear from the regression estimates in table 6.5. I argued earlier that both of these components are analytically distinct but central to the evaluation of organizational capacity. That this difference is also manifested empirically means that each of these components needs to be considered separately in the appraisal of national political performance.

In contrast, the third correlation is considerably higher. This stems in good part from the construction of the measure of generational age, which reflects the number of leaders in the current constitutional period. Such a design obviously builds a relationship into these two measures, especially for those states with older constitutions. Even so, the correlation is not perfect. Most notably, the size of this correlation masks considerable variance in constitutional age among chronologically young juridical states. Given my argument that the youngest states are the most fragile, this discrepancy between the two measures indicates that they are identifying different aspects of institutional age precisely in the most important range of country values. And this discrepancy was already apparent in the regression estimates in the second and third columns of table 6.5.

Legitimacy

At various points in this book I have argued that the analysis of legitimacy addresses the nature of the relationship between rulers and

---

7. These correlations are again calculated from the logarithms of the country scores for the 133 states included in table 6.2.

ruled. It is therefore essential to examine the behavior of both groups. With this in mind, I proposed in chapter 5 that there are two critical ingredients to political legitimacy: to what degree do authorities rely on physical coercion, and to what extent do challengers to those authorities employ violent tactics to advance their interests?

The Official Use of Physical Force

The large-scale analysis of the ways that states and governments repress challenges has grown in recent decades. Organizations as diverse as Amnesty International, the Freedom House, and the United States Department of State routinely collect data that bear on this general problem. These data are thus sometimes generated by extra-governmental groups that seek in a watchdog capacity to mobilize general awareness of the use of coercion, while at other times they are developed by governments, to be used presumably in the policy-making process. Attention to the issue increased substantially with the publicity afforded human rights in the late 1970s by the Carter administration.

My emphasis on the use of physical force parallels this interest in many ways, but it is not motivated by human rights concerns. Such considerations are too broad for present purposes and divert attention away from the use of power as I have defined it. For example, the Universal Declaration of Human Rights endorsed by the United Nations in 1947 stressed the provision of such factors as food, clothing, housing, and medical care sufficient to maintain a minimal living standard along with political rights. These are, of course, important and interesting issues in their own right, but they do not bear directly on the problem at hand.

Even when attention is confined to the use of physical force, my approach diverges from a political-rights orientation in the following way. Questions of legality necessarily bear on any evaluation of rights, and all regimes can legally employ physical force, albeit in varying degrees. Accordingly, the imposition of martial law or the detention of political opponents is usually justified as legal, and statutes bearing on "security" are typically invoked to advance such claims. Whether these proclamations are widely accepted is, of course, another matter, since it is generally unclear whose security is at issue. The important point, however, is that if such justifications can be sustained, then it is not clear that political rights have been violated, even though physical force has been employed. In contrast, questions of legality have no bearing on the interpretation of the use of physical force within the power framework that I have adopted. If officials employ force, that fact directly reflects a loss of power (and thus diminished political capacity) regardless of any legal justification that those officials are able to invoke. This distinguishes my approach from a human-rights perspective.

There are different ways of measuring the amount of force employed by officials. One might focus on the size of the state repressive apparatus and count either expenditures on internal security forces or the size (in terms of personnel) of those forces. The assumption here would be that states with larger internal security forces (standardized by population) rely more heavily on those forces. While this approach has much to recommend it, there are major practical difficulties in distinguishing internal from external security budgetary and personnel allocations. For example, although the imposition of martial law is typically defended on the grounds that it is an action designed to maximize internal security, martial law itself is usually administered by the military whose publicly announced purpose is to provide security against external threats to the state. The internal/external distinction is further clouded by the common use of appeals to internal security as a cover for the use of physical force against challengers and by the familiar claim by authorities that the challengers so acted against are agents of external forces.[8] Coupled with the political sensitivity of the information, these considerations make the relevant data hard to obtain.

But even without these problems of definition and information, it is important to recognize that measures of the size of internal security forces can never be more than incomplete proxies because they do not directly address the official *use* of force. Instead, on the presumption that size reflects strength, and disregarding questions of efficiency, they indicate at best the propensity of governments to employ force.

As an alternative gauge of the official use of force, one could transform the qualitative judgments of country experts into rankings of national differences. Perhaps the best-known efforts along these lines are the evaluations compiled by the Freedom House (Gastil 1985), which include ratings of political liberties, such as rights of political expression and organization. Although this series bears more on issues of liberal democratic performance than it does on legitimacy

---

8. As I argued in chapter 2, the idea of a national interest is difficult to sustain, especially when it is applied to domestic politics. This is what makes terms like *internal security threats* inherently ambiguous. That this ambiguity is recognized by many governments is reflected in recurrent attempts to discredit challengers by casting them as agents of external interests.

as I have defined it, data of this type would seem in principle to offer a more clear-cut measure of repressiveness than does the first approach. Again, however, practical difficulties remain. In the particular case of Gastil's data, there is some uncertainty in the coding criteria, and the basis for many of the qualitative judgments that underlie the overall country ratings is unclear (Bollen 1986). More generally, alleviating these problems with data of this form is difficult, given that they rely on qualitative judgments the bases of which are inherently ambiguous.[9] Laying these concerns to one side, the fact remains that ratings like Gastil's do not directly address the use of force.

Information that appears more directly linked to this question is available in the annual series on the application of official violence against the citizens of Third World countries assembled by World Priorities (Sivard 1986, 24–25). Activities included in this classification are "torture, brutality, disappearances, and political killings." The classification itself is based on the publications and files of such organizations as Amnesty International, the Washington Office on Latin America, Americas Watch, the U.S. Department of State's *Country Reports on Human Rights Practices*, and Human Rights Internet (Sivard 1986, 42). While this coverage of sources is broad, the fact that the kinds of activities included under the rubric of official violence are not clearly defined limits the value of the measure. Further, the classification has only three categories of official violence ("none," "some," and "frequent"), and again the criteria for assignment of a country to a particular category are somewhat obscure.

In light of these difficulties, the most promising approach is to focus on *events* that involve the official use of force. As I will make clear below, this does not resolve all of the practical obstacles to measurement. But because it does make an explicit distinction between those occasions in which governments employ physical force and those occasions in which they do not (regardless of the rationales they offer), it affords the most fruitful basis from which to proceed, given the available alternatives.

When considering the use of force, governments have an extensive menu of options at their disposal. The declaration of martial law is one stratagem to which I have already alluded. It is perhaps the broadest tactic under the rubric of which a host of more specific actions are commonly included and which is typically invoked to rationalize and provide a semblance of legality (if not the acceptance

---

9. The difficulties should not be overstated, and Gastil (1991) provides an interesting discussion of the approach. An alternative set of estimates of human rights is available in Humana (1992).

that comes with legitimacy) to those actions. But it is also the case that the use of force does not require a general proclamation of martial law, especially when governments are targeting particular groups rather than the population as a whole. A curfew may instead be imposed in selected geographic areas where specific opposition groups are the target. Even smaller groups or individuals may be targeted, in which case there is no purpose in designating geographic areas. Instead, political arrests are made, opponents are exiled, or newspapers are closed in apparently isolated fashion without resort to more general action by authorities.

The extensiveness of the menu of options available to authorities means that the set of activities one might designate as evidence of their use of physical force is necessarily heterogeneous. There is clearly a considerable variety in the *size* of the target groups. The range of forceful tactics (preemptive and reactive) employed against challengers is equally variegated. In other substantive settings, this heterogeneity might be a source of concern. For example, were one interested in tracing through a sequence of events in a given country, then the targets of particular actions, why they are targets, or the success of the action itself would become important considerations. Such an analytic focus might also require that attention be restricted to more homogeneous sets of activities. But despite their intrinsic significance and their manifest bearing on other analytic concerns, these issues are secondary in the evaluation of the general legitimacy of a regime. In any such evaluation, the question is not why a government decided to employ force in a given instance or how efficacious that action may have appeared to its initiators. The more fundamental issue centers on whether and to what degree national governments and their agents (states, if it helps) do actually employ physical force over a specified time interval, so that they can be compared according to the pervasiveness of their reliance on coercion.

The most extensive set of data that address the frequency with which states employ physical coercion is reported in the *World Handbook of Political and Social Indicators* (Taylor and Jodice 1983, 2:61–77). Under the rubric of state coercive behavior, this compendium lists figures on "government sanctions," which identify censorship of individuals or institutions, general restrictions on political activity, and other restrictions on social and political behavior.

> Censorship includes actions by the authorities to limit, curb, or intimidate the mass media, including newspapers, magazines, books, radio, and television. Typical examples of such action are the closing of a newspaper or journal, or the censoring of articles

in the domestic press or dispatches sent out of the country . . . . Restrictions on political behavior include general restrictive measures by authorities, such as the declaring of martial law, mobilizing troops for domestic security, and instituting a curfew. They also include actions specifically directed against an individual, a party, or other political organizations. Such specific actions include the removal of a government official reportedly because of his or her political beliefs and activities, the banning of a political party or acts of harassment against it, the arrest of opposition leaders on grounds of state security, the exiling or deportation of persons for engaging in political actions or for expressing opposition regarded as detrimental to the national interest, and the arrest or deportation of persons reportedly involved in political protest actions, including protest demonstration, riots, political strikes, armed attacks, and assassination attempts. Finally, restrictions on political behavior also encompass actions by the authorities against foreign espionage. (Taylor and Jodice 1983, 2:62-63)

Because this measure pertains to coercive behavior by the state, it refers only to events initiated by a formal government agency. Thus, in cases like Lebanon, where there has been little central authority since 1975, the coercive actions taken by the various private and externally supported militia are not counted. Similar considerations apply to the activities of the death squads in various Latin American countries, since, despite apparent associations with governmental elements, these do not constitute official agents.

Along with this information on government sanctions, Taylor and Jodice report a separate series on political executions.

A political execution is an event in which a person or group is put to death under orders of the national authorities while in their custody. Excluded are assassinations, even if known to have been arranged by the authorities, and persons killed in riots, armed attacks, strikes, and the like. Also excluded are executions for criminal offenses, such as murder, that are not reported to have political significance. Typically, a political execution is one in which the person executed is charged with activities threatening the security of the state, the regime, the government, or the leadership. (1983, 2:63)

Taylor and Jodice observe that the requirement that the execution be directly or indirectly instigated by national authorities sometimes created a practical difficulty in coding. For example, they note that the death of Steven Biko in a South African prison lacked the formalities of a court and a firing squad. Nonetheless, the event is coded as an execution, on the following grounds:

> The climate of opinion in the South African security services and their behavior in general was sufficient to determine that this was no accident. The aura of values and expectations emanating from the national political leadership encourages or discourages such treatment of political detainees. In South Africa, and in many other authoritarian systems, the burden of proof of noncomplicity is on the government. National leaders are responsible politically and morally for actions done in their names, even if they do not issue the specific orders. (1983, 2:63-72)

With respect to geographic and temporal coverage, the *World Handbook* data constitute the most comprehensive extant collection. They include information for over 140 countries for the thirty-five years starting in 1948 and ending in 1982.[10] In its complete form, this information is available in two series for each country. The first reports a daily count of political events, and the second is based on annual counts. For reasons that will become clearer below, the data based on aggregations of the annual series are preferable. Among other things, the annually compiled data smooth out very short-run fluctuations in the official use of physical coercion.

I have argued throughout this section that we need to focus on differences of orders of magnitude. I have also suggested that we should place more emphasis on differences between lower scores and to discount differences between higher ones. For example, the differences between (*a*) zero and ten and (*b*) fifty and one-hundred political executions are not of equivalent significance, even though each involves a doubling of the raw scores. The distinction between no executions and ten is of more momentous import because it involves crossing the threshold between zero and one event. While the movement from fifty to one-hundred executions is certainly profound for the additional individuals involved, the score of fifty indicates that authorities were already employing force in a massive manner. Given this, the most interpretable metric for the government sanctions data is

---

10. Taylor and Jodice (1983, vol. 2) report the data for the thirty years from 1948 to 1977. An updated version extending the series through the end of 1982 is available from the Inter-University Consortium for Political and Social Research, and further updates are in preparation.

generated by applying a natural logarithmic values of the raw scores.[11] As I pointed out earlier in this chapter, this transformation of the data preserves the original rank ordering, but attaches much more significance to differences between low values and minimizes differences between higher values.

I postpone a fuller discussion of the properties of these data and turn to the question of how the severity of challenges to states is best measured.

The Violence of Challenges

Over the last twenty-five years, the systematic empirical analysis of domestic political conflict in a comparative context has received a good deal of attention (see, e.g., Gurr 1970; and Hibbs 1973 for two well-known studies). Although different scholars have often employed distinctive explanatory arguments, their investigations have all shared a central concern with understanding the conditions under which those who challenge authority resort to violence. Thus, Gurr's book is titled *Why Men Rebel*. Further, these studies have devoted considerable effort to questions of measurement, from which we can profitably draw.

Hibbs argued that to be counted as challenges, the activities must meet three interrelated conditions. First, the behaviors in question need to have an anti-system nature, a condition that antigovernment protests meet, but progovernment parades do not. Second, they must have a clear and direct political significance, so that they "pose a threat of at least severe inconvenience to the normal operation of the political elite." This criterion excludes such incidents as "ordinary labor strikes," but includes "strikes with at least mildly threatening political objectives." Third, the behaviors must involve a collective endeavor, which stipulation is intended to exclude criminal activities like murder and armed robbery (1973, 7).

Employing these criteria in a dimensional analysis with data from over one hundred countries for the years 1948 through 1967, Hibbs concluded that "mass political violence" has two general components: collective protest and internal war. The first of these reflects milder forms of violence, and includes antigovernment demonstrations, political strikes, and riots. Internal war refers to the escalated form, and encompasses deaths from political violence, "armed attacks," and political assassinations. Since it more clearly addresses variations in

---

11. As a practical matter, since there are several instances where the raw score is zero for which the logarithm is undefined, 1 should be added to all raw scores prior to the transformation.

the severity of the violence with which challenges to regimes are mounted, internal war appears to be the more suitable general component for present purposes.[12]

Even so, it is not clear that all three of the variables identified by Hibbs bear equally on the question of internal war. As Hibbs himself points out (1973, 11), a good case can be mounted against including assassinations under the rubric of *mass* violence. At best, there is considerable uncertainty surrounding the political meaning, antisystem character, and collective significance of assassinations (Taylor and Jodice 1983, 2:43), which means that they do not necessarily meet the criteria specified for inclusion. I believe that a similar ambiguity surrounds the interpretation of the events labeled as "armed attacks," and indeed Hibbs's empirical results suggest that these events do not fit cleanly on the internal war dimension.

These considerations suggest that the violence or severity of challenges is best measured by a single variable, the number of deaths from political violence. This approach has at least three advantages. First, a single variable is more readily interpretable than a composite variable. Death counts are less subject to the ambiguities just discussed because they reflect the severity of collectively based events with clear political significance. While some of these deaths stem from intergroup violence, most of them are caused by official or unofficial government agents.[13] Second, if we conceive of violent challenges as activities with high potential costs to the participants, death counts provide the most direct available estimate of the costs that were actually incurred. Finally, and on a more practical level, there is a variety of evidence to indicate that, because of their visibility, deaths are much more likely to be considered newsworthy than the more specific events (riots, armed attacks, etc.) considered by Hibbs. They consequently tend to be more completely reported (on this point, see especially Snyder and Kelly 1977; Rosenblum 1981; Weede 1981).[14]

As was the case with the use of state physical coercion, the most

---

12. I exclude the behaviors labeled "everyday forms of peasant resistance" by Scott (1985, 1990) and Colburn (1989) because these behaviors seem to represent more a form of accommodation than of resistance. Besides, the efficacy of these behaviors as challenges is far from clear (for a similar conclusion, see the essay by Esman in Colburn 1989).

13. For example, Gurr and Lichbach (1979) estimated that for the deadly political conflict that occurred in fifty countries from 1966 through 1970 the ratio of deaths among challengers to deaths among soldiers and police was about 2.5 to 1.

14. This is not, of course, to suggest that they are recorded without error. Instead, I am making the more modest and simpler claim that deaths from violence are more likely to

comprehensive set of data on deaths from domestic political violence is reported in the *World Handbook of Political and Social Indicators* (Taylor and Jodice 1983, 2:48–51). These figures refer to the deaths that occurred in different kinds of specific events, including protests, riots, and armed attack events. "The category includes nationals who are casualties of foreign interventions in the country, but excludes deaths of foreigners. Also excluded are political executions, deaths in enemy prisons, deaths in international war, and deaths in border incidents with other countries, as well as homicide victims" (Taylor and Jodice 1983, 2:43). Information is again available for over 140 countries covering the thirty-five years from 1948 through 1982.

Paralleling my use of the information about coercion, these data on the severity of challengers are best treated in terms of the natural logarithmic values of the raw country scores. As I indicated earlier, this transformation places declining weight on country values as they increase. For instance, there were more reported casualties in the Nigerian civil war than in Indonesia in the 1960s, but the important point is that fatalities were massive in both countries.

Characteristics of the Data on Legitimacy

How well do these data reflect the official use of violence and the severity of challenges to authorities? In evaluating this question several issues need to be addressed. I consider, in turn, problems of reliability and validity, issues of aggregation, and possible standardizations of the data.

The compilers of the *World Handbook* data devoted a good deal of attention to the reliability of the conflict data they collected. Indeed, their concern in this regard is exemplary (see especially Taylor and Jodice 1983, 2, chaps. 1 and 6). Information for each country was coded from two sources, the *New York Times* and one other (where possible, this second source was a regionally specific one). The available evidence indicates that the procedure is reasonable in the sense that additional sources tend to yield little new information (see, e.g., Jackman and Boyd 1979). Further, Taylor and Jodice provide considerable information on intercoder reliability. Of course, neither they nor I would claim that the data are without error. But the reliability of

be reported than the other events under discussion. It is interesting to note that in his original analysis Hibbs suggested death counts as the single variable most representative of his internal war dimension.

these data appears to be good, in the sense that they reasonably reflect the information available in the original documents.

Turning to the issue of validity, it is important to understand that these data reflect *reported* behavior, that is, events and casualties that the press deemed newsworthy. Even where there are no restrictions on the press, it is evident that news typically stresses the extraordinary and downplays the routine. Although some believe that this reflects a preference for "bad" over "good" events, nothing sinister or mysterious is involved. Just as fires are plainly more newsworthy than everyday trips to the market at the local level, assassinations attract more attention than, say, minor-to-moderate revisions to national budgets. There is thus every reason for the press to be more likely to cover and report events that assume a more spectacular form (Rosenblum 1981). In this connection, the counts I am employing are relatively dramatic. Deaths from violence are much more likely to be reported than a minor peaceful protest. Similarly, there is considerable evidence to indicate that the imposition of repressive measures is more widely covered than their relaxation (Rosenblum 1981; Taylor and Jodice 1983).

Even so, attention paid by the press to different countries does vary in the absence of severe restrictions on the press. Some countries may receive more attention because they are regarded as more strategically important or problematic. For example, reporting on El Salvador (a small country) increased notably after 1981 with concern that the country might become another Vietnam (Taylor and Jodice 1983, 2:178–79). Other evidence indicates that national governments can take steps to increase at least minimally the volume of coverage accorded their country in the international press (Manheim and Albritton 1984).

The problem is of course exacerbated when governments systematically conceal information and restrict the press. Such efforts are common in states as diverse as the former Soviet Union and South Africa. During the middle 1970s they gained momentum and apparent respectability in some quarters of the Third World with the UNESCO-sponsored effort to create a "New International Information Order." Among other things, this was described by its proponents as an attempt to place limits on Western control over the international media and to place more emphasis on "positive" rather than "negative" news.[15] The complaints of many non-Western participants are well

15. For a discussion of the issues involved and the views of the major protagonists, see the essays in Richstad and Anderson 1981.

summarized in the statement by Narinder K. Aggarwala (an official in the United Nations Development Program at the time) that rights to information are "fundamental but not absolute" (in Richstad and Anderson 1981, xvii). Aggarwala continued:

> The process of establishing equations and corelationships be-tween various fundamental rights is going on throughout the world all the time, much more so in the Third World where the concepts of fundamental rights are being defined and interpreted *by the powers that be* in terms of each country's own national, historical, and cultural needs. While the media leaders are justi-fied in striving for the maximum freedom of the press, the degree of freedom enjoyed by the press in a given country *will depend entirely on its leaders' perception of the country's political and security needs*. Examples can be found in the Western world as well. Media freedom is treated differently by various Western countries, according to their own historical development. (Em-phasis added)

The relativism and authoritarianism of this argument is self-evident. Given that the way in which leaders perceive their country's political and security needs is inextricably bound up with their own aspirations to retain office, the purpose of the proposed changes is also transpar-ent.

Obviously, data on legitimacy are sensitive and therefore difficult to collect, and the obstacles increase with governmental efforts to conceal those data. But while we should be aware of these difficulties, their existence is hardly a brief for abandoning the available data. We need to remember that governments attempt to conceal information on the use of violence precisely because that information bears directly on their legitimacy. And, of course, material on censorship is included in the measure of government sanctions. While there is always room for refinement, I conclude that these data provide important informa-tion on the use of force by both officials and challengers.

Beyond the issues of reliability and validity, it is evident that the data are aggregated summaries of events and casualties. It is clearly difficult to draw inferences about the motivational forces behind the use of violence or about sequences of violence from information of this form. That fact may be a real constraint in some settings, as Snyder (1978), Tilly (1978), DeNardo (1985), Lichbach (1987), and others have pointed out. For example, data like these cannot be used to analyze tactical calculations made by those who decide to engage in violence, whether officials or challengers.

But my focus is on variations in the overall legitimacy of regimes or states, not on issues having to do with tactics of those who employ violent tactics. The question then is not why or how violence was used in one particular setting and not in another, but the degree to which violence was employed, if at all. Aggregated data would seem both necessary and desirable for comparisons along these lines, because the substantive question is itself cast in aggregated terms. Further, I earlier emphasized the importance of examining the *use* rather than the threat of force, since all governments (states) have the capacity to employ violence. These data reflect that emphasis, because they deal with counts of events and casualties.

Of course, there are different ways in which these data can be usefully aggregated. Two issues are germane here. First, I have already pointed out that the measure of the use of government sanctions includes a relatively heterogeneous set of events, which reflects among other things the variety of repressive techniques that is available to governments. But it may be useful for some purposes to disaggregate these data further, by distinguishing repression aimed at individuals (e.g., arrests) from that targeted at groups (e.g., declarations of martial law or censorship). Repression against individuals tends to be more discrete, while that against groups is generally more open-ended in terms of its duration. While recognizing the onset of repression targeted at groups is relatively straightforward, identifying the completion of the event is more difficult. Distinguishing repression according to the two basic kinds of target involved would reduce the heterogeneity in the measure of government sanctions.[16] The resulting series on sanctions against individuals would also more closely parallel the separate series on political executions.

Second, I have suggested that the annually based data series is preferable to the series generated from daily counts because the latter are oversensitive to very short-run fluctuations. Nothing mystical is implied by this suggestion, and indeed other analysts have used longer periods (for example, Hibbs [1973] employed ten-year intervals). However, some have claimed that any such intervals are excessively long. Sanders (1978, 1981), for example, has proposed instead that attention be restricted to data aggregated over monthly intervals. Once this is done, he reports that very few general patterns emerge. While I

---

16. Such a disaggregation would also alleviate the problem of the boundary in time of the sanctions events discussed by Taylor and Jodice (1983, 2:76).

am not arguing that any particular aggregation is optimal for all purposes, Sanders's specific proposal is unsatisfactory.

In choosing a decent interval, it is important to understand that with very short intervals, analyses become extremely sensitive to short-term fluctuations of little substantive significance. Indeed, the shorter the interval, the less reliable the measure (Allison 1977). As a result, the analyses come increasingly to reflect noise, which accounts for Sanders's conclusion that there were few general patterns to report. That reliability should decrease with the length of the period over which the data are aggregated will come as no surprise to those who have coded conflict data. Even a cursory examination of the sources reveals that press reports often date events in a very general way, with statements like "It is estimated that 200 civilians were killed in ethnic conflict in the past several months." In the case of the *World Handbook* data, this is why the annual series are to be preferred over the daily series (used by Sanders).[17]

Finally, my discussion to this point refers to raw total event counts that have not been standardized in any manner. This usage is not meant to suggest that they should never be standardized, however, and for some purposes certain adjustments may be useful. Consider three of the alternatives.

First, some might argue that these data could profitably be standardized by population size, given the wide variability in the latter across nation-states. On closer inspection, however, the case for an automatic population control is hardly overwhelming. There is little to recommend the procedure with the data on government sanctions targeted against groups, because events such as proclamations of martial law are typically directed at whole populations or subsets of them, defined for example by geographic region. The case for standardization by population size remains ambiguous when applied to official violence against individuals. Would the significance of the summary executions after the 1980 coup in Liberia have been appreciably altered had they occurred in the same number in much more populous Nigeria? Would the detention of twenty individuals for political activities be regarded as more momentous in New Zealand than in the United States? The ambiguity persists with the data on deaths in domestic political violence. Even though the population at risk of death in violence expands in some sense with population size, it is not self-evident that the political significance of deaths increases in the

---

17. For the deaths from domestic violence data, the annual series is also superior because it includes information from summary reports in addition to the daily reports (Taylor and Jodice 1983, 2:47).

same manner. These ambiguities preclude any routine decision to standardize by population size. Where there may be reason to anticipate that population size is germane, that variable is best treated as a separate control variable whose effects can then be estimated rather than assumed a priori.[18]

Second, Bollen (1980, 1986) raises an interesting issue concerning the measure of government sanctions. These data, of course, include repression against groups, in the form of press censorship, declarations of martial law, and the like. Where restrictions on the press were severe *before* the beginning of the series, however, there may be few further restrictions that could afterwards be placed on the press, even if authorities were inclined to do so. Similarly, if a state of emergency had been declared prior to the beginning of the series, there would be no need for a repressive regime to impose martial law subsequently. Given these possibilities, the official use of force may be underestimated for some countries in this series unless further adjustments are made, and Bollen adjusted the series directly.[19] An alternative approach is to include appropriate adjustments as control variables, and estimate their effects. While the specific nature of any such controls will depend on the nature of the empirical model under consideration, the general goal would be to include the pervasiveness of restrictions in place at the beginning of the data series.

The third possible standardization that has been suggested (in assorted guises) stems from the proposition that raw counts of events cannot be compared directly because different political systems have differing traditions of violence. For example, Duvall and Shamir (1980) generated a measure of the coercive propensity of states from the residuals obtained by regressing the use of coercion on antigovernment protests. The official use of force is thus standardized by the extensiveness of challenges to regimes to yield a measure of the degree to which authorities over- or underreact to challenges. A very small residual is presumably taken as evidence that severe sanctions are justifiable because they were a response to a severe challenge. Sanders has made a parallel argument that levels of violence need to be "contextualized," because "'normal' patterns of political interaction vary from country to country" (1981, 74). He therefore proposed that the use of violence (by officials or by challengers) be standardized

---

18. This is the procedure employed by Hibbs (1973). For a useful survey of the use of ratio variables and their alternatives, see Firebaugh and Gibbs (1985).

19. Bollen used the government sanctions data as one component of his well-known index of political democracy. The adjustment he applied (1980, 376) involves subtracting the number of negative sanctions from a liberties index, formed by averaging measures of press freedom and the ability of groups to organize opposition groups.

by prior levels of violence. Sanders's premise seems to be that violence loses much of its import if it is common or habitual. The implication is odd. Because it has a history of violence, high current levels of violence in country A do not signify a notable degree of instability; although it has much lower current levels of violence, country B is deemed more unstable simply because it has a history of even lower rates of violence.

Whether we consider the suggestion by Duvall and Shamir or that by Sanders, this third standardization is perverse. Although these authors seem unaware of the fact, these proposals come very close to a justification of the use of force.[20] They also confuse the use of force with the exercise of power. True, violence may beget violence, but such patterns are best modelled explicitly as has been done in many studies (e.g., Hibbs 1973; Duff and McCamant 1975; Weede 1981). There is no basis for normalizing various forms of violence against either each other or their own prior levels.

To summarize briefly, the data on legitimacy can be arranged in a number of ways. In particular, decisions about the optimal manner in which they should be aggregated will depend on the goals of specific analyses. The same is true for decisions concerning standardization, whether by population size or by prior degrees of legitimacy. While they are not immune to error, these data offer a reasonable representation of the use of force by national governments and their challengers in the period. It is possible, of course, to envisage improvements that might be made to the series, but it should also be recognized that such improvements will require a major effort. Part of my purpose in this book has been to offer substantive justification for this endeavor and to underscore the payoffs it will yield.

Implications

In this chapter I have offered definitions and measures of national political capacity conceived in terms of institutional capacity and legitimacy. The former was measured in terms of the age of the juridical state and the current constitutional form and the number of national executives in the prevailing constitutional period. The measurement of legitimacy was informed by my treatment of the distinction between power and force, introduced in chapter 2. There, I

---

20. The implicit justification takes the following form. Official coercion is reasonable if officials were challenged; in fact, if there is a negative residual (little coercion/high challenge) they underreacted and presumably should have coerced more. High civilian casualties are not particularly momentous in countries with a history (culture?) of violence.

argued that legitimate regimes are those that can induce compliance without resort to force and that are not challenged with violence. Measurement is necessarily inexact, of course, but the data discussed in this chapter do allow broad comparisons of national political capacity across states. While these comparisons involve general orders of magnitude, national political capacity is always a matter of degree.

My goal has been to provide a sharper focus to the discussion of national political capacity by linking general definitions to clear operational indicators. Many of the earlier approaches to development were not cast in a manner that led readily to systematic measurement, while much of the more current research on state strength has deliberately avoided questions of measurement altogether. My approach is predicated on the view that such a tactic is counterproductive. Not measuring a concept in a consistent manner (or not measuring it at all) is far too imprecise, more likely to lead to a false sense of confidence and to false conclusions. Recent assertions to the contrary (e.g., Evans, Rueschemeyer, and Skocpol 1985; Mitchell 1991), before we can make any general statements about national political capacity or state strength we need to have a clear set of empirical referents by which we can judge the process.[21] Of course, as I have emphasized throughout, the identification of systematic measures helps reduce but hardly eliminates all definitional ambiguities, and errors remain. But the merit of the process is that it forces one to confront and address those problems directly.

At various points in this book, I have stressed the ways in which the approach I have adopted builds on or departs from previous analyses. In the final chapter, I pursue these issues by casting my argument in broader terms and placing it in context.

---

21. General statements include, of course, propositions that no useful generalizations are possible, or that each state is unique and can only be analyzed within the context of the idiosyncrasies of its own history.

CHAPTER 7

Conclusions

"Write that down," the King said to the jury, and the jury eagerly wrote down all three dates on their slates, and then added them up, and reduced the answer to shillings and pence.
—Lewis Carroll, *Alice's Adventures in Wonderland*

My purpose in this book has been to offer a fresh brief for the study of national political development or capacity. The topic received a good deal of attention throughout the 1960s and for part of the 1970s. Starting in the early 1970s, however, analyses of political development came under increasing fire. As noted in the first chapter, they were attacked on ideological grounds as conservative, naive, and ethnocentric. They were simultaneously assailed for empirical shortcomings, and it was alleged that the world did not conform to the models adopted in studies of political development.

These criticisms appear less compelling in retrospect. First, it has become evident that the critics have not generated an alternative research program capable of addressing the issues more fruitfully. Most notably, despite the revival of interest in the state, that concept remains mired in definitional confusion. The confusion has permeated all efforts to produce a novel approach, so that the critics can recommend little more than a retreat to historicism, a denial that generalization is feasible or even desirable. Second, a reading of the development studies that were attacked indicates that those studies were often stereotyped by the critics. Development studies were cast as part of the modernization school that saw development as inexorable and inevitable, which ignored political conflict, and which assumed that countries of the Third World could reasonably be expected to follow the path of the industrial states of the West. But this general portrait is no more than a stereotype, and a highly misleading one at that.

I do not mean to endorse the early development studies in their entirety. As is the case with any new field of inquiry, those inquiries raised many more questions than they were able to answer, and they did, of course, contain a number of false starts. Their relative optimism about the prospects for political development in the Third World coincided with a more widespread enthusiasm associated with decolonization that events since have eroded. And agreement on how development should be defined and measured proved elusive.[1] But this is a far cry from the critics' insistence that the earlier studies of political development are wholly misdirected and should therefore be abandoned altogether. Instead, it is more promising to recognize that, despite several problems, they continue to include an interesting set of ideas on which we can profitably draw.[2]

Further, the history of the last thirty years underscores the importance of those ideas. If many of the earlier studies inclined toward optimism, the circumstances of more recent years have reminded us of the fragility of political orders. In states as diverse as Iran, Lebanon, South Africa, and Sri Lanka, along with the remnants of the former Soviet Union and its proteges, political capacity is limited. That is, the ability to accommodate contending interests in a political manner is restricted. States are prone instead to resort to physical force as a mechanism for conflict resolution, and the more they do so, the greater the erosion of their power to accommodate interests. The pervasiveness of the problem is manifested by the youth of so many current constitutional orders documented in chapter 6. Whether or not one is discouraged by those data, they do highlight the proposition that many states are so politically weak that they cannot be effectively governed. That this involves real issues is self-evident.

I have argued that political capacity has two general interrelated components: organizational age and legitimacy. In broad terms, this means that I have been concerned both with institutions conceived in organizational terms and with the amount of compliance and consent that leaders are able to engender. My emphasis on each component reflects the view that political life centers on the exercise of power, and that, unlike physical force, power is intrinsically relational. Although all states have the capability to inflict physical sanctions, their ability to exercise power is the key element of their political capacity. In this context, the prolonged use of force reflects a loss of power and is fundamentally apolitical, because it indicates a deterioration in the relationship between rulers and ruled.

This rudimentary proposition, discussed in chapter 2, has an

---

1. In this context, the criticism that development studies were wanting because they were too scientific and parsimonious (Valenzuela and Valenzuela 1978) is pure caricature.

2. For a similar conclusion, drawn from quite different premises, see Wiarda (1989–90). Indeed, it is informative to compare this more recent and reasonable essay with Wiarda's earlier commentary (1981) that I discussed in chapter 1.

immediate bearing on how we go about the definition and measurement of political capacity. Organizational age becomes important because it reflects the adaptability of institutions. Not only are older organizations more likely to survive, but they are also more likely to be accepted by the relevant population to the extent that they are perceived as having always existed. In this sense, age bears indirectly on consent. But age alone does not imply capacity, and the measures of legitimacy are intended to address the issue of consent more directly. Where regimes employ force or repression on a large scale, we have evidence that they are unable to induce compliance by less costly means. By the same token, where challengers use irregular channels to pursue their interests, that fact indicates a lack of confidence in the efficacy of less costly regular political channels.

If we entertain a rough distinction between rulers and the ruled, these variables cast political capacity in relational terms by focusing on the behavior of both groups. With the measures of organizational age, the casting is implicit; with legitimacy, it is explicit. The fact remains, of course, that these measures do not address the means by which consent is generated, but that is beside the point given the variety of means that might be employed. I argued in chapter 5 that the more fundamental issue is the degree to which consent has been generated at all, which is precisely the quantity that these variables are intended to identify.

I have made clear throughout that my approach draws on earlier studies of development. After all, political capacity was often cast as part of the syndrome (Pye 1966; Coleman 1971) and adaptability was seen as a key element of institutionalization (Huntington 1968). Institutional durability, civil order, legitimacy, and "decisional efficacy" were similarly taken by Eckstein (1971) to define national political performance. In much the same tradition, Young (1982) has suggested that development or performance has six components: economic growth, equality, national autonomy and self-reliance, the preservation of human dignity (as reflected in the absence of state repression), participation, and "societal" capacity.[3]

But the continuity should not be overstated. The earlier studies typically included a broader range of characteristics under the general rubric of political development. In contrast, I have been more concerned with separating the issue of political capacity both from

---

3. Oddly, given the obvious parallels between their two approaches, Young (1982, 14) questions Eckstein's inclusion of durability and civil order as components of performance in light of authoritarian regimes. However, Eckstein's analysis implies that durability and civil order are relevant only in the context of legitimate political orders.

changes associated with industrialization (like complexity and differentiation) and from policy outcomes (such as economic growth and equality). In this sense, my approach is more sharply delimited than most of the earlier proposals, even though it also includes a number of components. Of course, national political capacity would seem to have clear implications for questions of public policy and social change, but that is not a license for conflating it with those questions. Capacity centers simply on the degree of government, and needs to be treated in its own terms.

Although I examined differences in organizational age by geographic region and by national wealth for descriptive purposes and to show that age is not a simple linear function of national wealth, I have obviously resisted attempting to model national political capacity in a systematic manner. Such efforts would center on the relationships among the components of political capacity themselves, as opposed to averaging the various elements into a simple index of "overall capacity."[4] In addition, they would examine the preconditions and consequences of those components. Analyses along these lines have much to offer. That I have refrained from pursuing them reflects three considerations.

First, as indicated in chapter 6, there is reason to believe that in principle, at least, the quality of the data could be improved. This is particularly true for the information on the use of government sanctions taken as an indicator of state repression. An advantage of this measure is its sensitivity to short-run fluctuations in legitimacy, which is particularly helpful in identifying weaknesses in authority among the older states. By the same token, the measure may be less responsive to more systematic, long-term differences in the use of physical force across states. But as I also pointed out, the collection of more extensive data on repressiveness is difficult, a result in good part of the political sensitivity of the material involved.[5] This sensitivity, in turn, reflects the efforts of regimes to conceal the use of physical repression precisely because it is widely recognized that such activity signals an inability to resolve conflict politically through channels that are regarded as legitimate. And even with its difficulties, the measure

---

4. In the present context, the latter strategy would distort the information in an unacceptable way. There is no justification for the view that development as I have conceived it can be reduced to a single number for each country. The issue is best broached instead by examining the relationships among the component measures of development, a procedure that recognizes that the phenomenon is a multidimensional process.

5. Taylor and Jodice (1983, vol. 2, chap. 3) provide an excellent discussion of the practical difficulties involved here, and I certainly do not mean to minimize the considerable effort and thought that went into the construction of their measures.

of government sanctions is certainly superior to a measure of repressiveness based on impressionistic criteria that tend to penalize one's least favored regimes and advantage one's favorites.

Second, considerable efforts have already been made at modeling aspects of national political capacity. For instance, there is an extensive empirical literature on mass political violence in comparative perspective (examples include Russett 1964; Gurr 1968, 1970; Hibbs 1973; Weede 1981; Muller 1985; Muller and Seligson 1987). Many of these studies have also examined linkages between violent political challenges and regime repressiveness. The role of the military in politics has also received a good deal of attention (e.g., Jackman 1976, 1978; Zuk and Thompson 1982; Hanneman and Steinback 1990; Londregan and Poole 1990). Since successful military coups instance the disruption of constitutional orders, analyses along these lines bear directly on the question of organizational age as I have conceived it.[6] The existing empirical studies of mass and elite political violence thus provide us with important information from which we can proceed. But those studies were motivated largely by the sheer frequency of political violence at all levels and by a desire to address what was seen (correctly, in several cases) as the neglected underbelly of many political orders. The framework I have offered provides a broader substantive context within which such analyses can be located.

Finally, I have refrained from constructing an empirical model of political capacity because the criteria I have developed can be used in a variety of ways, each of which would imply different kinds of models. These criteria can, for example, be adopted in the framework of a broad comparative analysis that seeks to document relatively general patterns. But they are equally appropriate for more historical studies restricted to one or two cases. And there are many other potential applications in between. For example, while my measures of organizational age refer to the institutions in place at the end of 1985, it is easy to conceive of other purposes for which more data on the age of various political eras will need to be collected. Indeed, recent events in the member states of the former Warsaw Pact have yielded a new set of constitutional orders. My purpose in this book has not been to pursue the variety of ways in which the data can be used, but rather to address the general issues involved in the definition and measurement of national political capacity.

---

6. Useful surveys and evaluations of these studies include Snyder (1978), the essays in Gurr (1980), and Zimmermann (1983).

At various points, I have emphasized that political capacity needs to be viewed in continuous terms, that it is always a matter of degree. It follows that there is no such thing as a fully developed polity, and it makes little sense to conceive of such a polity, even in principle. Discussions of economic development do not imply the potential existence of a fully developed economy, but simply that states can be ranked according to their economic capacity. The same is true of political capacity. Where economic capacity refers to the production of goods and services (and the efficiency with which they are produced), political capacity refers to the ability to resolve conflict among competing interests without resort to physical force. Phrased differently, it identifies the ability to make problems go away.

That political capacity is always a matter of degree is a simple point that would be banal, were it not for the common penchant among comparativists for taxonomies that classify states into discrete, ranked categories, and a general proclivity to view the most highly ranked category as representing some absolute end point. When combined with the familiar suggestion that the use of the term *development* is teleological, this penchant has led many to conceive of development as an all-or-nothing matter. Such urges are best repressed. The term political development is most fruitfully treated as synonymous with political capacity, as I have done throughout this book.

Coupled with my relational approach, the treatment of political capacity of states as continuous reminds us that it is fragile. Within given states, it is a quantity that is likely to fluctuate considerably over time, even under relatively normal circumstances. And as is apparent from the data discussed in chapter 6, the collapse of national political orders is not infrequent. Again, the use of the term does not imply an inexorable and irreversible process.

Some may see parallels between my argument and the discussion of political decay by Huntington (1968), and it is true that both perspectives attach great weight to political institutions and emphasize the fragility of those institutions. Recall that Huntington specified decay as a function of the ratio of participation to institutionalization, with decay occurring when the former outstrips the latter. The key, then, to maintaining stability is to ensure that levels of participation and institutionalization are balanced. This emphasis on balance would appear to share some elements with my stress on the relational nature of political capacity.

Despite these parallels, however, my approach diverges sharply from Huntington's in its distinction between power and force and in its treatment of political participation. I have argued that the exercise of power presupposes a degree of acceptance and legitimacy, and that a sustained reliance on force is fundamentally apolitical. In contrast, Huntington asserts that the military—the organization that epitomizes the use of force in all political orders—can play a distinctive and positive role. Consider the following:

> Military intervention . . . often marks the end of a sequence of violence in politics. It is, in this sense, significantly different from the tactics employed by other social groups . . . . The military . . . do possess some capacity for generating at least transitory order in a radical praetorian society. The coup is the extreme exercise of direct action against political authority, but it is also the means of ending other types of action against that authority and potentially the means of reconstituting political authority . . . . The seizure of power, in this sense, represents the end of a political struggle and the recording of its results, just as takes place on election day in a democratic country (Huntington 1968, 216–19).

The statement is, of course, qualified by terms like "transitory": obviously, Huntington does not cast the military as invincible. Even so, his conclusion does imply that military coups and the repressive juntas that typically follow can forcefully impose political solutions and thereby succeed where others fail. My approach implies the quite different judgment that "solutions" forcefully imposed by the military constitute no meaningful political solutions at all, especially in the longer term. And, indeed, the available evidence suggests that leaders installed by a coup experience a shorter tenure than others and are also more likely to be removed by a coup (e.g., Hanneman and Steinback 1990). This is why most military juntas must ultimately be judged as failures.

The two approaches also diverge radically over the meaning of mass political participation. Huntington's analysis implies that where institutions are weak, participation by people representing different social groups needs to be contained and curbed to avoid excesses. Excessive participation, goes the argument, simply leads to political decay and praetorianism. As I noted in chapter 5, this conclusion is predicated on Durkheimian assumptions which cast political violence as irrational and anomic. But these assumptions are misleading, particularly because they ignore the costs of political violence that accrue to those who adopt the strategy. In fact, they do not conceive of violence as a strategy at all. Thus, these premises are best abandoned in favor of a perspective that treats political violence as a tactic associated with a variety of costs and potential benefits. Violence no longer represents disorganized expressions of anomie under this alternative but is instead construed as the behavior of those who think that despite the costs, benefits may accrue from the tactic. Seen in this light, the occurrence of violence signifies that sizeable elements of the national community lack confidence in normal political channels and hence represents a failure of national political capacity.

Given these differences, it is obvious that the two approaches have distinctive policy implications. Both, of course, stress the importance of the chronological and generational age of institutions, but these are quantities that cannot be created rapidly, even in principle. How then is political capacity built in the short to medium term? Huntington's argument implies that mobilization needs to be contained so that excessive demands are avoided. But it needs to be recognized that the term *containment* is euphemistic, because efforts at containing rapidly degenerate into repression, a scenario that is particularly likely when the military actively and directly engages in national political life.

My analysis implies that if one is really concerned with *political* capacity, then the containment strategy is largely counterproductive. Legitimacy is instead the quantity that needs to be maximized in the short term for new states. Since decisions to employ repressive tactics are primarily in the hands of regimes, maximizing legitimacy means that those regimes should avoid the use of physical coercion. As I have indicated, consent can be induced in a variety of ways involving different combinations of material and symbolic incentives. Even so, the difficulties of manufacturing legitimacy are not to be underestimated. Because of these difficulties, mine is not an optimistic prognosis. But it does remind us of the fragility of most national political orders and, in so doing, it helps account for the political weakness of so many contemporary states.

Appendix: Country Values for the Chronological Age of National Political Institutions and the Generational Age of the Top National Political Leadership

	Year of Independence	Year of Constitution Effective at End of 1985	Number of Leaders in Current Constitutional Period
United States	1776	1787	39
Canada	1867	1867	17
Cuba	1901	1959	1
Haiti	1840	1957	2
Dominican Republic	1844	1966	3
Jamaica	1962	1962	5
Trinidad and Tobago	1962	1962	2
Barbados	1966	1966	3
Mexico	1820	1917	14
Guatemala	1813	1983	1
Honduras	1838	1982	1
El Salvador	1838	1983	1
Nicaragua	1838	1979	1
Costa Rica	1838	1949	8
Panama	1903	1972	2
Colombia	1819	1958	7
Venezuela	1830	1958	6
Guyana	1966	1966	2
Ecuador	1830	1978	3
Peru	1821	1980	2
Brazil	1822	1984	1
Bolivia	1825	1982	1
Paraguay	1811	1967	1
Chile	1818	1980	1
Argentina	1816	1983	1
Uruguay	1828	1984	1
United Kingdom	1775	1832	20
Ireland	1921	1937	7
Netherlands	1775	1814	25
Belgium	1831	1831	33
Luxembourg	1890	1868	13
France	1775	1958	4
Switzerland	1775	1874	61
Spain	1775	1978	2
Portugal	1775	1976	2
West Germany	1871*	1949	6

(continued)

	Year of Independence	Year of Constitution Effective at End of 1985	Number of Leaders in Current Constitutional Period
East Germany	1871*	1949	2
Poland	1918	1952	6
Austria	1775	1945	7
Hungary	1918	1949	3
Czechoslovakia	1918	1948	4
Italy	1861*	1948	16
Malta	1964	1964	3
Albania	1912	1946	2
Yugoslavia	1878	1946	6
Greece	1830	1975	2
Cyprus	1960	1960	2
Bulgaria	1908	1947	4
Rumania	1878	1948	2
Soviet Union	1775	1936	8
Finland	1918	1919	38
Sweden	1775	1809	26
Norway	1905	1814	27
Denmark	1775	1849	27
Iceland	1918	1944	13
Gambia	1965	1965	1
Mali	1960	1974	1
Senegal	1960	1963	2
Benin	1960	1977	1
Mauritania	1960	1984	1
Niger	1960	1974	1
Ivory Coast	1960	1960	1
Guinea	1958	1984	1
Burkina Faso	1960	1983	1
Liberia	1847	1980	1
Sierra Leone	1961	1978	2
Ghana	1957	1981	1
Togo	1960	1980	1
Cameroon	1960	1961	2
Nigeria	1960	1984	1
Gabon	1960	1960	2
Central African Republic	1960	1981	1
Chad	1960	1982	1
Congo	1960	1979	1
Zaire	1960	1965	1
Uganda	1962	1985	1
Kenya	1963	1963	2
Tanzania	1961	1965	1
Burundi	1962	1976	1
Rwanda	1962	1978	1
Somalia	1960	1979	1
Ethiopia	1775	1977	1

	Year of Independence	Year of Constitution Effective at End of 1985	Number of Leaders in Current Constitutional Period
Angola	1975*	1975	2
Mozambique	1975*	1975	1
Zambia	1964	1964	1
Zimbabwe	1980*	1980	1
Malawi	1964	1966	1
South Africa	1910	1910	3
Lesotho	1966	1966	1
Botswana	1966	1965	2
Madagascar	1960	1975	1
Mauritius	1968	1968	3
Morocco	1956	1956	2
Algeria	1962	1979	1
Tunisia	1956	1959	1
Libya	1951	1977	1
Sudan	1956	1985	1
Iran	1775	1981	1
Turkey	1775	1982	1
Iraq	1932	1970	2
Egypt	1922	1971	2
Syria	1943	1973	1
Lebanon	1943	1926	10
Jordan	1946	1951	1
Israel	1948	1948	6
Saudi Arabia	1925	1962	3
Yemen	1918	1974	3
Yemen (PDR)	1967	1985	1
Kuwait	1961	1961	2
Afghanistan	1919*	1978	1
China	1775	1954	2
Mongolia	1921	1960	2
Taiwan	1949	1950	3
North Korea	1945	1948	1
South Korea	1945	1980	1
Japan	1775	1947	14
India	1947	1950	5
Pakistan	1947	1973	2
Bangladesh	1972	1983	1
Burma	1948	1974	2
Sri Lanka	1947	1948	7
Maldive Islands	1965	1968	
Nepal	1775	1962	2
Thailand	1775	1979	1
Kampuchea	1954	1981	1
Laos	1954	1975	1
Vietnam	1954	1976	1
Malaysia	1957	1957	4

(*continued*)

	Year of Independence	Year of Constitution Effective at End of 1985	Number of Leaders in Current Constitutional Period
Singapore	1965	1965	1
Philippines	1946	1973	1
Indonesia	1949	1949	2
Australia	1901	1900	23
Papua New Guinea	1975*	1975	3
New Zealand	1907	1852	19

Note: Countries are listed in the order used in Taylor and Jodice (1983). The two measures of chronological age are based initially on information available in Rustow (1967) and Taylor and Hudson (1972). Modifications are derived from information in the following compendia, as is the count of the number of national political leaders in the constitutional era effective at the end of 1985: Banks (1986); Jackson and Rosberg (1982b, 288–304); Spuler (1953); and Spuler, Allen, and Saunders (1977). Materials from these compendia were supplemented by data from the following yearbooks: *Europa Yearbook* (London: Europa Publications, various years); *Information Please Almanac, Atlas and Yearbook,* 40th ed. (Boston: Houghton Mifflin, 1987); *Keesing's Contemporary Archives* (London: Longman's Group, various years); *The Statesman's Yearbook* (New York: St. Martin's Press, various years).

*Change from Rustow

Bibliography

Abernethy, David B. 1969. *The Political Dilemma of Popular Education: An African Case*. Stanford: Stanford University Press.

Ake, Claude. 1974. "Modernization and political instability: A theoretical exploration." *World Politics* 26 (July): 576–91.

Aldrich, Howard E. 1979. *Organizations and Environments*. Englewood Cliffs, N.J.: Prentice-Hall.

Aldrich, John H. 1993. "Turnout and rational choice." *American Journal of Political Science* 37 (February): 246–78.

Allison, Paul D. 1977. "The reliability of variables measured as the number of events in an interval of time." In Karl F. Schuessler, ed., *Sociological Methodology 1978*, 238–53. San Francisco: Jossey-Bass.

Almond, Gabriel A. 1965. "A developmental approach to political systems." *World Politics* 17 (January): 183–214.

———. 1987. "The development of political development." In Myron Weiner and Samuel P. Huntington, eds., *Understanding Political Development*, 437–90. Boston: Little, Brown.

Almond, Gabriel A., and James S. Coleman, eds. 1960. *The Politics of the Developing Areas*. Princeton: Princeton University Press.

Almond, Gabriel A., and G. Bingham Powell, Jr. 1966. *Comparative Politics: A Developmental Approach*. Boston: Little, Brown.

Ames, Barry. 1987. *Political Survival: Politicians and Public Policy in Latin America*. Berkeley and Los Angeles: University of California Press.

Anderson, Benedict R. O'G. 1972. "The idea of power in Javanese culture." In Claire Holt, Benedict R. O'G. Anderson, and James Siegel, eds., *Culture and Politics in Indonesia*, 1–69. Ithaca, N.Y.: Cornell University Press.

———. 1991. *Imagined Communities: Reflections on the Origins and Spread of Nationalism*. Rev. ed. New York: Verso.

Apter, David E. 1963. "Political religion in the new nations." In Clifford Geertz, ed., *Old Societies and New States: The Quest for Modernity in Asia and Africa*, 57–104. New York: Free Press.

Ardant, Gabriel. 1975. "Financial policy and economic infrastructure of modern states and nations." In Charles Tilly (ed.), *The Formation of National States in Western Europe*, 164–242. Princeton: Princeton University Press.

Arendt, Hannah. 1970. *On Violence*. New York: Harcourt, Brace, Jovanovich.

Armstrong, John A. 1982. *Nations before Nationalism*. Chapel Hill: University of North Carolina Press.

Arndt, H. W. 1987. *Economic Development: The History of an Idea*. Chicago: University of Chicago Press.

Bachrach, Peter, and Morton S. Baratz. 1970. *Power and Poverty: Theory and Practice*. New York: Oxford University Press.

167

Badie, Bertrand, and Pierre Birnbaum. 1983. *The Sociology of the State*. Chicago: University of Chicago Press.

Bahry, Donna. 1983. "The USSR and Eastern Europe, II." In Charles L. Taylor, ed., *Why Governments Grow: Measuring Public Sector Size*, 117–35. Beverly Hills, Calif.: Sage Publications.

Bahry, Donna, and Brian D. Silver. 1987. "The intimidation factor in Soviet politics: The symbolic uses of terror." *American Political Science Review* 81 (December): 1065–98.

Baldwin, David A. 1979. "Power analysis and world politics: New trends versus old tendencies." *World Politics* 31 (January): 161–94.

Banks, Arthur S. 1986. *Political Handbook of the World*. Binghamton, N.Y.: C.S.A. Publications.

Baran, Paul A. 1957. *The Political Economy of Growth*. New York: Monthly Review Press.

Bates, Robert H. 1981. *Markets and States in Tropical Africa: The Political Basis of Agricultural Policies*. Berkeley and Los Angeles: University of California Press.

Baum, Joel A. C., and Christine Oliver. 1991. "Institutional linkages and organizational mortality." *Administrative Science Quarterly* 36 (June): 187–218.

Beetham, David. 1991. *The Legitimation of Power*. Atlantic Highlands, N.J.: Humanities Press International.

Bellamy, Edward. 1887. *Looking Backward: 2000–1887*. New York: Doubleday.

Bendix, John, Bartholomew H. Sparrow, Bertell Ollman, and Timothy Mitchell. 1992. "Controversy: Going beyond the state?" *American Political Science Review* 86 (December): 1007–20.

Bendix, Reinhard. 1978. *Kings or People: Power and the Mandate to Rule*. Berkeley and Los Angeles: University of California Press.

Benjamin, Roger, and Stephen L. Elkin, eds. 1985. *The Democratic State*. Lawrence: University Press of Kansas.

Bennett, Douglas C., and Kenneth E. Sharpe. 1979. "Agenda setting and bargaining power: The Mexican state versus transnational automobile corporations." *World Politics* 32 (October): 57–89.

Berube, Allan. 1990. *Coming Out under Fire: The History of Gay Men and Women in World War Two*. New York: Free Press.

Bienen, Henry S., and Nicholas van de Walle. 1991. *Of Time and Power: Leadership Duration in the Modern World*. Stanford: Stanford University Press.

Binder, Leonard. 1986. "The natural history of development theory." *Comparative Studies in Society and History* 28 (January): 3–33.

Black, C. E. 1966. *The Dynamics of Modernization: A Study in Comparative History*. New York: Harper and Row.

Blau, Peter M. 1963. "Critical remarks on Weber's theory of authority." *American Political Science Review* 57 (June): 305–16.

Bollen, Kenneth A. 1980. "Issues in the comparative measurement of political democracy." *American Sociological Review* 45 (June): 370–90.

———. 1986. "Political rights and political liberties in nations: An evaluation of human rights measures, 1950 to 1984." *Human Rights Quarterly* 8 (November): 567–91.

Bollen, Kenneth A., and Robert W. Jackman. 1985. "Political democracy and the size distribution of income." *American Sociological Review* 50 (August): 438–57.

Bourdieu, Pierre. 1977. *Outline of a Theory of Practice*. Cambridge: Cambridge University Press.

Bright, Charles, and Susan Harding. 1984. "Processes of statemaking and popular protest." In Charles Bright and Susan Harding, eds., *Statemaking and Social Movements: Essays in History and Theory*, 1–15. Ann Arbor: University of Michigan Press.

Brownlie, Ian. 1979. *Principles of Public International Law*. 3d ed. Oxford: Clarendon Press.

Bruderl, Josef, and Rudolf Schussler. 1990. "Organizational mortality: The liabilities of newness and adolescence." *Administrative Science Quarterly* 35 (September): 530–47.

Brunk, Gregory G., Gregory A. Caldeira, and Michael S. Lewis-Beck. 1987. "Capitalism, socialism, and democracy: An empirical inquiry." *European Journal of Political Research* 15, no. 4: 459–70.

Bueno de Mesquita, Bruce. 1981. *The War Trap*. New Haven: Yale University Press.

Bueno de Mesquita, Bruce, and David Lalman. 1992. *War and Reason: Domestic and International Imperatives*. New Haven: Yale University Press.

Bueno de Mesquita, Bruce, David Newman, and Alvin Rabushka. 1985. *Forecasting Political Events: The Future of Hong Kong*. New Haven: Yale University Press.

Bueno de Mesquita, Bruce, Randolph M. Siverson, and Gary Woller. 1992. "War and the fate of regimes." *American Political Science Review* 86 (September): 638–46.

Bull, Hedley. 1979. "The state's positive role in world affairs." *Daedalus* 108 (Fall): 111–23.

Bull, Hedley, and Adam Watson. 1984. *The Expansion of International Society*. Oxford: Clarendon Press.

Burke, Edmund. [1775] 1908. "On conciliation with the colonies." In *Speeches and Letters on American Affairs*, 76–141. London: J.M. Dent and Sons.

Burling, Robbins. 1974. *The Passage of Power: Studies in Political Succession*. New York: Academic Press.

Calvert, Peter. 1987. *The Process of Political Succession*. London: Macmillan.

Cameron, David R. 1982. "On the limits of the public economy." *The Annals* 459 (January): 46–62.

Cardoso, Fernando Henrique, and Enzo Faletto. 1978. *Dependency and Development in Latin America*. Berkeley and Los Angeles: University of California Press.

Carnoy, Martin. 1984. *The State and Political Theory*. Princeton: Princeton University Press.

Carroll, Glenn R. 1983. "A stochastic model of organizational mortality: Review and reanalysis." *Social Science Research* 12 (December): 303–29.

Carroll, Glenn R., and Jacques Delacroix. 1982. "Organizational mortality in the newspaper industries of Argentina and Ireland: An ecological approach." *Administrative Science Quarterly* 27 (June): 169–98.

Chazan, Naomi. 1988. "Patterns of state-society incorporation and disengagement in Africa." In Donald Rothchild and Naomi Chazan, eds., *The Precarious Balance: State and Society in Africa*, 121–48. Boulder, Colo.: Westview Press.

Chenery, Hollis, and Moises Syrquin. 1975. *Patterns of Development: 1950–1970*. New York: Oxford University Press.

Chilcote, Ronald H. 1981. *Theories of Comparative Politics: The Search for a Paradigm*. Boulder, Colo.: Westview Press.

Chirot, Daniel. 1977. *Social Change in the Twentieth Century*. New York: Harcourt, Brace, Jovanovich.

———. 1985. "The rise of the West." *American Sociological Review* 50 (April): 181–95.

———. 1986. *Social Change in the Modern Era*. New York: Harcourt, Brace, Jovanovich.

Clapham, Christopher. 1985. *Third World Politics*. Madison: University of Wisconsin Press.

Cohen, Benjamin J. 1973. *The Question of Imperialism: The Political Economy of Dominance and Dependence*. New York: Basic Books.

Cohen, Youseff, Brian R. Brown, and A. F. K. Organski. 1981. "The paradoxical nature of state-making: The violent creation of order." *American Political Science Review* 75 (December): 901–10.

Colburn, Forrest D., ed.. 1989. *Everyday Forms of Peasant Resistance*. Armonk, N.Y.: M. E. Sharpe.

Coleman, James S. 1971. "The development syndrome: Differentiation-equality-capacity." In Leonard Binder et al., *Crises and Sequences in Political Development*, 73–100. Princeton: Princeton University Press.

Collier, Ruth Berins. 1982. *Regimes in Tropical Africa: Changing Forms of Supremacy*. Berkeley and Los Angeles: University of California Press.

Connally, William E. 1972. "On 'interests' in politics." *Politics and Society* 2 (Summer): 459–77.

Connor, Walker. 1972. "Nation-building or nation-destroying?" *World Politics* 24 (April): 319–55.

———. 1987. "Ethnonationalism." In Myron Weiner and Samuel P. Huntington, eds., *Understanding Political Development*, 196–220. Boston: Little, Brown.

———. 1990. "When is a nation?" *Ethnic and Racial Studies* 13 (January): 92–103.

Crozier, Michel, and Erhard Friedberg. 1980. *Actors and Systems: The Politics of Collective Action*. Chicago: University of Chicago Press.

Dahl, Robert A. 1961. *Who Governs?* New Haven: Yale University Press.

Davis, Lance E., and Robert A. Huttenback. 1986. *Mammon and the Pursuit of Empire: The Political Economy of British Imperialism, 1860–1912*. New York: Cambridge University Press.

Dekmejian, Richard H., and Margaret J. Wyszomirski. 1972. "Charismatic leadership in Islam: The Mahdi of the Sudan." *Comparative Studies in Society and History* 14 (March): 193–214.

DeNardo, James. 1985. *Power in Numbers: The Political Strategy of Protest and Rebellion*. Princeton: Princeton University Press.

de Schweinitz, Karl. 1970. "Growth, development, and political modernization." *World Politics* 22 (July): 518–40.

Deutsch, Karl W. 1961. "Social mobilization and political development." *American Political Science Review* 55 (September): 493–514.

———. 1981. "The crisis of the state." *Government and Opposition* 16 (Summer): 331–43.

Dominguez, Jorge I. 1987. "Political change: Central America, South America and the Caribbean." In Myron Weiner and Samuel P. Huntington, eds., *Understanding Political Development*, 65–99. Boston: Little, Brown.

Donnelly, Jack. 1984. "Human rights and development: Complementary or competing concerns?" *World Politics* 36 (January): 255–83.

Downs, Anthony. 1957. *An Economic Theory of Democracy*. New York: Harper and Row.

Duff, Ernest, and John McCamant. 1975. *Violence and Repression in Latin America: A Quantitative and Historical Analysis*. New York: Free Press.

Durkheim, Emile. 1951. *Suicide*. New York: Free Press.

Duvall, Raymond, and Michal Shamir. 1980. "Indicators from errors: Cross-national, time-serial measures of the repressive disposition of governments." In Charles L. Taylor, ed., *Indicator Systems for Political, Economic, and Social Analysis*, 155–82. Cambridge, Mass.: Oelgeschlager, Gunn, and Hain.

Easton, David. 1957. "An approach to the analysis of political systems." *World Politics* 9 (April): 383–400.

———. 1965. *A Systems Analysis of Political Life*. New York: John Wiley & Sons.

———. 1981. "The political system beseiged by the state." *Political Theory* 9 (August): 303–25.

Eatwell, John, Murray Milgate, and Peter Newman. 1989. *The New Palgrave: Economic Development*. New York: W. W. Norton.

Eckstein, Harry. 1963. "A perspective on comparative politics, past and present." In Harry Eckstein and David Apter, eds., *Comparative Politics: A Reader*, 3–32. New York: Free Press.

———. 1971. *The Evaluation of Political Performance: Problems and Dimensions*. Beverly Hills, Calif.: Sage Publications.

———. 1979. "On the 'science' of the state." *Daedalus* 108 (Fall): 1–20.

———. 1980. "Theoretical approaches to explaining collective political violence." In Ted Robert Gurr, ed., *Handbook of Political Conflict: Theory and Research*, 135-66. New York: Free Press.

———. 1982. "The idea of political development: From dignity to efficiency." *World Politics* 34 (July): 451–86.

———. 1992. "Rationality and frustration." In Harry Eckstein, ed., *Regarding Politics: Essays on Political Theory, Stability, and Change*, 378–95. Berkeley and Los Angeles: University of California Press.

Edelman, Murray. 1964. *The Symbolic Uses of Politics*. Urbana: University of Illinois Press.

Eisenstadt, S. N. 1968. "Introduction." In Max Weber, *On Charisma and Institution Building*, ed. S. N. Eisenstadt, ix–lvi. Chicago: University of Chicago Press.

Emerson, Rupert. 1960. *From Empire to Nation: The Rise to Self-Assertion of Asian and African Peoples*. Cambridge: Harvard University Press.

Epstein, Edward C. 1984. "Legitimacy, institutionalization, and opposition in exclusionary bureaucratic-authoritarian regimes: The situation of the 1980s." *Comparative Politics* 17 (October): 37–54.

Evans, Peter B. 1979. *Dependent Development: The Alliance of Multinational, State, and Local Capital in Brazil*. Princeton: Princeton University Press.

Evans, Peter B., Dietrich Rueschemeyer, and Theda Skocpol, eds. 1985. *Bringing the State Back In*. New York: Cambridge University Press.

Fearon, James D. 1991. "Counterfactuals and hypothesis testing in political science." *World Politics* 43 (January): 169–95.

Femia, Joseph. 1975. "Hegemony and consciousness in the thought of Antonio Gramsci." *Political Studies* 23 (March): 29–48.

Fichman, Mark, and Daniel A. Levinthal. 1991. "Honeymoons and the liability of adolescence: A new perspective on duration dependence in social and organizational relationships." *Academy of Management Review* 16 (April): 442–68.

Fieldhouse, D. K. 1982. *The Colonial Empires: A Comparative Study from the Eighteenth Century*. 2d ed. London: Macmillan.

———. 1986. *Black Africa 1945–1980: Economic Decolonization and Arrested Development*. London: Allen and Unwin.

Finer, Samuel E. 1975. "State- and nation-building in Europe: The role of the military." In Charles Tilly, ed., *The Formation of National States in Western Europe*, 84–163. Princeton: Princeton University Press.

Fiorina, Morris P. 1990. "Information and rationality in elections." In John Ferejohn and James Kuklinski, eds., *Information and Democratic Processes*, 329-42. Urbana: University of Illinois Press.

Firebaugh, Glenn. 1992. "Growth effects of foreign and domestic investment." *American Journal of Sociology* 98 (July): 105–30.

Firebaugh, Glenn, and Jack P. Gibbs. 1985. "User's guide to ratio variables." *American Sociological Review* 50 (October): 713–22.

Fireman, Bruce, and William A. Gamson. 1979. "Utilitarian logic in the resource mobilization perspective." In Mayer N. Zald and John D. McCarthy, eds., *The Dynamics of Social Movements: Resource Mobilization, Social Control, and Tactics*, 8–44. Cambridge, Mass.: Winthrop.

Fogel, Robert W. 1989. *Without Consent or Contract: The Rise and Fall of American Slavery*. New York: W. W. Norton.

Fogel, Robert W., and Stanley L. Engerman. 1974. *Time on the Cross: The Economics of American Negro Slavery*. Boston: Little, Brown.

Frank, Andre Gunder. 1969. *Capitalism and Underdevelopment in Latin America: Historical Studies of Chile and Brazil*. New York: Monthly Review Press.

Freeman, John, Glenn R. Carroll, and Michael T. Hannan. 1983. "The liability of newness: Age dependence in organizational death rates." *American Sociological Review* 48 (October): 692–710.

Friedrich, Carl J. 1961. "Political leadership and the problem of charismatic power." *Journal of Politics* 23 (February): 3–24.

———, ed.. 1962. *The Public Interest*, NOMOS V. New York: Atherton Press.

Furtado, Celso. 1964. *Development and Underdevelopment*. Berkeley and Los Angeles: University of California Press.

Galbraith, John S. 1968. "The 'turbulent frontier' as a factor in British expansion." *Comparative Studies in Society and History* 2 (2): 150–68.

Gastil, Raymond D. 1985. *Freedom in the World: Political Rights and Civil Liberties, 1984-1985.* Westport, Conn.: Greenwood Press.

———. 1991. "The comparative study of freedom: Experiences and suggestions." In Alex Inkeles, ed., *On Measuring Democracy: Consequences and Concomitants,* 21–46. New Brunswick, N.J.: Transaction Books.

Geddes, Barbara. 1991. "Paradigms and sandcastles in comparative politics of developing areas." In William Crotty, ed., *Political Science: Looking to the Future.* Vol. 2: *Comparative Politics, Policy, and International Relations,* 45–75. Evanston: Northwestern University Press.

Geertz, Clifford. 1963. "The integrative revolution: Primordial sentiments and civil politics in the new states." In Clifford Geertz, ed., *Old Societies and New States: The Quest for Modernity in Asia and Africa,* 105–57. New York: Free Press.

———. 1972. "Afterword: The politics of meaning." In Claire Holt, Benedict R. O'G. Anderson, and James Siegel, eds., *Culture and Politics in Indonesia,* 319–35. Ithaca, N.Y.: Cornell University Press.

———. 1977. "The judging of nations: Some comments on the assessment of regimes in the new states." *European Journal of Sociology* 18, no. 2: 245–61.

Gellner, Ernest. 1983. *Nations and Nationalism.* Ithaca, N.Y.: Cornell University Press.

———. 1985. *Relativism and the Social Sciences.* Cambridge: Cambridge University Press.

Goodin, Robert E. 1980. *Manipulatory Politics.* New Haven: Yale University Press.

Gourevitch, Peter. 1978. "The international system and regime formation." *Comparative Politics* 10 (April): 419–38.

Gramsci, Antonio. 1971. *Selections from the Prison Notebooks,* trans. Quintin Hoare and Geoffrey Nowell Smith. New York: International Publishers.

Gurr, Ted Robert. 1968. "A causal model of civil strife: A comparative analysis using new indices." *American Political Science Review* 62 (December): 1104–24.

———. 1970. *Why Men Rebel.* Princeton: Princeton University Press.

———, ed. 1980. *Handbook of Political Conflict: Theory and Research.* New York: Free Press.

———. 1986a. "The political origins of state violence and terror: A theoretical analysis." In Michael Stohl and George A. Lopez, eds., *Government Violence and Repression,* 45–71. Westport, Conn.: Greenwood Press.

———. 1986b. "Persisting patterns of repression and rebellion: Foundations for a general theory of political coercion." In Margaret P. Karns, ed., *Persisting Patterns and Emerging Structures in a Waning Century,* 149–68. New York: Praeger.

Gurr, Ted Robert, and Mark Irving Lichbach. 1979. "Forecasting domestic political conflict." In J. David Singer and Michael D. Wallace, eds., *To Augur Well: Early Warning Indicators in World Politics,* 153–93. Beverly Hills, Calif.: Sage Publications.

Gusfield, Joseph R. 1967. "Tradition and modernity: Misplaced polarities in the study of social change." *American Journal of Sociology* 72 (January): 351–62.

Haggard, Stephan. 1986. "The newly industrializing countries in the international system." *World Politics* 38 (January): 343–70.

———. 1990. *Pathways from the Periphery: The Politics of Growth in the Newly Industrializing Countries*. Ithaca, N.Y.: Cornell University Press.

Hall, John A., and G. John Ikenberry. 1989. *The State*. Minneapolis: University of Minnesota Press.

Hannan, Michael T., and John Freeman. 1984. "Structural inertia and organizational change." *American Sociological Review* 49 (April): 149–64.

———. 1989. *Organizational Ecology*. Cambridge: Harvard University Press.

Hanneman, Robert A., and Robin L. Steinback. 1990. "Military involvement and political instability: An event history analysis 1940–60." *Journal of Political and Military Sociology* 18 (Summer): 1–23.

Harris, Nigel. 1986. *The End of the Third World: Newly Industrializing Countries and the End of Ideology*. New York: Penguin Books.

Hart, H. L. A. 1961. *The Concept of Law*. Oxford: Clarendon Press.

Hechter, Michael. 1987. *Principles of Group Solidarity*. Berkeley and Los Angeles: University of California Press.

Hermassi, Elbaki. 1978. "Changing patterns in research on the Third World." *Annual Review of Sociology* 4: 239–57.

Hibbs, Douglas A., Jr. 1973. *Mass Political Violence: A Cross-National Causal Analysis*. New York: Wiley-Interscience.

Hobsbawm, E. J. 1990. *Nations and Nationalism since 1780: Programme, Myth, Reality*. Cambridge: Cambridge University Press.

Hobsbawm, Eric, and Terence Ranger. 1983. *The Invention of Tradition*. Cambridge: Cambridge University Press.

Holt, Robert T., and John E. Turner. 1975. "Crises and sequences in collective theory development." *American Political Science Review* 69 (September): 979–94.

Hopkins, Raymond F. 1972. "Securing authority: The view from the top." *World Politics* 24 (January): 271–92.

Horowitz, Donald L. 1985. *Ethnic Groups in Conflict*. Berkeley and Los Angeles: University of California Press.

Howard, Rhoda E., and Jack Donnelly. 1986. "Human dignity, human rights, and political regimes." *American Political Science Review* 80 (September): 801–17.

Humana, Charles. 1992. *World Human Rights Guide*. 3d ed. New York: Oxford University Press.

Huntington, Samuel P. 1968. *Political Order in Changing Societies*. New Haven: Yale University Press.

———. 1971. "The change to change: Modernization, development, and politics." *Comparative Politics* 3 (April): 283–322.

———. 1987. "The goals of development." In Myron Weiner and Samuel P. Huntington, eds., *Understanding Political Development*, 3–32. Boston: Little, Brown.

Huntington, Samuel P., and Joan M. Nelson. 1976. *No Easy Choice: Political Participation in Developing Countries*. Cambridge: Harvard University Press.

Hutchcroft, Paul D. 1991. "Oligarchs and cronies in the Philippine state: The politics of patrimonial plunder." *World Politics* 43 (April): 414–50.

Ikenberry, G. John. 1986a. "The state and strategies of international adjustment." *World Politics* 39 (October): 53–77.

———. 1986b. "The irony of state strength: Comparative responses to the oil shocks in the 1970s." *International Organization* 40 (Winter): 105–37.

Jackman, Mary R. 1993. *Paternalism and Conflict: Ideology and Coercion in Gender, Class, and Race Relations*. Berkeley and Los Angeles: University of California Press.

Jackman, Robert W. 1976. "Politicians in uniform: Military governments and social change in the Third World." *American Political Science Review* 70 (December): 1078–97.

———. 1978. "The predictability of coups d'etat: A model with African data." *American Political Science Review* 72 (December): 1262–75.

———. 1982. "Dependence on foreign investment and economic growth in the Third World." *World Politics* 34 (January): 175–96.

———. 1985. "Cross-national statistical research and the study of comparative politics." *American Journal of Political Science* 29 (February): 161–82.

———. 1986. "Elections and the democratic class struggle." *World Politics* 39 (October): 123–46.

———. 1987. "Political institutions and voter turnout in the industrial democracies." *American Political Science Review* 81 (June): 405–23.

———. 1993. "Rationality and political participation." *American Journal of Political Science* 37 (February): 279–90.

Jackman, Robert W., and William A. Boyd. 1979. "Multiple sources in the collection of data on political conflict." *American Journal of Political Science* 23 (May): 434–58.

Jackson, Robert H. 1990. *Quasi-States: Sovereignty, International Relations, and the Third World*. New York: Cambridge University Press.

Jackson, Robert H., and Carl G. Rosberg. 1982a. "Why Africa's weak states persist: The empirical and juridical in statehood." *World Politics* 35 (October): 1–24.

———. 1982b. *Personal Rule in Black Africa: Prince, Autocrat, Prophet, Tyrant*. Berkeley and Los Angeles: University of California Press.

———. 1984a. "Popular legitimacy in African multi-ethnic states." *Journal of Modern African Studies* 22 (June): 177–98.

———. 1984b. "Personal rule: Theory and practice in Africa." *Comparative Politics* 16 (July): 421–42.

Janos, Andrew C. 1986. *Politics and Paradigms: Changing Theories of Change in Social Science*. Stanford: Stanford University Press.

Johnson, Chalmers. 1982a. *MITI and the Japanese Miracle: The Growth of Industrial Policy, 1925–1975*. Stanford: Stanford University Press.

———. 1982b. *Revolutionary Change*. 2d ed. Stanford: Stanford University Press.

Kalleberg, Arthur L. 1966. "The logic of comparison: A methodological note on the comparative study of political systems." *World Politics* 19 (October): 68–82.

Katzenstein, Peter J. 1978. "Conclusion: Domestic structures and strategies of foreign economic policy." In Peter J. Katzenstein, ed., *Between Power and Plenty: Foreign Economic Policies of Advanced Industrial States*, 295–336. Madison: University of Wisconsin Press.

————. 1985. "Small nations in an open international economy: The converging balance of state and society in Switzerland and Austria." In Peter B. Evans, Dietrich Rueschemeyer, and Theda Skocpol, eds., *Bringing the State Back In*, 227–51. New York: Cambridge University Press.

Kesselman, Mark. 1973. "Order or movement? The literature of political development as ideology." *World Politics* 26 (October): 139–54.

Key, V. O., Jr. 1949. *Southern Politics in State and Nation*. New York: Knopf.

Kiser, Edgar, and Michael Hechter. 1991. "The role of general theory in comparative-historical sociology." *American Journal of Sociology* 97 (July): 1–30.

Kohli, Atul. 1986. "Introduction." In Atul Kohli, ed., *The State and Development in the Third World*, 3–21. Princeton: Princeton University Press.

Kornhauser, William. 1959. *The Politics of Mass Society*. Glencoe, Ill.: Free Press.

Korpi, Walter. 1983. *The Democratic Class Struggle*. London: Routledge and Kegan Paul.

Krasner, Stephen D. 1978. "United States commercial and monetary policy: Unravelling the paradox of external strength and internal weakness." In Peter J. Katzenstein, ed., *Between Power and Plenty: Foreign Economic Policies of Advanced Industrial States*, 51–87. Madison: University of Wisconsin Press.

————. 1984. "Approaches to the state: Alternative conceptions and historical dynamics." *Comparative Politics* 16 (January): 223–46.

Kravis, Irving B., Alan Heston, and Robert Summers. 1982. *World Product and Income*. Baltimore: Johns Hopkins University Press.

Kuhn, Thomas S. 1962. *The Structure of Scientific Revolutions*. Chicago: University of Chicago Press.

Kuznets, Simon. 1951. "The state as a unit in the study of economic growth." *Journal of Economic History* 11 (Winter): 25–41.

Lakatos, Imre. 1978. *The Methodology of Scientific Research Programmes*, Philosophical Papers, vol. 1, ed. John Worrall and Gregory Currie. Cambridge: Cambridge University Press.

Lamborn, Alan C. 1983. "Power and the politics of extraction." *International Studies Quarterly* 27 (June): 125–46.

Lane, Christel. 1984. "Legitimacy and power in the Soviet Union through socialist ritual." *British Journal of Political Science* 14 (April): 207–17.

Lasswell, Harold D. 1936. *Politics: Who Gets What, When, How*. New York: McGraw-Hill.

Lentner, Howard H. 1984. "The concept of the state." *Comparative Politics* 16 (April): 367–77.

Levi, Margaret. 1988. *Of Rule and Revenue*. Berkeley and Los Angeles: University of California Press.

Levinthal, Daniel. 1991. "Random walks and organizational mortality." *Administrative Science Quarterly* 36 (September): 397–420.

Levy, Marion J., Jr. 1966. *Modernization and the Structure of Societies*. Princeton: Princeton University Press.

Leys, Colin. 1975. *Underdevelopment in Kenya: The Political Economy of Neo-Colonialism 1964-1971*. London: Heinemann.

Lichbach, Mark I. 1987. "Deterrence or escalation? The puzzle of aggregate studies of repression and dissent." *Journal of Conflict Resolution* 31 (June): 266–97.

————. 1990. "Will rational people rebel against inequality? Samson's choice." *American Journal of Political Science* 34 (November): 1049–76.

Lieberson, Stanley. 1991. "Small N's and big conclusions: An examination of the reasoning in comparative studies based on a small number of cases." *Social Forces* 70 (December): 307–20.

Lindblom, Charles E. 1982. "Another state of mind." *American Political Science Review* 76 (March): 9–21.

Linz, Juan J. 1978. *The Breakdown of Democratic Regimes.* Baltimore: Johns Hopkins University Press.

Lipset, Seymour Martin. 1960. *Political Man: The Social Bases of Politics.* London: Heineman.

Lipsky, Michael. 1968. "Protest as a political resource." *American Political Science Review* 62 (December): 1144–58.

Londregan, John B., and Keith T. Poole. 1990. "Poverty, the coup trap, and the seizure of executive power." *World Politics* 42 (January): 151–83.

Low, D. A. 1982. "The Asian mirror to tropical Africa's independence." In Prosser Gifford and William Roger Louis, eds., *The Transfer of Power in Africa: Decolonization 1940–1960*, 1–29. New Haven: Yale University Press.

Lukes, Stephen. 1974. *Power: A Radical View.* London: Macmillan.

————, ed.. 1986. *Power.* Oxford: Basil Blackwell.

Machiavelli, Niccolo. [1513] 1985. *The Prince*, trans. Harvey C. Mansfield, Jr. Chicago: University of Chicago Press.

Mackenzie, W. J. M. 1960. "Some conclusions." In W. J. M. Mackenzie and Kenneth Robinson, eds, *Five Elections in Africa: A Group of Electoral Studies*, 462-88. Oxford: Clarendon Press.

McNeill, William H. 1982. *The Pursuit of Power: Technology, Armed Force, and Society since A.D. 1000.* Chicago: University of Chicago Press.

Mair, Lucy. 1977. *Primitive Government: A Study of Traditional Political Systems in Eastern Africa.* Bloomington: Indiana University Press.

Manheim, Jarol B., and Robert B. Albritton. 1984. "Changing national images: International public relations and media agenda setting." *American Political Science Review* 78 (September): 641–57.

Mann, Michael. 1986. "The autonomous power of the state: Its origins, mechanisms and results." In John A. Hall, ed., *States in History*, 109–36. Cambridge: Basil Blackwell.

March, James G., and Johan P. Olsen. 1976. *Ambiguity and Choice in Organizations.* Bergen, Norway: Universitetsforlaget.

Mason, T. David, and Dale A. Krane. 1989. "The political economy of death squads: Toward a theory of the impact of state-sanctioned terror." *International Studies Quarterly* 33 (June): 175–98.

Mastanduno, Michael, David A. Lake, and G. John Ikenberry. 1989. "Toward a realist theory of state action." *International Studies Quarterly* 33 (December): 457–74.

Melson, Robert, and Howard Wolpe. 1970. "Modernization and the politics of communalism: A theoretical perspective." *American Political Science Review* 64 (December): 1112–30.

Merriam, Charles E. 1934. *Political Power*. New York: McGraw Hill.

Merritt, Richard L. 1966. *Symbols of American Community, 1735–75*. New Haven: Yale University Press.

Michels, Roberto. [1915] 1958. *Political Parties: A Sociological Study of the Oligarchical Tendencies of Modern Democracy*. New York: Dover Books.

———. 1927. "Some reflections on the sociological character of political parties." *American Political Science Review* 21 (November): 753–72.

Migdal, Joel S. 1987. "Strong states, weak states: Power and accomodation." In Myron Weiner and Samuel P. Huntington, eds., *Understanding Political Development*, 391-434. Boston: Little, Brown.

Miliband, Ralph. 1969. *The State in Capitalist Society*. New York: Basic Books.

Mill, John Stuart. 1861. *Considerations on Representative Government*. New York: Harper and Brothers.

Milne, R. S. 1981. *Politics in Ethnically Bipolar States: Guyana, Malaysia, Fiji*. Vancouver: University of British Columbia Press.

Mitchell, Timothy. 1991. "The limits of the state: Beyond statist approaches and their critics." *American Political Science Review* 85 (March): 77–96.

Mommsen, Wolfgang J. 1980. *Theories of Imperialism*. Chicago: University of Chicago Press.

———. 1989. *The Political and Social Theory of Max Weber*. Cambridge: Polity Press.

Moore, Will H. 1989. "Rational rebels: Overcoming the free-rider problem." Paper presented at the annual meeting of the American Political Science Association, Atlanta.

Moon, Bruce E., and William J. Dixon. 1985. "Politics, the state, and basic human needs: A cross-national study." *American Journal of Political Science* 29 (November): 661–94.

Muller, Edward N. 1985. "Income inequality, regime repressiveness, and political violence." *American Sociological Review* 50 (February): 47–61.

Muller, Edward N., and Mitchell A. Seligson. 1987. "Inequality and insurgency." *American Political Science Review* 81 (June): 425–51.

Nelson, Daniel L. 1984. "Charisma, control, and coercion: The dilemma of communist leadership." *Comparative Politics* 17 (October): 1–15.

Nelson, Richard R., and Sidney G. Winter. 1982. *An Evolutionary Theory of Economic Change*. Cambridge: Harvard University Press.

Nettl, J. P. 1967. *Political Mobilization: A Sociological Analysis of Methods and Concepts*. New York: Basic Books.

———. 1968. "The state as a conceptual variable." *World Politics* 20 (July): 559–92.

Newman, Saul. 1991. "Does modernization breed ethnic political conflict?" *World Politics* 43 (April): 451–78.

Nielsen, Francois. 1985. "Toward a theory of ethnic solidarity in modern societies." *American Sociological Review* 50 (April): 133–49.

Nkrumah, Kwame. 1965. *Neo-Colonialism: The Last Stage of Imperialism*. London: Nelson.

Nordlinger, Eric A. 1970. "Soldiers in mufti: The impact of military rule upon economic and social change in the non-Western states." *American Political Science Review* 64 (December): 1131–48.

————. 1981. *On the Autonomy of the Democratic State*. Cambridge: Harvard University Press.

————. 1987. "Taking the state seriously." In Myron Weiner and Samuel P. Huntington, eds., *Understanding Political Development*, 353–90. Boston: Little, Brown.

North, Douglass C. 1990. *Institutions, Institutional Change, and Economic Performance*. New York: Cambridge University Press.

O'Brien, Donal Cruise. 1972. "Modernization, order, and the erosion of a democratic ideal: American political science 1960–70." *Journal of Development Studies* 8 (July): 351–78.

O'Brien, Patrick. 1982. "European economic development: The contribution of the periphery." *Economic History Review*, series 2, 35 (February): 1–18.

Olson, Mancur. 1963. "Rapid economic growth as a destabilizing force." *Journal of Economic History* 23 (December): 529–52.

————. 1982. *The Rise and Decline of Nations: Economic Growth, Stagflation, and Social Rigidities*. New Haven: Yale University Press.

Organski, A. F. K., and Jacek Kugler. 1980. *The War Ledger*. Chicago: University of Chicago Press.

Organski, A. F. K., Jacek Kugler, J. Timothy Johnson, and Youseff Cohen. 1984. *Births, Deaths, and Taxes: The Demographic and Political Transitions*. Chicago: University of Chicago Press.

Packenham, Robert A. 1992. *The Dependency Movement: Scholarship and Politics in Development Studies*. Cambridge: Harvard University Press.

Page, Benjamin. 1983. *Who Gets What from Government*. Berkeley and Los Angeles: University of California Press.

Parkin, Frank. 1979. *Marxism and Class Theory: A Bourgeois Critique*. New York: Columbia University Press.

————. 1982. *Max Weber*. London: Tavistock.

Pempel, T. J. 1978. "Japanese foreign economic policy: the domestic bases for international behavior." In Peter J. Katzenstein, ed., *Between Power and Plenty: Foreign Economic Policies of Advanced Industrial States*, 139–90. Madison: University of Wisconsin Press.

Perrow, Charles. 1968. "Organizational goals." In David L. Sills, ed., *International Encyclopedia of the Social Sciences*, 11:305–11. New York: Free Press.

————. 1986. *Complex Organizations: A Critical Essay*. 3d ed. New York: Random House.

Philip, George. 1990. "The political economy of development." *Political Studies* 58 (September): 485–501.

Poggi, Gianfranco. 1978. *The Development of the Modern State: A Sociological Introduction*. Stanford: Stanford University Press.

Polsby, Nelson W. 1980. *Community Power and Political Theory*. 2d ed. New Haven: Yale University Press.

Popkin, Samuel. 1979. *The Rational Peasant: The Political Economy of Rural Society in Vietnam*. Berkeley and Los Angeles: University of California Press.

Portes, Alejandro. 1972. "Rationality in the slum: An essay on interpretive sociology." *Comparative Studies in Society and History* 14 (June): 268–86.

Poulantzas, Nicos. 1978. *State, Power, Socialism*. London: New Left Books.

Pryor, Frederic L. 1968. *Public Expenditures in Communist and Capitalist Nations*. Homewood, Ill.: Richard D. Irwin.

Putnam, Hilary. 1981. *Reason, Truth, and History*. New York: Cambridge University Press.

Pye, Lucian W. 1962. "Armies in the process of political modernization." In John J. Johnson, ed., *The Role of the Military in Underdeveloped Countries*, 69–89. Princeton: Princeton University Press.

———. 1966. *Aspects of Political Development*. Boston: Little, Brown.

———. 1985. *Asian Power and Politics: The Cultural Dimensions of Authority*. Cambridge: Harvard University Press.

Rabushka, Alvina, and Kenneth A. Shepsle. 1972. *Politics in Plural Societies: A Theory of Democratic Instability*. Columbus, Ohio: Charles Merrill.

Ragin, Charles C. 1987. *The Comparative Method: Moving Beyond Qualitative and Quantitative Strategies*. Berkeley and Los Angeles: University of California Press.

———. 1992. "Introduction: Cases of 'What is a Case.'" In Charles C. Ragin and Howard S. Becker, eds., *What is a Case? Exploring the Foundations of Social Inquiry*, 1–17. New York: Cambridge University Press.

Randall, Vicky, and Robin Theobold. 1985. *Political Change and Underdevelopment: A Critical Introduction to Third World Politics*. Durham, N.C.: Duke University Press.

Ratnam, K. J. 1964. "Charisma and political leadership." *Political Studies* 12 (October): 341–54.

Raz, Joseph. 1980. *The Concept of a Legal System: An Introduction to the Theory of Legal Systems*, 2d ed. Oxford: Clarendon Press.

Richstad, Jim, and Michael H. Anderson. 1981. *Crisis in International News: Policies and Prospects*. New York: Columbia University Press.

Rigby, T. H. 1984. "Dominant and subsidiary modes of political legitimation in the USSR." *British Journal of Political Science* 14 (April): 219–22.

Rogowski, Ronald. 1988. "Structure, growth, and power: Three rationalist accounts." In Robert H. Bates, ed., *Toward a Political Economy of Development: A Rational Choice Perspective*, 300–30. Berkeley and Los Angeles: University of California Press.

Rokkan, Stein. 1975. "Dimensions of state formation and nation-building: A possible paradigm for research on variations within Europe." In Charles Tilly, ed., *The Formation of National States in Western Europe*, 562–600. Princeton: Princeton University Press.

Rosenblum, Mort. 1981. *Coups and Earthquakes: Reporting the World for America*. New York: Harper and Row.

Roth, Guenther. 1968. "Personal rulership, patrimonialism, and empire-building in the new states." *World Politics* 20 (January): 194–206.

Rouyer, Alwyn R. 1987. "Political capacity and the decline of fertility in India." *American Political Science Review* 81 (June): 453–70.

Rubinson, Richard. 1976. "The world economy and the distribution of income within states." *American Sociological Review* 41 (August): 638–59.

———. 1977. "Dependence, government revenue, and economic growth." *Studies in Comparative International Development* 12 (Summer): 3–28.

Rubinson, Richard, and Daniel Quinlan. 1977. "Democracy and social inequality: A reanalysis." *American Sociological Review* 42 (August): 611–23.
Rudolph, Lloyd I., and Susanne Hoeber Rudolph. 1979. "Authority and power in bureaucratic and patrimonial administration: A revisionist interpretation of Weber on bureaucracy." *World Politics* 31 (January): 195–227.
Rueschemeyer, Dietrich, and Peter B. Evans. 1985. "The state and economic transformation: Toward an analysis of the conditions underlying effective intervention." In Peter B. Evans, Dietrich Rueschemeyer, and Theda Skocpol, eds., *Bringing the State Back In*, 44–77. New York: Cambridge University Press.
Rule, James B. 1988. *Theories of Civil Violence*. Berkeley and Los Angeles: University of California Press.
Russell, Bertrand. 1938. *Power: A New Social Analysis*. New York: W. W. Norton.
Russett, Bruce M. 1964. "Inequality and instability: The relation of land tenure to politics." *World Politics* 16 (April): 442–54.
Rustow, Dankwart A. 1967. *A World of Nations: Problems of Political Modernization*. Washington, D.C.: Brookings Institution.
Ruttan, Vernon W. 1991. "What happened to political development?" *Economic Development and Cultural Change* 39 (January): 265–92.
Sabine, George H. 1934. "State." In Edwin R. A. Seligman and Alvin Johnson, eds., *Encylopedia of the Social Sciences*, 14:328–32. New York: Macmillan.
Sanders, David. 1978. "Away from a general model of mass political violence: Evaluating Hibbs." *Quality and Quantity* 12 (June): 103–29.
———. 1981. *Patterns of Political Instability*. New York: St. Martin's.
Sartori, Giovanni. 1970. "Concept misformation in comparative politics." *American Political Science Review* 64 (December): 1033–53.
Schaffer, B. B. 1965. "The concept of preparation: Some questions about the transfer of systems of government." *World Politics* 18 (October): 42–67.
Schattschneider, E. E. 1960. *The Semi-Sovereign People*. New York: Holt, Rinehart and Winston.
Schlesinger, Joseph A. 1991. *Political Parties and the Winning of Office*. Ann Arbor: University of Michigan Press.
Schmidt, Steffen W., Laura Guasti, Carl H. Lande, and James C. Scott. 1977. *Friends, Followers, and Factions: A Reader in Political Clientelism*. Berkeley and Los Angeles: University of California Press.
Scott, James C. 1985. *Weapons of the Weak: Everyday Forms of Peasant Resistance*. New Haven: Yale University Press.
———. 1990. *Domination and the Arts of Resistance: Hidden Transcripts*. New Haven: Yale University Press.
Scott, Robert E. 1963. "Nation-building in Latin America." In Karl W. Deutsch and William J. Foltz, eds., *Nation-Building*, 73–83. New York: Atherton Press.
Shils, Edward. 1963. "On the comparative study of the new states." In Clifford Geertz, ed., *Old Societies and New States: The Quest for Modernity in Asia and Africa*, 1–26. New York: Free Press.
———. 1964. "The fortunes of constitutional government in the political devel-

opment of the new states." In John H. Hallowell, ed., *Development: For What?*, 103–43. Durham, N.C.: Duke University Press.

Siegfried, Andre. 1956. "Stable instability in France." *Foreign Affairs* 34: 394–404.

Sills, David L. 1957. *The Volunteers*. Glencoe, Ill.: Free Press.

Silver, Brian D. 1974. "Social mobilization and the russification of Soviet nationalities." *American Political Science Review* 68 (March): 45–66.

———. 1987. "Political beliefs of the Soviet citizen: Sources of support for regime norms." In James R. Millar, ed., *Politics, Work, and Daily Life in the USSR: A Survey of Former Soviet Citizens*, 100–41. New York: Cambridge University Press.

Simon, Herbert A. 1976. *Administrative Behavior*. 3d ed. New York: Free Press.

Singh, Jitendra, David J. Tucker, and Robert J. House. 1986. "Organizational legitimacy and the liability of newness." *Administrative Science Quarterly* 31 (June): 171–93.

Sivard, Ruth Leger. 1986. *World Military and Social Expenditures*. 11th ed. Washington, D.C.: World Priorities.

Skocpol, Theda. 1977. "Wallerstein's world capitalist system: A theoretical and historical critique." *American Journal of Sociology* 82 (March): 1075–90.

———. 1985. "Bringing the state back in: Strategies of analysis in current research." In Peter B. Evans, Dietrich Rueschemeyer, and Theda Skocpol, eds., *Bringing the State Back In*, 3–37. New York: Cambridge University Press.

Smith, Adam. [1789] 1976. *An Inquiry into the Nature and Causes of the Wealth of Nations*. Chicago: University of Chicago Press.

Smith, Anthony D. 1986. "State-making and nation-building." In John A. Hall, ed., *States in History*, 228–63. Cambridge: Basil Blackwell.

———. 1987. *The Ethnic Origins of Nations*. Cambridge: Basil Blackwell.

———. 1988. "The myth of the 'modern nation' and the myths of nations." *Ethnic and Racial Studies* 11 (January): 1–26.

Smith, Tony, ed. 1975. *The End of the European Empire: Decolonization after World War II*. Lexington, Mass.: D. C. Heath.

———. 1978. "A comparative study of French and British decolonization." *Comparative Studies in Society and History* 20 (January): 70–102.

———. 1979. "The underdevelopment of development literature: The case of dependency theory." *World Politics* 31 (January): 247–88.

———. 1985. "Requiem or new agenda for Third World studies?" *World Politics* 37 (July): 532–61.

Snider, Lewis W. 1987. "Identifying the elements of state power: Where do we begin?" *Comparative Political Studies* 20 (October): 314–56.

Snyder, David. 1978. "Collective violence: A research agenda and some strategic considerations." *Journal of Conflict Resolution* 22 (September): 499–534.

Snyder, David, and William R. Kelly. 1977. "Conflict intensity, media sensitivity, and the validity of newspaper data." *American Sociological Review* 42 (February): 105–23.

Somjee, A. H. 1982. *Political Capacity in Developing Societies*. New York: St. Martin's.

———. 1986. *Parallels and Actuals of Political Development*. London: Macmillan.

Southall, Aidan. 1968. "Stateless society." In David L. Sills, ed., *International Encyclopedia of the Social Sciences*, 15:157–68. New York: Free Press.

Spuler, Bertold. 1953. *Regenten und Regierungen der Welt*. Wurzburg: A. G. Ploetz Verlag.

Spuler, Bertold, C. G. Allen, and Neil Saunders. 1977. *Rulers and Governments of the World*, vol. 3. London: Bowker.

Staniland, Martin. 1985. *What Is Political Economy? A Study of Social Theory and Underdevelopment*. New Haven: Yale University Press.

Starbuck, William H. 1965. "Organizational growth and development." In James G. March, ed., *Handbook of Organizations*, 451–533. Chicago: Rand McNally.

———. 1983. "Organizations as action generators." *American Sociological Review* 48 (February): 91–102.

Stepan, Alfred. 1978. *The State and Society: Peru in Comparative Perspective*. Princeton: Princeton University Press.

———. 1985. "State power and the strength of civil society in the southern cone of Latin America." In Peter B. Evans, Dietrich Rueschemeyer, and Theda Skocpol, eds., *Bringing the State Back In*, 317–43. New York: Cambridge University Press.

Stinchcombe, Arthur L. 1965. "Social structure and organizations." In James G. March, ed., *Handbook of Organizations*, 142–93. Chicago: Rand McNally.

Strang, David. 1990. "From dependency to sovereignty: An event history analysis of decolonization 1870–1987." *American Sociological Review* 55 (December): 846–60.

Summers, Robert, and Alan Heston. 1988. "A new set of international comparisons of real product and price levels: Estimates for 130 countries, 1950–1985." *Review of Income and Wealth* 34 (March): 1–25, and three accompanying diskettes.

———. 1991. "The Penn world table (Mark 5): An expanded set of international comparisons." *Quarterly Journal of Economics* 106 (May): 327–68.

Suppe, Frederick. 1977. *The Structure of Scientific Theories*. 2d ed. Urbana: University of Illinois Press.

Taylor, Charles L., and Michael C. Hudson. 1972. *World Handbook of Political and Social Indicators*. 2d ed. New Haven: Yale University Press.

Taylor, Charles L., and David A. Jodice. 1983. *World Handbook of Political and Social Indicators*. 3d ed. 2 vols. New Haven: Yale University Press.

Taylor, Michael. 1988. "Rationality and revolutionary collective action." In Michael Taylor, ed., *Rationality and Revolution*, 63–97. New York: Cambridge University Press.

Theobold, Robin. 1978. "A charisma too versatile?" *European Journal of Sociology* 19, no. 1: 192–98.

———. 1982. "Patrimonialism." *World Politics* 34 (July): 548–59.

———. 1990. *Corruption, Development, and Underdevelopment*. Durham, N.C.: Duke University Press.

Thompson, James D. 1967. *Organizations in Action*. New York: McGraw-Hill.

Tilly, Charles. 1975. "Reflections on the history of European state-making." In Charles Tilly, ed., *The Formation of National States in Western Europe*, 3–83. Princeton: Princeton University Press.

————. 1978. *From Mobilization to Revolution*. Reading, Mass.: Addison-Wesley.

————. 1985. "War making and state making as organized crime." In Peter B. Evans, Dietrich Rueschemeyer, and Theda Skocpol, eds., *Bringing the State Back In*, 169–91. New York: Cambridge University Press.

————. 1986. "The replay of politics." *Comparative Studies in Society and History* 28 (January): 114–18.

————. 1990. *Coercion, Capital, and European States, AD 990–1990*. Cambridge: Basil Blackwell.

Tilly, Charles, Louise Tilly, and Richard Tilly. 1975. *The Rebellious Century: 1830–1930*. Cambridge: Harvard University Press.

Tiryakian, Edward A. 1991. "Modernization: Exhumetur in pace." *International Sociology* 6 (June): 165–80.

Tomich, Dale W. 1990. *Slavery in the Circuit of Sugar: Martinique and the World Economy 1830–1848*. Baltimore: Johns Hopkins University Press.

Tong, James. 1992. *Disorder under Heaven: Collective Violence in the Ming Dynasty*. Stanford: Stanford University Press.

United States Arms Control and Disarmament Agency. 1990. *World Military Expenditures and Arms Transfers, 1989*. Washington, D.C.: USACDA.

Valenzuela, J. Samuel, and Arturo Valenzuela. 1978. "Modernization and dependency: Alternative perspectives on the study of Latin American underdevelopment." *Comparative Politics* 10 (July): 543–57.

van den Berghe, Pierre L. 1983. "Class, race, and ethnicity in Africa." *Ethnic and Racial Studies* 6 (April): 221–36.

Veliz, Claudio. 1980. *The Centralist Tradition in Latin America*. Princeton: Princeton University Press.

von Beyme, Klaus. 1985. "The role of the state and the growth of government." *International Political Science Review* 6:11–34.

Wallerstein, Immanuel. 1974a. *The Modern World System: Capitalist Agriculture and the Origins of the European World Economy in the Sixteenth Century*. New York: Academic Press.

————. 1974b. "The rise and future demise of the capitalist world system: Concepts for comparative analysis." *Comparative Studies in Society and History* 16 (September): 387–415.

————. 1976. "Modernization: Requiescat in pace." In Lewis A. Coser and Otto N. Larsen, eds., *The Uses of Controversy in Sociology*, 131–35. New York: Free Press.

Walsh, James P., and Gerardo Rivera Ungson. 1991. "Organizational memory." *Academy of Management Review* 16 (January): 57–91.

Watkins, Frederick M. 1968. "State: The concept." In David L. Sills, ed., *International Encyclopedia of the Social Sciences*, 15:150–57. New York: Free Press.

Weber, Max. 1946. "Politics as a vocation." In H. H. Gerth and C. Wright Mills, eds., *From Max Weber: Essays in Sociology*, 77–128. New York: Oxford University Press.

————. 1947. *The Theory of Social and Economic Organization*, trans. A. M. Henderson and Talcott Parsons. Glencoe, Ill.: Free Press.

Weede, Erich. 1980. "Beyond misspecification in sociological analyses of income inequality." *American Sociological Review* 45 (June): 497–501.

———. 1981. Income inequality, average income, and domestic violence." *Journal of Conflict Resolution* 25 (December): 639–53.

Weede, Erich, and Horst Tiefenbach. 1981. "Some recent explanations of income inequality." *International Studies Quarterly* 25 (June): 255–82.

Weiner, Myron. 1965. "Political integration and political development." *The Annals* 358 (March): 52–64.

———. 1987. "Political change: Asia, Africa, and the Middle East." In Myron Weiner and Samuel P. Huntington, eds., *Understanding Political Development*, 33–64. Boston: Little, Brown.

White, Stephen. 1986. "Economic performance and communist legitimacy" *World Politics* 38 (April): 462–82.

Wiarda, Howard. 1981. "The ethnocentrism of the social sciences: Implications for research and policy." *Review of Politics* 42 (April): 163–97.

———. 1989–90. "Rethinking political development: A look backward over thirty years, and a look ahead." *Studies in Comparative International Development* 24 (Winter): 65–82.

Williams, Gwyn A. 1960. "The concept of 'egemonia' in the thought of Antonio Gramsci: Some notes on interpretation." *Journal of the History of Ideas* 21 (October-December): 586–99.

Willner, Ann Ruth. 1984. *The Spellbinders: Charismatic Political Leadership*. New Haven: Yale University Press.

Wilson, James Q. 1973. *Political Organizations*. New York: Basic Books.

World Bank. 1983. *World Tables*. 3d ed. Baltimore: Johns Hopkins University Press.

———. 1987. *World Development Report 1987*. New York: Oxford University Press.

Young, Crawford. 1976. *The Politics of Cultural Pluralism*. Madison: University of Wisconsin Press.

———. 1982. *Ideology and Development in Africa*. New Haven: Yale University Press.

———. 1988. "The African colonial state and its political legacy." In Donald Rothchild and Naomi Chazan, eds., *The Precarious Balance: State and Society in Africa*, 25–66. Boulder, Colo.: Westview Press.

Zeitlin, Irving. 1990. *Ideology and the Development of Sociological Theory*. 4th ed. Englewood Cliffs, N.J.: Prentice-Hall.

Zimmermann, Ekkart. 1983. *Political Violence, Crises, and Revolutions*. Cambridge, Mass.: Schenkman.

Zolberg, Aristide R. 1966. *Creating Political Order: The Party-States of West Africa*. Chicago: Rand McNally.

———. 1981. "Origins of the modern world system: A missing link." *World Politics* 33 (January): 253–81.

Zuk, Gary, and William R. Thompson. 1982. "The post-coup military spending question." *American Political Science Review* 76 (March): 60–74.

Index